S0-BKT-332

INTRODUCTION TO MASS COMMUNICATIONS RESEARCH

JOURNALISM MONOGRAPHS
NUMBER SIX

JOURNALISM MONOGRAPHS

Published under the auspices of the

COUNCIL ON COMMUNICATIONS RESEARCH

Association for Education in Journalism

OTHER TITLES IN THE SERIES:

Free Circulation
By Charles L. Allen

Jefferson and the Press
By Frank Luther Mott

Management of Newspaper Correspondents
By C. F. Smith and Kathryn M. Rheuark

An Introduction to Journalism Research
Edited by Ralph O. Nafziger and Marcus M. Wilkerson

Bovard of the Post-Dispatch
By James W. Markham

Introduction to Mass Communications Research

EDITED BY

RALPH O. NAFZIGER

AND

DAVID M. WHITE

LOUISIANA STATE UNIVERSITY PRESS

BATON ROUGE

Revised Edition 1963

Second Printing 1966

Third Printing 1968

Library of Congress Catalog Card Number: 63-8223

Printed in the United States of America by
Cushing-Malloy, Inc.

Preface

FIFTEEN YEARS AGO the Council on Research authorized a short handbook on journalism research which would serve primarily as a pathfinder for beginning graduate students. Since the last edition of this monograph appeared in 1958, new methodological advances in communication research have made necessary a new edition of this introduction to the subject. Moreover, increasing interest among journalism teachers in this area of research method has required an expansion in the range of subject matter.

This volume is confined to a more specific area of method and research than was treated in the earlier book. Limits were placed on its scope in order to concentrate on research methods in mass communication from a behavioral point of view. This delimitation of the many fruitful fields of journalism research was decided on to emphasize and to answer relevant questions about approaches and methods which are new to many students of journalism. The Council and the editors did not undervalue the continuing importance of other areas, such as the method and application of historiography to journalism. Rather, they decided that the essence of these tried and well-known approaches was more readily accessible to students of journalism than the procedures which have been applied more recently to our problems.

An essential addition to the present volume is the new chapter on content analysis by Wayne A. Danielson. A comparison of this chapter with the discussion of content analysis in the first edition of the monograph shows the recent advances in the scope of this specialized research method. It has been necessary also to revise thoroughly several other chapters, especially those on research planning, field methods, and statistical analysis of mass communications data.

Further discussion of the research area to which this monograph is confined is carried on throughout the book. In summary, communication research is the main part of journalism research, but our field has no exclusive claim to the broad area of communication studies. The methods which are defined in this monograph are not unique to journalism but are common to students in the social sciences who are cultivating the fields of human behavior and, more specifically, of communication research. But in view of our special orientation in the problems of the mass media and our practical understanding of the development, practices, and procedures of the mass media, we are and should be equipped uniquely to apply new methods for attacking our data and to arrive at general principles which can contribute to a theory of communications.

As we pointed out in the 1958 edition, this volume attempts to introduce the beginner to a stimulating area of research. It does not pretend to serve as a comprehensive textbook or as a manual on details of research techniques. It is our hope that a textbook or a series of books dealing with details of the different fields of mass communications research outlined in this monograph will soon appear on the market.

R. O. N.
D. M. W.

Contents

Authors

John E. Alman, Director of Statistical and Research Services, and Lecturer on Education, Boston University

Roy E. Carter, Jr., Professor of Journalism and Sociology, and Director, Communications Research Division, School of Journalism, University of Minnesota

Wayne A. Danielson, Associate Professor of Journalism, School of Journalism, University of North Carolina

Paul J. Deutschmann, Director, Communications Research Center, Michigan State University

Malcolm S. MacLean, Jr., Professor, Communications Research Center, Michigan State University

Ralph O. Nafziger, Professor of Journalism and Director of the School of Journalism, University of Wisconsin

Wilbur Schramm, Janet M. Peck Professor of International Communications and Director, Institute for Communications Research, Stanford University

Percy H. Tannenbaum, Professor of Journalism and Director, Mass Communications Research Center, University of Wisconsin

Bruce H. Westley, Associate Professor of Journalism and Research Co-ordinator, Television Laboratory, University of Wisconsin

David Manning White, Professor of Journalism, School of Public Relations and Communications, Boston University

INTRODUCTION TO MASS COMMUNICATIONS RESEARCH

The Challenge to Communication Research

WILBUR SCHRAMM

LET US AT the very beginning rid ourselves of the hampering and erroneous notion that there is somewhere a sharp border and a guarded frontier between journalism research and communication research or between communication research and *mass* communication research.

Twenty-five years ago it might have been possible to say that journalism research is *newspaper* research, but the schools of journalism themselves have taken care of that by interesting themselves in radio, television, photography, magazines, and advertising and by adding research institutes and programs whose interests range over the entire field of communication. Therefore, the notion that journalism research is limited to one medium, whereas communication research covers the whole field, is manifestly unsound.

Sometimes scholars who should know better speak in terms of a distinction in method: i. e., journalism research is the "simpler" research; it uses the simpler methods and tools and concerns itself with the more applied and less theoretical questions. In this vein one hears journalism research talked about as being typified by questionnaires about advertising rates and by readership surveys. And yet the full-day quantitative research section which has now become a part of the annual journalism convention would do credit in method and sophistication to any of the learned societies in the field of behavioral science. Furthermore, when one looks at the variety of research actually under way at the schools and their related institutes, it seems to compare very well in level and range with that of communication research anywhere. A brief look at research in progress or recently completed at the schools and their associated institutes reveals such projects as: the performance of newspapers in the 1960 election campaign; the effect of TV on children; factors by which meaning is expressed in different cultures; how knowledge of science is diffused through the public; the content of foreign news given the American public; communication between schools and their communities; communication in economic and social development; mass media in Latin American countries. This is a small sample, but an impressive one.

Journalism research is sometimes distinguished from communication research in terms of mass media: i.e., journalism research is concerned primarily with the mass media of communication, whereas communication research deals with the communication process. No one has ever explained very clearly just how one could study the mass media without concerning oneself with the communication process. In any active communication research program these two concerns usually blend imperceptibly. For example, at Illinois during the years 1952 to 1955 researchers were thinking about the "indexing process" by which mass media enable their audiences to scan media offerings and to focus attention on what particularly interests them. These indexing devices include headlines in newspapers, captions on pictures, cue words in radio news announcements, etc. Several articles were published on the subject, and Percy Tannenbaum, in the *Public Opinion Quarterly,* tried to state an acceptable psychological theory for the indexing process.[1] Now, was this journalism research or communication research? It was clearly focused on the mass media and yet concerned centrally with process. Our experience has been that only by this blending of institutional interest with process interest has it been possible to understand what goes on in the mass media and how they have an effect.

I have heard the distinction put in terms of origin: journalism research is done in schools and departments of journalism, whereas communication research is done in social science departments outside journalism. This is logically defensible but not very useful. Some of the people at Illinois who were working on the indexing process had appointments in journalism, some did not. They were all concerned with the same problem. Morris Janowitz, a professor of sociology at the University of Michigan, writes on the suburban newspaper.[2] Paul Deutschmann, head of communications research at Michigan State University, wrote his dissertation at Stanford on the process of selective perception.[3] What does it tell us, then, to know that one of these scholars is in a school of journalism, the other outside a school of journalism?

The truth is that there is no frontier. There is only communication research. All parts of it are related to all other parts, and the landscape is marked off only by the fact that some scholars are centrally interested in one part, some in another. In the last decade, by exploring here and there in the broad domain of communication research, the schools of journalism and their related institutes have begun to define more sharply their own central interests. And it is seen to be true that the communication research interests of journalism are actually somewhat broader than those of the other behavioral sciences. For whereas communication research as a small part of psychology, of economics, of anthropology, of law, of sociology, of political science, it is the main part of journalism research.

Thus, the journalist shares with the psychologist, the sociologist, and the anthropologist joint responsibility for exploring the broad problems of the communication process. We realize now that we shall never fully understand mass communication without understanding person-to-person and small-group communication. Indeed, such books as Richard LaPiere's *Theory of Social Control* and Elihu Katz's and Paul Lazarsfeld's *Personal Influence*[4] only emphasize how important it is to bring into one conceptual framework what we know about person-to-person, small-group, and mass media communication. Without doing so we shall never arrive at a satisfactory estimate of expectation of effects.

But journalism has also a peculiar and primary obligation for exploring *mass* communication, a responsibility which is shared only in small part by the political scientist, the economist, and the institutional sociologist. That is to say, journalism has a particular obligation for studying:

1. Mass communication as a social institution—its organization, its social control, its place in social structure and function, its content, its audiences, its responsibilities and performance.

2. The conditions of its effectiveness—the choice of channels, the nature of messages, the self-selection of the audiences, the nature of

attention, the problem of transmitting meaning, the relation of group structure and predispositions to effect.

3. The nature and evidence of effects—what mass communication does to the individual life and what it contributes to social change or lack of change.

Call this journalism research or communication research; it does not matter. It is a huge task. It will not be made easier by setting up an artificial barrier between journalism research and communication research or between journalism school research and research in other departments. The task ahead is rather to break down such barriers as already exist; to cross the imaginary borders (as the best researchers do now, with ease and acceptance); to make use of the training of the psychologist, the sociologist, and others; to draw on the insights of the learning theorist, the psycholinguist, the psychiatrist, the specialist in small-group research, the student of propaganda and public opinion, the student of decision theory, and all the others who have some contribution to make to these problems; and to share with them our own particular insights, including our somewhat more informed knowledge of the working of the mass media. This is no time for secluding or restricting our research interests and our field, but rather for the widest possible exploration in other fields where our problems are under study, and for the maximum number of interchanges and alliances, with other scholars working on these problems.

In this essay the term *journalism* research is used simply to mean communication research as practiced by the schools and departments of journalism and their related institutes and research units. It is not implied that there is any essential difference between the communication research that goes on inside these schools, departments, and institutes and outside them—or that there should be.

Trends in Journalism Research

Several trends have made themselves clear in journalism research. For one, there is the trend of growth. It is an exciting experience to leaf through the *Journalism Quarterly* for the last thirty years and observe the burgeoning and maturing of research. As a matter of fact, the 1931 volume is a good place to begin because it carries a full report of the annual convention and the first attempt at a full report of research under way in schools and departments of journalism.[5] The *Quarterly* itself contains only a small proportion of what today would be thought of as research, and most of this material is in the history or law of the press. The convention gave no time to research talks, but it did receive a report on current research from Dean Eric W. Allen of Oregon. He listed 187 items, a very respectable total, although many of the topics are listed only as "planned," some of them came from outside the schools, and a surprisingly large number of the projects would not be listed as research today. Of these, more will be said later. The list contains many of the names we have come to know well: Frank Luther Mott (the first volume of *A History of American Magazines* had been published the year before); Ralph D. Casey (he was expanding his material on political propaganda in the 1928 campaign); Chilton R. Bush (*Newspaper Reporting of Public Affairs* had been published); Ralph O. Nafziger (with one of the early journalism field researches, a survey of the reading and buying habits of Madison, Wisconsin); Kenneth E. Olson (*Typography and Mechanics of the Newspaper*); and so on. But perhaps the most interesting feature of the list is the nature of the research reported. Here are a few examples: "Checking Louisiana newspapers to determine the number of agriculture editorials by them in 1930"; "College campus journalism, how it differs from regular newspaper work"; "Copyreading laboratory exercises"; "Country weekly profits"; "Sportwriting text"; "Folklore in the works of Mark Twain." This is not an attempt to poke fun at the list, for there were giants in those days as in all days. But it is an attempt to suggest the nature of the change that has come to schools and departments of journalism in thirty years: a great increase in the number of students and the proportion of faculty engaged in research; a general lifting of sights as to what constitutes research and how a serious research man in journalism can make a contribution to knowledge.

To see the full dimension of that change, look at the 1961 volume of the *Journalism Quarterly*. There is no reason to believe it is either the best or the worst of the last five volumes that have appeared. But what a change it represents from 1931! History is represented in both volumes, and rather well. In both there are articles on legal and political problems of the media, and three out of the four issues of 1961 have symposia on journalism teaching. But the leading articles in the 1961 volume, unlike the articles of 1931, tend to be quantitative. Two of the four issues lead off with quantitative studies of press performance in the 1961 campaign, a third with a summary of trends in press ownership and intermedia competition, and the fourth with a study of trends in Sunday newspaper content. There are a number of articles which would have been strange and out of place in the 1931 volume: for example, an article on how perceived distance differs from actual distance in the news, one on the effect of bylines on attitude change, still another on a new medium and the process of cultural change. Beyond these, however, it is the tone of the 1961 volume that contrasts so sharply with that of 1931. For whereas this earlier volume is thoughtful, graceful of phrase, and often wise, the tone of the later volume is investigative, skeptical, and tough. The young scholars who wrote in 1961 were concerned with taking a good hard look at the communication processes and products around them. They were examining the performance of the media—in elections, in using wire news, in reporting teen-ager problems, in representing foreign countries and international relations, in maintaining a free market place of ideas. They were looking hard at other national communication systems—Burma, Liberia, Latin America, West Germany, and the Soviet Union—and were willing to compare the performance of foreign systems with that of our own. For example, one article in the 1961 volume reported the far from reassuring news that the New York Times concentrated mainly on "procedural" news of a UN session, whereas the Hungarian national press concentrated on "substantive" questions. And the scholars who published in 1961 were deeply concerned with what the media do to their users. They were measuring, for example, the effect of cigarette and cancer news on readers' smoking habits. An article of this kind would never have appeared in the 1931 volume, if for no other reason than because few of the contributors to the 1931 *Journalism Quarterly* would have had the methodological tools to handle it.

There were no statistics to speak of in the 1931 volume, and only a few years ago the *Journalism Quarterly* typically carried no more sophisticated statistics than percentages, comparisons of means, and standard errors of proportions. But more than half the articles in the 1961 volume depend on quantitative data, and about half of *those* use statistics. In the 1961 and nearby volumes regular use is made of t-tests, Chi-squares, nonparametric measures, scaling techniques, factor analysis, multiple correlations, complex analysis of variance.

That this would be worth mentioning at all may seem ridiculous to a habitual reader of, say, the psychological journals where such statistics have been in use for a long time. But that is the very point. Journalism researchers lagged behind the psychologists and sociologists in feeling the need of these quantitative techniques, and only recently, with the introduction of the new quantitative research doctorates, have these techniques blossomed out in the journals and at the annual conventions. Perhaps the first appearance of analysis of variance in the *Quarterly*—used by a journalist who had just taken his degree in psychology—was something of a sensation.[6] That was eighteen years ago. It would be very interesting to know how many journalism schools even owned calculating machines eighteen years ago. Now, a number of them have access to and make frequent use of the great electronic computers. It is worth noting that the chief mathematical models useful in communication research—such as learning theory, scaling theory, and information theory—all have arisen in other fields, but within the last ten years they have been put to good use by journalism researchers. If the development has come slowly and late, it has nevertheless come strongly.

In the last dozen years journalism research, which for a long time had been contributing to research in the humanities, has carved out an area for itself within behavioral science. In the last five years, for the first time, the schools and institutes have had a significant number of young research men, trained in the methods of the behavioral sciences. Fourteen doctorates have been given since 1955 in the tough Stanford program in mass communication research. Somewhat smaller numbers of graduates have come from a few other such doctoral programs, and a few persons well trained in psychology or sociology have allied themselves with schools of journalism or institutes of communication research. These new additions have already made a great difference, and the difference will probably be felt more dramatically in the years to come.

The Need for Theory

But this will be the case only if this new generation of research men seizes the opportunity presented to them—to plan and use their research to contribute to theory.

A very large proportion of journalism research has been descriptive, and the analysis that accompanied the description has not often been of the kind to contribute to theory. By theory here is meant a set of related statements, at a high level of abstraction, from which propositions can be generated that are testable by scientific measurements and on the basis of which predictions can be made about behavior. It is safe to say that we are now out of the great age of description, characterized chiefly by a large number of audience studies. Journalism researchers contributed heavily to the perfecting of readership measurement technique, somewhat less to the technique of estimating listenership. The disappointing feature about this age was the immense proportion of effort that was expended without contributing to theory: survey after survey, resulting only in information on what percentage of male or what percentage of female readers reads a particular item in a particular paper.

Lazarsfeld's dicovery in 1939—that, whereas radio survey results had always been used to tell something about programs, they actually told more about the audiences—had too little effect on readership surveys. We kept our eyes closely on the paper, delineating the readership of editorials, of the classified ads, of the paper above the fold, of news pictures, of the best-read story, etc. If in every survey we had collected merely one different, additional, and related set of facts; if we had turned our attention to the readers and asked *why* they read, and *what kind* of people read *what,* and how reading related to other behavior, we should have made much more use of all this fine technique and great enrgy. But actually the first article that is still quoted on the correlates of newspaper reading (in this case, age, sex, education, and economic status) appeared only in 1949.[7] Nafziger completed his Office of Naval Research work at Minnesota about the same time, correlating newspaper reading with a number of other behaviors and kinds of knowledge.[8] Since that time there has been a considerable activity in describing the motivations and dynamics of reading, listening, and viewing; and this work has merged—as it inevitably must—into studies of the effects of reading, listening, and viewing. From the schools and their related institutes there has lately been a very satisfactory indication of work in this field that promises to have generality of application and to merge into the broader understanding of human motivation and behavior.

But it is significant that the two publications most people would list as the most significant ones in communication research during the last few years depended only in a very small degree on work done in schools of journalism. I am referring to the important summer 1960 number of the *Public Opinion Quarterly,* edited by Daniel Katz, and the related Yale volume on *Attitude Organization and Change,* edited by D. Rosenberg, C. Hovland, *et al.*[9] These two publications represent a highly important convergence of theory which goes much farther than ever before toward permitting us to understand the cognitive processes which intervene between a communication and the resulting attitude change and behavior. For the most part these two books are built on close, careful experiments done in departments of psychology, a large number of them at Yale under the late Carl Hovland.

Journalism research has not been noted for finishing its jobs. Nowhere in journalism has there been a continuing program aimed at clearing away the miasma from a whole area of communication research, a program, for example, like that of Hovland at Yale wherein component after component is systematically varied while others are held constant, with the idea that after a certain amount of these efforts a working model of the interrelationships will emerge.[10] We have done a great deal of describing, and here and there we have performed an experiment (like Tannenbaum's congruity experiment with attitude change)[11] which has cast a bright, if momentary, light over an area of the field. But we have never put any large number of these together in a meaningful way. One of the consummations devoutly to be desired from co-operative research among communication researchers is a few well-thought-out programs which will indeed try to clear out an area related to good behavioral science theory, beginning with the descriptive tools (the surveys and factor analysis), moving then into cleancut experiments (in which, as Roy Carter points out, the statistical techniques may actually be simpler than in the early work), replicating, and feeding the results back into a developing theory. Unless we in this field develop some continuing theoretically oriented research programs of this sort, our progress is going to be very slow and quite unworthy of the skills we now have at our command.

One thing, however, should be clear. Although we have been talking mostly in terms of quantitative research and describing a trend from an almost purely qualitative journalism research of thirty years ago toward a balance today that is slightly on the quantitative side, still what we have written is in no sense a death march for qualitative research. The better the quantitative research, the more qualitative thinking is likely to have gone into it. The more use history, propaganda study, foreign communications system description, and other such chiefly qualitative fields make of quantitative methods, the better they are likely to be. No one wants the kind of development toward quantitative research that inspired one scholar to say to another, "How are you doing, now that you have learned to count and ceased to think?"

Furthermore, it is the very quality of mind which characterizes the best qualitative researchers that is needed by the quantitative researchers if they are to contribute in any important way to theory. That is, they must be able to think broadly, to perceive relationships, to sketch the world on a broad canvas, in order to do really significant work with their quantitative tools. They have not learned to count in order to stop thinking; rather, they must think all the harder because of all the new data they are able to generate. The test of our new quantitative research capacity during the next ten years will be whether it results only in displays of virtuosity or of real understanding. And if it accomplishes the latter, I think we shall find that the insights and thought-patterns of the historian and political scientist and other "nonquantitative" scholars have contributed their share along with the insight and skills of the quantitative behavioral researcher.

On the other hand, it is a distinctly healthy sign that some of our political scientists and historians are now learning to count, and even to count responses in the field. In organizations like the Bureau of Applied Social Research and in many of the communication institutes, qualitative men can co-operate to mutual benefit with quantitative men, and the whole program of the organization can move smoothly from case studies into sample surveys, and thence into experiments and back to qualitative analysis. In a communication research organization which knows its business there is a close relationship between studies of mass media responsibility and mass media effect, although one is necessarily qualitative and the other quantitative. And because this kind of relationship exists throughout the spectrum of communication study, expectation is not that quantitative research will crowd out quantitative or that the two will necessarily live in worlds of their own, but rather that they will go forward together on the road to an adequate theory of communication.

The Need for Co-operative Research

It has been remarked that the incidence of co-operative research in different fields of knowledge correlates quite closely with the difficulty of research at a particular time in a particular field. The more difficult the stage, the more likely it is that groups, rather than individuals, will be able to do what needs doing.

In the case of the mass media, the enormous amount of data gathering and analysis involved, the importance of broad samples, the need of replicating many experiments in this difficult area, and the closeness of contact of the journalism researchers—all these point to the usefulness and desirability of co-operative research. There have been some movements in this direction and will doubtless be more as the supply of highly trained research men is distributed more widely over the country. This co-operation has taken a number of forms. Two or more schools have joined forces to get a field sample. Several schools have informally collaborated to study the content of a sample of newspapers. A number of schools, under the leadership of Minnesota, made the content analyses of newspapers which went into the International Press Institute survey. Formally or informally, research personnel from two schools have sometimes met together to exchange information and plans. Illinois lent its great electronic digital computer, the Iliac, to help Stanford with a large computational problem, at a time before Stanford had similar facilities. On frequent occasions research men in various institutes or departments have replicated experiments or planned them together so that the results would be mutally helpful.

In the years to come this kind of co-operation will continue to be useful but will not be enough. It will be necessary to assemble interdisciplinary teams appropriate to given interdisciplinary problems. For example, suppose that the problem is how communication serves economic and social development in a new nation. To do adequate research of that kind would require at least an economist and an anthropologist, and perhaps a political scientist, in addition to a communication researcher. Research on the nature of meaning would require help from psychology, linguistics, and perhaps logic or philosophy. A study of the organization of a newspaper or a television network would benefit from the aid and advice of a sociologist and perhaps an economist. A study of the social effects of communication might benefit from co-operation with any of the social sciences, depending on the nature of the problem. A study of communication networks may well benefit from the help of a mathematician.

Communication research, studying as it does the basic social process, must thus expect to draw on the co-operation of other scholars with special insights into human interaction. The time is already at hand when many of these problems are too big or too complex for one man working by himself. Therefore, the challenge is to interest other scholars from the appropriate disciplines and to learn to work with them—not on all problems, but on certain key problems, and in many continuing research programs.

Inviting Fields for Research

The trends we have been describing project into the future. But within them what priorities, what areas of special need and promise can we discern? What are the targets for tomorrow?

That is a hard question. The whole field calls. None of H. D. Lasswell's five questions has been answered in general enough terms.[12] None of the great problems is really solved. Communication theory is incomplete and tenuous. Almost anywhere in the broad areas of communication process, institutions, and effect a researcher can stake his claim and begin to dig and, if he digs deep enough, count on striking gold.

Here are a few areas which are not necessarily the top priority ones but, on the other hand, are not chosen quite at random. They are at least interesting, promising, and demanding. And they look like territory in which some of the precious metal lies relatively near the surface.

The Reference Group in the Communication Process

We realize now that one reason we have had difficulty predicting and explaining the apparent effects of mass communication is that we have not taken into account the group structure of the audience. We quickly got rid of the idea that the recipient at the end of the communication chain is an undifferentiated mass, and we began to work on the proposition that the audience of mass communication is composed of individuals. By collecting the usual demographic variables, we found out comparatively little about these individuals and their use of communication. In fact, the United States Army experimenters who reported their results in *Experiments on Mass Com-*

munication[13] concluded that such objective demographic characteristics as age, marital status, rank, length of service, religious affiliation, region of birth, etc., were almost uniformly unrelated to the effects of the films they were testing. Education *was* related. Variables of attitude and motivation were obviously related and helpful. But there was still something missing, something which played an important part in what happened at the end of the communication chain.

A glimmer of this situation came from R. Merton's study of opinion leaders.[14] After identifying these leaders by an elaborate and sophisticated method, he discovered that about half the leaders did, and half did not, read the news magazines which were the commercial reason for his study. None of the elaborate material which had been collected on the leaders served to explain why these two groups should be differentiated, until almost by accident it was noticed that some of the leaders were prone to answer questions largely in terms of the local community, others in terms that extended far beyond the local setting. By a little deeper probing Merton was able to divide his leaders into "locals" and "cosmopolitans," in terms of whether they were oriented to the local social structure or the larger society. When this division was made, then the fact of whether they did or did not read news magazines began to make sense, for it became apparent that one group had far greater social need for news magazines than did the other.

Some time later John and Matilda Riley began an interesting series of experiments with teen-age children[15] in which they discovered that the children's sense of belonging or not belonging to peer groups made great differences in their use of mass communication—for example, in their liking for programs of action and violence and in the kind of comic strips they selected. On the basis of this they posed the hypothesis that the peer group members appeared "to judge media in terms of a criterion which we might call *social utility*, to select media materials which will in some way be immediately useful for group living."

In 1955 Claire Zimmerman and Raymond Bauer found that audiences tended to remember the parts of a communication which would be acceptable to another audience with whom they would later have to communicate, even though that audience held a viewpoint far different from their own.[16] This experiment was replicated, with some changes in design, at Stanford, and with the same result.[17] It was found also that the attitude of this anticipated reference group apparently had some effect on the attitude change brought about in the original receiver of the communication. In other words, the groups an individual thinks he may have to communicate with in the future (the club he will have to address, the fellow workers with whom he will talk, his family) have a powerful effect in what he selects from mass communication, what he remembers, and even the attitudes he takes toward those items.

It is apparent that the audience at the end of the mass communication chain is neither an undifferentiated mass nor an aggregate of completely differentiated individuals. It is rather a complex of overlapping groups. The group relations of every receiver will affect his communication behavior and the results of it.

Now this is a promising shaft sunk into the dark mountain of communication effects. It suggests a basis on which to reconcile the theoretically oriented viewpoint of a scholar like La Piere, which is simply that mass communication has no part in social control, with the practical observation of a man like President John F. Kennedy who complains that political life is becoming "saturated with the tremendous power of mass communication."[18] This problem is not settled, however. Indeed, we are merely beginning to get insights into the part that group relationships play in communication effects. There are probably thirty or forty important experiments clearly called for in this area. But it is clear that there *are* important relationships here and that when we understand them clearly we shall be much nearer to understanding mass communication.

The Communicator

It is hard to explain why journalism researchers, who of all scholars have the most right to believe they know what happens in the act of producing newspapers, magazines, and radio and television programs, have not contributed more than they have to the analysis of these communicators and what they do. This does not imply that we have not written about the communicators of the past (indeed, our journalism histories have been chiefly the shadows of men), or that we have not described for beginning students what newspaper life and work is like, or that we have not collected figures on the annual balance sheets of country weeklies, etc. But how many solid analyses of mass media as social institutions have we produced?

When we think of studies of communicators, we think of Leo Rosten's *The Washington Correspondents.*[19] This was done in the middle 1930's and needs to be done again. The same kind of thing needs to be done for other groups in mass communication: the columnists and commentators, the wire services, the foreign correspondents, the network executives, the film directors and producers, among others. We have an interesting study of the Milwaukee *Journal* staff.[20] This kind of treatment could be applied to other papers and other kinds of communication organizations.

But what we need even more than this last kind of study is a closer analysis of what goes on in a mass communication organization. Perhaps the best example we have is Warren Breed's Columbia Ph. D. dissertation analyzing social relationships and communication processes in a newsroom.[21] A newspaper or a broadcasting station, a magazine office or a film studio, as has been pointed out elsewhere, is itself a communication network. Actually it is a very complex network with many overlapping and related work groups and a complicated system of status, authority, and influence. In fact, when you look at a newspaper in that way and see the complexity of its operation, it seems a little daily miracle that the paper ever gets out. Yet decisions of great importance to us are being made in a newspaper every minute of the day, and it behooves us to know something about the decision process: the flow of the news through the organization, the points at which decisions are made, the pattern of authority and influence, the kind of values and standards that come into use in given places and under given conditions.

Participant observer studies are clearly called for. In the late 1940's David M. White persuaded a telegraph operator to set aside, over a considerable period of time, all the wire copy he rejected and to try to reproduce for White the reasons for rejection.[22] There were certain difficulties with the study. For one thing, the editor became skittish and refused permission for an important part of the material to be published. There was also the technical problem of how to relate the given reasons to what must have been the real reasons. But the study is a kind that could well be done, many times over, with other "gatekeepers," before the gatekeeping process is understood. Another hopeful approach is the critical incident technique. For instance, in 1956 we collected instances from working newspaper men of decisions they had to make or had seen made, within a recent one-

or two-day period, involving some question of professional ethics or responsibility. Adequately done, this kind of thing would reveal not only the existing patterns of communication ethics and practice but also some of the reasons for them and effects of them.

International Communication

Important work in international communication has been done during the last decade at M. I. T., to which the Ford Foundation gave over a million dollars for this purpose; at the laboratory of Hadley Cantril and Lloyd Free, which is financed on a comparable scale; and in a number of universities and research organizations which are not so well financed. Where in the field of nongovernmental research can journalism make its greatest contribution?

So far, journalism's chief contribution has been descriptive: articles on the press of different foreign countries and on the function and organization of the wire services.[23] These have been useful. Whatever one may think of the way the International Press Institute researches were conducted, one must admit that they were in a good and useful direction, for they gave us some picture of the flow of political news between countries and the kind of impression which one country was getting of another. The contribution that schools of journalism made to these studies was not wasted. Furthermore, incomplete though the UNESCO books on the mass media may be, they are still our best source of quick data on the communication systems of different countries,[24] and the contribution of journalism researchers to the technical needs reports and other facts behind these volumes have been valuable.

Nonetheless, when Bruce Smith reviewed ten years of international communication research in the *Public Opinion Quarterly* in the spring of 1956, he concluded that "with due deference to all these developments, it seems to the writer that no very adequate *general* theoretical model of the *international* communication process has yet developed.[25] In other words, he felt that all this work on international communication was not yet quite adding up. And this is the general impression one has as one looks over the rather impressive contribution of journalism to this area—that all this work is not quite adding up.

Take, for instance, the communication systems of various countries. Obviously we need more straight descriptive matter, but preferably in some context which permits comparison and an understanding of the import of the differences. *Four Theories of the Press*[26] attempts to set down four political philosophies into which most of the national communication systems of the world can be classified, and it helps to explain certain important features of the way they function. This is one way in which separate descriptive studies can be made to add up. A similar service could be done in terms of economics and human resources. If one looks at a book like *World Communications,* or *One Day in the World's Press,*[27] or at twenty articles in the *Journalism Quarterly* on twenty countries and their press, it is perfectly apparent that the literacy of each country, the gross national product, the distribution of wealth and population, and other elements are instrumentally related in some way to the pattern by which the press systems have developed. But exactly how? A cross-country study of some of these variables in relation to communication systems would be revealing. Or take the matter of news. It is evident that several different concepts of news exist in the world. For example, the difference between the Soviet concept of news and our own is a key to understanding the media of the two countries and their attempts at communication with each other. How do the concepts of news differ throughout the world? In different countries, what different expectations do people have of their mass communications and how do these communications enter into their daily lives? I am suggesting only a few of the many topics which fall into what one might call a second level of abstraction—that is, more general than the kind of description we have been mostly accustomed to, and pointing toward the kind of general theory of which Bruce Smith laments the lack.

Journalism research has made and doubtless will continue to make important contributions to the understanding of the flow of news and opinion between countries. Here, too, we need a great deal more description. Some of this can be on the general order of the International Press Institute studies. For example, a multilingual student recently made a study of the coverage of the Bandung Conference in six countries of Asia and the West,[28] and the different pictures of that conference were startling. But perhaps more important is a better understanding of the gatekeepers who stand astride the flow of international news and of the kinds of stereotypes and areas of ignorance which determine how that news will be received and interpreted at its destination. One hardly needs to say that it is not necessary in all cases to work with a foreign language or a foreign communication system on this kind of topic. What are we hearing, in our own communities, about foreign countries that are important to us? What concepts of these countries and peoples do we hold, and how have we formed them?

One of the most important communication questions in the world at this moment is how communication can contribute most effectively to the economic and social development of new nations. This is a problem where the economist, the political scientist, the educator, and the communication research man come together. It is one of the problems where theory is desperately needed and in short supply, one of the areas where results can be quickly seen and where insightful findings can be dramatically rewarded.[29]

Studies of Media Performance

It is, of course, a matter of keen regret that the large co-operative study of press performance in the 1956 presidential election could not be made. But this is clearly a temporary setback. Media performance has been and will continue to be described and evaluated. There has been a long tradition of literary and drama criticism, which has carried over to films. Jack Gould, John Crosby, A. J. Liebling, Don Hollenbeck, and others have made some attempt to extend this tradition to newspaper and magazine. Media performance has been studied in a more scholarly vein by persons like S. M. Kingsbury and H. Hart;[30] cases of special-event coverage have been recorded, as for example the press coverage of the Heirens murder trial;[31] Mitchell Charnley has demonstrated a perfectly good way to check up on news accuracy;[32] C. R. Bush, Granville Price, and others, building on a solid foundation of content study by such men as H. D. Lasswell, A. Kaplan, N. Leites, B. Berelson, and I. Pool, have demonstrated feasible ways of measuring the imbalance of political content during an election campaign.[33]

In other words, in this area we are in good shape to describe performance but not so well equipped to evaluate. We have the uneasy feeling that any realistic measurement of political content should be weighted for certain factors—position in the paper, display, pictorial display, etc. That is, it seems that when an editor puts article A on the front page and article B on page 13, or when he puts a banner head on article A and a one-column 18-point head on article B, he is discriminating between those two items just as much as though he were giving them different lengths or emphasizing different aspects of the content. But how does one weight different positions or displays, if, indeed, one should weight them at all? This becomes a problem in effect and can be illuminated by split-run or matched-sample experiments. Again we know that any fair evaluation of media performance must take into account the circumstances of the performance. Why was the decision made? Perhaps there is good reason—or what seemed to the communicator good reason—for an imbalance or an omission, or an inaccuracy. To know more about this selection we have to know more about what goes on in the process of decision-making within the media, and this calls for participant observer and other such studies as mentioned earlier.

Finally, it seems clear that any full understanding of media performance would include a considerable knowledge of what the media mean to the people, how they use them, what they expect of them, and what degree of imbalance is really serious. The Stanford scale of attitudes towards the newspaper is a promising tool of this kind; more about this general topic shall be said in the next section.

But given the caveat that we are better equipped in this area to describe than to interpret and evaluate, still the great questions of a democratic communication system are demanding answers: Are we getting a true and balanced picture of reality? Are we getting the kind and amount of information which is necessary if a "free market place of ideas" is to function? Are we getting the kind and amount of information we need in order to function wisely as citizens in this complex and difficult age?

Mass Communication in the Life of the Individual

Perhaps, as we have suggested before, the pleasant fiction of audience measurements—program ratings, readership percentages, etc.—have tended to cloud up for us what really happens at the end of the communication chain and to keep us from digging into some of the harder questions. Yet there is enough evidence on the motivations and gratifications of mass media use to show what a really exciting field this can be. Why has there been so little development based on Bernard Berelson's stimulating study of "What Missing the Newspaper Means"?[34] Here is an excellent way for getting at the why and how of mass media use—and there are others. Herta Herzog's paper on the use of radio daytime serials[35] was based on straight interviews without the added stimulus of having the medium withdrawn, and the results were extremely provocative. In a chapter of the 1956 yearbook for the National Society for the Study of Education I have summarized some of the work of W. S. Gray, B. Berelson, D. Waples, and K. Tyler in this field, and in an early article I suggested immediate and delayed reward as a tentative patterning for reader choice.[36] This stands neither proved nor disproved. M. S. MacLean's study of factors in news picture interest,[37] and the few studies of factors in news interest, are helpful preliminary explorations. But the area calls for more attention. We owe a better explanation of why people read a newspaper than the pablum about sex, conflict, children, animals, etc., with which baby reporters are fed.

Let us take another side road in this almost limitless area. A very large part of modern mass communication is popular art. This is by no means the same as folk art, for it does not grow out of the people but comes from commercial sources and tends thus to be controlled by the top rather than the bottom of the hierarchy. What is the effect of this popular art on the life of the individual? What is the effect on public taste? Leo Lowenthal has demonstrated the ancient roots of this debate over the effect of commercial entertainment on public taste and values,[39] and Lyman Bryson and others have written penetratingly about popular art.[40] But what does it mean to us, and what changes is it bringing about in us? Is there any connection demonstrable between the violence of popular art and the violence of juvenile crime? What is the connection between "rock 'n roll" and the teenagers' riots that have been occuring when "rock 'n roll" bands play?

One more bypath. We suspect that mass communication has the power to reshape one's picture of environment in spectacular fashion. It seems, for example, that the mass media have the power of conferring great status on individuals who use the media and even of projecting for these individuals a personality which is sometimes at variance with what the facts appear to be. An example of this is the "mother martyr" personality which Kate Smith appeared to project during her bond marathon.[41] Dorothy Kilgallen provides another example of what the mass media can do to give great familiarity and prestige to one of their users. Senator Estes Kefauver is another who, in his crime hearings, experienced the status-conferring power of the media. Another power of the media is to remake the effective geography of its audience; for example, for many individuals in the United States, Hollywood has seemed nearer than the next county. In addition, the media have the power to replace with their mediated experience much of the direct experience with environment which individuals used to get in the small town and the simpler society. For example, many city dwellers now can thank television and print for their only contacts with the growing of food. How does this process work, and how are the media remaking our maps of environment? These are two of the most important questions we can ask.

Mass Communication in the Collective Decision

We started this sample survey of research areas by talking about the group in the communication chain. Now let us return to the same sector and talk about mass communication and the larger group —the state and society. We have several excellent books on election campaigns, all of which throw considerable light on the media in those campaigns. Among these are such volumes as those of Lazarsfeld, Berelson, and Gaudet;[42] Berelson, Lazarsfeld, and McPhee;[43] and A. Campbell.[44] We have some record of what the media can do in disaster situations—what we can abstract from the United States Strategic Bombing Survey and from the disaster projects. We are beginning to pile up enough evidence to understand how the mass media work in some cases of smaller civic decision, especially in the fluoridation elections which, because of their emotional quality and other characteristics, are especially tempting to mass communication researchers. We have some studies of the use of the media by persons with deliberate intent to influence civic decision, all the way from Hitler to Father Coughlin to McCarthy to editorial advertisers. If we could get out some of the material locked in advertising agency files, we should have some extremely useful analyses of the tactics, successes, and failures of the public relations directors who have commanded the last several presidential and congressional elections.

This is a basis for understanding one of the most important aspects of mass communication, but only a basis. These studies do not quite add up. We can yet make with confidence comparatively few generalized statements about how the media function in times of collective decision. Here is an area where the journalism researcher certainly has a special interest and probably a special competence. With his understanding of the media and their audiences, and his constant curiosity about effects, should he not be studying these campaigns, trying to unravel the difficult skein of causation? It is not necessary even to study national campaigns. The fluoridation problem comes to most towns. There are always school bond fights and public relations campaigns, and occasionally an alert researcher can take advantage of an unexpected traumatic event (like the Orson Welles broadcast, Pearl Harbor, the death of a president, or some other news event which will change the lives of people) and go into the field to examine what happened and why.

But, you are saying, these are not the only areas worth working in, probably not even the most important ones. You are absolutely right. There are many areas to work in. There is no shortage of problems. There is only a shortage of people and of time, and sometimes of insight and technique, and above all of the combination at one place and one hour of people, time, insight, and technique. And in the future of journalism research we shall have fewer such shortages.

The Need for Method and Methodological Tools

Basically the tools of communication research derive from the methods of behavioral science, chiefly psychology and sociology. There is more available in the way of method than is commonly used either in the *Journalism Quarterly* or in the research programs of the schools. But there is always a need for tools and instruments which are especially adapted to the study of communication. And the question we want to raise is whether journalism researchers should not take a more active part in filling this need.

Judging from the *Journalism Quarterly*, the quantitative method most germane to journalism research is content analysis; about half the quantitative articles in recent issues have been content studies. But this method was developed in the late 30's and 40's under the leadership of a political scientist, Harold Lasswell; and the chief contributions to it recently have been made by the political scientists, psychologists, linguists, and historians assembled at the Allerton conference of 1955.[45]

The most exciting new methodological development of the last decade has been the semantic differential, developed by Charles Osgood, a psychologist who was appointed to the Illinois Institute of Communications Research and who has been the director of that Institute since 1955.[46] As a tool for the measurement of meaning and for the study of attitudes, the differential has been very widely used. But Dr. Osgood's work on it considerably antedates his work in a communication research institute, and most of the work of development was carried out by psychologists and linguists.

Some of the most original contributions to tool-making by journalism researchers have been in the use of Guttman scaling, for example in the making by Bush, Brinton, and others of the scale of attitudes toward the press.[47] But even this useful instrument has never been developed to the point of establishing an attitudinal base line.

It is worth asking, therefore, whether the development of communication research at the necessary rate will not require more attention to the methodology and instruments of research and whether one objective of schools, departments, and institutes should not be the making of a series of measuring instruments uniquely suited to the study of communication. If we wait for others to make these, we may wait a long time or forever. If we get them when we need them, we shall probably have to make them. Add this, therefore, to the tasks ahead.

Obligations of Research

The basic task of journalism research is that of all research: to contribute to the knowledge which is the common property of men everywhere. This is the basic and general obligation. There can be no doubt about its meaning, and no need to discuss it further. But journalism research, by virtue of its location in or around a quasi-professional school, has at least one obligation of a restrictive and special nature: to serve the profession's needs for research knowledge. Let us look briefly at this latter obligation.

What is the research obligation of a professional school to its profession? What, for example, do medical schools, law schools, and engineering schools do about it? For one thing, they concern themselves with the great problems which confront the professions: they study the cancers, the schizophrenias, the viruses. In the second place, they try to establish ways by which the members of the profession can solve the smaller problems that keep recurring: how to diagnose a given disease or cut into a given area. They feel it is their obligation to work on the *hardest* problems, not the less significant ones; and they find ways *for the profession to solve* the smaller recurring problems. They may show how a disease may be diagnosed, but they do not keep on making all the diagnoses. In the third place, they serve a highly important interpretive function. They play the part of a middleman between the practitioners, on the one hand, and the basic scientists, on the other. They interpret the needs of the profession to the basic scientists, the findings of the scientists to the professionals.

Considering the professional difference between mass communication and these older callings and considering the different relationships of journalism schools with their profession, we can still say that our obligation to the profession is quite closely parallel to that of the older schools. We have an obligation to face the great problems. We have been talking about many of them: why people read and what mass communication means in their lives; the relation of mass communication to delinquency and other social phenomena; the part mass communication plays in the collective decision. We also have some responsibility to find how to solve some of the smaller recurring problems. For example, if most bias in news handling is unconscious bias which comes out under time pressure or other tension, we have an obligation to demonstrate that fact to the news handlers. If there is a better way to measure audiences, we have an obligation to show the profession how to do it. But just as the medical school is not supposed to keep on making all the diagnoses, so the school of journalism is not necessarily expected to keep on making audience measurements once it has demonstrated how. And finally, like the medical and engineering schools, the journalism school should in theory be a middleman to represent the profession in interpreting the research needs of mass communication to other social scientists and in interpreting the relevant findings of social science to the profession.

It is true that mass communication does not ask the schools for a great deal of research. Compared with the older professions like medicine, it does not really use a lot of research. The kind it does use is chiefly market research of one kind or another, to determine the size and makeup of audiences and their program preferences and to support advertising. The advertising branches of mass communication have some interest in studying the communication process, and the technical units have a large research program of their own—for example, in color television or in typesetting by photographic processes.

Second only to our obligation to advance knowledge is the obligation to interpret and convey research knowledge. We have never asumed very seriously the middleman role, and it is fascinating to consider what might happen if we did. For example, hundreds of important mass communicators in this country ought to be excited if they really understood what social science now knows about some of the topics mentioned previously: for example, the part the group plays in the communication process (which amounts to a brand new way of thinking of the audience); why people read (and what the newspaper, TV, radio, film, and magazine really mean to them); how gatekeepers work in mass communication; and the way mass communication can have an effect on society, and how much effect in what kind of situation. Furthermore, if they did understand the relevance of these findings, they ought to be urging us and other researchers to work day and night to push knowledge a little further in these areas. This assumes that they understand these findings and can see the relevance to their public responsibility and professional accomplishment. But is that a fair assumption? And if it is not, how much of the fault is ours for not interpreting these findings in their terms?

Now look at the middleman's job from the other side. How well do we really know the research needs of mass communication—not the market research needs, but the deeper, more substantial needs? Consider the difference between the situations in one of the older professions and in this one. When a doctor enters the practice of internal medicine, he has at hand a book or a series of books which, in effect, codify the field in which he will be working. Here are the diseases known to medical science, their etiology, their symptomology, their prevention, prognosis, and therapy, if any. Now the making of that kind of book was an intellectual achievement of high magnitude. The entire field of internal medicine had to be mapped out, analyzed, and the great needs made very clear. When these needs were known, then all the knowledge of science had to be matched with them, and science had to be put to work to fill in the remaining blanks as soon as possible—to understand the disease of diabetes, for example, to produce an insulin to control it, and to test that treatment and establish a new prognosis. In the field of mass communication there has been no effort comparable to the effort of codifying human diseases in medicine or similar activities in others of the older professions. Is it too fanciful to think that perhaps this kind of thing is part of the job of journalism research? Should we not be studying, far more intensively and systematically than we do, the research needs of mass communication, helping the profession to express its own problems, then interpreting those needs in terms with which social science can deal, and finally matching up the needs with the knowledge in such a way as to illuminate bit by bit the dark areas of practice which even the kleig lights of Hollywood have not been able to touch?

Perhaps this has an overambitious tone, in view of present relationships, but we are talking about *the future* of journalism research, and it will not sound so fantastic ten years from now. In fact, one suspects that in the next two or three decades it will turn out to be one of our greater responsibilities. At the very least, this should be said: as *journalism* researchers we have certain special responsibilities for interpreting our research and other social research to the profession, and that is a responsibility which we have not yet discharged very effectively.

Let us remind ourselves again of the dual responsibility which journalism research holds and will continue to hold in the future. By virtue of its relation to a quasi-professional school, it has a research responsibility to the profession. By virtue of being that part of the university most directly concerned with mass communication, it has also a research responsibility to the public, to science, and to knowledge in general. Many of the great questions about mass communication still need answering, quite enough to keep journalism research busy for a long time. In fact, the future looks very busy indeed.

REFERENCES

1. P. H. Tannenbaum, "The Indexing Process in Communication," *Public Opinion Quarterly*, 19 (1955), 292–302.
2. M. Janowitz, *The Community Press in an Urban Setting* (Glencoe, Ill.: The Free Press, 1952).
3. P. J. Deutschmann, "The Effect of Interest upon Visual Perception of Headline Type Stimuli" (Ph. D. dissertation, Stanford University, 1955).
4. R. T. LaPiere, *Theory of Social Control* (New York: McGraw-Hill, 1954);

P. Lazarsfeld and E. Katz, *Personal Influence* (Glencoe, Ill.: The Free Press, 1955).

5. See *Journalism Quarterly*, Vol. 8, No. 1 (March, 1931).
6. E. English, "A Study of the Readability of Four Newspaper Headline Types," *Journalism Quarterly*, 21 (1944), 217–29.
7. W. Schramm and D. M. White, "Age, Education, and Economic Status: Factors in Newspaper Reading," *Journalism Quarterly*, 26 (1949), 149–66.
8. R. Nafziger, *Newspapers and Their Readers* (2 vols.; Minneapolis: Research Division, University of Minnesota School of Journalism, 1948, 1949, *mimeo.*).
9. D. Katz (ed.), *Attitude Change*, special number of the *Public Opinion Quarterly* (summer, 1960).

   D. Rosenberg, C. Hovland, *et al.*, *Attitude Organization and Change* (New Haven: Yale University Press, 1960).
10. C. I. Hovland, I. L. Janis, and H. H. Kelley, *Communication and Persuasion* (New Haven: Yale University Press, 1953).
11. Tannenbaum's Illinois thesis on this subject was first paraphrased in W. Schramm, *The Process and Effects of Mass Communication* (Urbana: University of Illinois Press, 1954), and later in the *Psychological Review*.
12. Who, says what, in which channel, to whom, with what effect? Lasswell asked these questions in a paper entitled "The Structure and Function of Communication in Society," first published in L. Bryson (ed.), *The Communication of Ideas* (New York: Harper, 1948).
13. C. Hovland, A. Lumsdaine, and F. Sheffield, *Experiments on Mass Communication* (Princeton: Princeton University Press, 1949).
14. R. Merton, "Patterns of Influence," in P. F. Lazarsfeld and F. N. Stanton (eds.), *Communications Research, 1948–49* (New York: Harper, 1949), 180–222.
15. M. W. Riley and J. W. Riley, Jr., "A Sociological Approach to Communications Research," *Public Opinion Quarterly*, 15 (1951), 445–60.
16. C. Zimmerman and R. A. Bauer, "The Effect of an Audience upon What Is Remembered," *Public Opinion Quarterly*, 20 (1956), 238–48.
17. W. Schramm and W. Danielson, "Anticipated Audiences as Determinants of Recall," *Journal of Abnormal and Social Psychology*, 56 (1958), 282–83.
18. LaPiere, *Theory of Social Control*; J. F. Kennedy, in *New York Times Magazine*, February 26, 1956.
19. Leo Rosten, *The Washington Correspondents* (New York: Harcourt, Brace, 1937).
20. F. V. Prugger, "The Social Composition and Training of the Milwaukee *Journal* News Staff," *Journalism Quarterly*, 19 (1941), 231–44.
21. Warren Breed, "The Newspaperman, News, and Society" (Ph. D. dissertation, Columbia University, 1952). For a selection, see Wilbur Schramm, *Mass Communications* (Urbana: University of Illinois, 1960).

22. D. M. White, "The 'Gatekeeper'; A Case Study in the Selection of News," *Journalism Quarterly*, 27 (1950), 383–90.
23. International Press Institute (Zurich, Switzerland): *The Flow of the News* (1953); *As Others See Us* (1954); *Government Pressures on the Press* (1955).
24. E. g., *World Communications*, news agencies, reports of the Technical Needs Commission, etc.
25. B. L. Smith, "Trends in Research on International Communication and Opinion, 1945–55," *Public Opinion Quarterly*, 20 (1956), 182–96.
26. F. Siebert, T. B. Peterson, and W. Schramm, *Four Theories of the Press* (Urbana: University of Illinois Press, 1956).
27. *World Communications* (5th ed.; Paris: UNESCO, 1962). Wilbur Schramm, *One Day in the World's Press* (Stanford: Stanford University Press, 1959).
28. I. Burney, "Newspaper Coverage of the Bandung Conference" (Master's thesis, Stanford University, 1956).
29. One part of this problem of special interest to communication researchers is the social and individual effect of some of the news media and devices of communication.
30. S. M. Kingsbury, H. Hart, *et al.*, *Newspapers and the News* (New York: Putnam, 1937).
31. L. Gottlieb, "Radio and Newspaper Reports of the Heirens Murder Case," *Journalism Quarterly*, 24 (1947), 97–108.
32. Mitchell V. Charnley, "A Study of Newspaper Accuracy," *Journalism Quarterly*, 13 (1936), 394–401.
33. C. R. Bush, "The Analysis of Political Campaign News," *Journalism Quarterly*, 28 (1951), 250–52; Granville Price, "A Method for Analyzing Newspaper Campaign Coverage," *Journalism Quarterly*, 31 (1954), 447–58; D. Lasswell, N. Leites, *et al.*, *Language of Politics* (New York: Stewart, 1949); Bernard Berelson, *Content Analysis as a Tool of Communications Research* (Glencoe, Ill.: The Free Press, 1952); I. Pool, *The Prestige Papers* (Stanford: Hoover Library and Institute, 1952).
34. Bernard Berelson, "What Missing the Newspaper Means," in P. F. Lazarsfeld and F. N. Stanton (eds.), *Communications Research, 1948–49* (New York: Harper, 1949).
35. Herta Herzog, "Motivations and Gratifications in Daily Serial Listening," in P. F. Lazarsfeld and F. N. Stanton (eds.), *Radio Research* (New York: Duell, Sloan, and Pearce, 1944).
36. W. Schramm, "Why Adults Read," in N. Henry (ed.), *Adult Reading*, yearbook of the National Society for the Study of Education (Chicago: University of Chicago Press, 1956), and "The Nature of Jews," *Journalism Quarterly*, 26 (1949), 259–69.
37. M. S. MacLean and W. R. Hazard, "Women's Interest in Pictures: The Badger Village Study," *Journalism Quarterly*, 30 (1953), 139–62.
38. Factor analyses, applications of motivational theory, and other techniques are now beginning to be used on this problem. Some of the results are very promising.

39. L. Lowenthal, "Historical Perspectives of Popular Culture," *American Journal of Sociology*, 55 (1950), 323–32.
40. L. Bryson, "Popular Art," in L. Bryson (ed.), *The Communication of Ideas* (New York: Harper, 1948). See also David M. White and Bernard Rosenberg (eds.), *Mass Culture: The Popular Arts in America* (Glencoe, Ill.: The Free Press, 1957).
41. R. Merton, *Mass Persuasion* (New York: Harper, 1946).
42. P. F. Lazarsfeld, B. Berelson, and H. Gaudet, *The People's Choice* (New York: Columbia University Press, 1946).
43. B. Berelson, P. F. Lazarsfeld, and W. McPhee, *Voting* (Chicago: University of Chicago Press, 1954).
44. A. Campbell, *et al.*, *The Voter Decides* (Evanston: Row, Peterson, 1954).
45. H. D. Lasswell, *et al.*, *The Language of Politics* (New York, George W. Stewart, 1949). Ithiel de Sola Pool (ed.), *Trends in Content Analysis* (Urbana: University of Illinois Press, 1959).
46. C. E. Osgood, G. J. Suci, P. H. Tannenbaum. *The Measurement of Meaning* (Urbana: University of Illinois Press, 1957).
47. See J. E. Brinton, C. R. Bush, T. M. Newell, *The Newspaper and Its Public* (Stanford: Institute for Communication Research, 1957).

2

Research Planning

MALCOLM S. MACLEAN, JR.

A RESEARCHER without a design is like a house-builder without a plan or a ship's navigator without a chart. Just as the navigator might go off course and flounder on a shoal or the builder construct something which he then must tear down to rebuild, the researcher without a design may miss some of the most valuable possibilities of his research problem. Fruitful hypotheses will likely go by the board. So will analytic schemes. Measurement techniques will tend to be superficial. He will finish with only the barest kind of interpretation of his findings, because he did not really think through in the first place where he was going, what he was after, and how alternative results might contribute to the theory and practical activity which generated the original problem. When this happens in a study that has the outward trimmings of a systematic, "quantitative" piece of research, an injustice is done to behavioral research itself.

Not having planned his study, the researcher may find the data piling higher than he ever imagined they could. He scoops up the piles and rushes to the nearest statistician or research "expert" to ask, "Now, what should I do with it all?" He can only hope that his research "doctor" has a kindly disposition.

However, there seem to be cases where too much attention to planning might have seriously inhibited some very important creative work. There are many communication problems of which we have so little knowledge of the complex processes involved that a good deal of relatively haphazard trial-and-error effort can be fruitful.

For example, a Michigan State doctoral candidate, Albert Talbott, was asked by the manager of an educational televsion station to study people's reactions to different sets of call letters with a view to making a change. Talbott decided to use Stephenson's Q methodology, a method based on having people sort objects on a scale from high to low according to various characteristics.[1] He constructed ninety-six unused call-letter combinations and got a variety of people to sort them in terms of how much they would like them and consider them appropriate for an educational station. His analysis indicated three major types of people: those who liked some combination with the letters TV or 10 (for Channel 10), those who liked sets which spelled some meaningful word, and those who liked letter repetitions, such as WQQQ. His next step was to develop a broader survey of the public in which he would ask respondents their preferences among the sets ranked highest in the Q study. Another phase of the study would determine the kinds and intensities of associations they stimulate.

This is not a case of no planning at all. Nevertheless, this and many other similar incidents show that asking "what would happen if we did so and so" can lead to promising results—and studies like these can be lots of fun. *Sometimes,* as they push into little explored, puzzling problems, they bear more fruit than studies which are planned in every detail.

The Place of Planning in Research.

There seem to be some kinds of studies and some aspects of almost any study which can and should be carefully planned.

Two Approaches to Communication Research

In mass communication research, and indeed all research, two somewhat different approaches are relevant to the planning problem. Some researchers are seeking, rather directly, solutions to practical everyday communication problems. For example, David K. Berlo, Thomas Danbury, and the writer are conducting a study to assist Civil Defense in developing communication strategies.

On the other hand, there are many researchers who focus on one or two particular variables and explore how these operate in different situations and how they relate to other variables which might help to explain them. Here, the congruity studies of Charles E. Osgood, Percy H. Tannenbaum, and others who have followed them are excellent examples.[2] Such studies can be highly practical in the long run where they help to develop principles which can be used by communicators in many different situations.

These two approaches are not independent; they feed into each other. In fact, the same researcher often uses both approaches at the same time. For example, the idea of "local" versus "cosmopolitan" influentials, now widely recognized as a significant variable in communication research, was originally developed out of a practical field study by Robert K. Merton for *Time* magazine.[3]

Problem-Oriented Research

In problem orientation, researchers frequently "feel out" the problem quite unsystematically before proceeding to more carefully planned stages. For example, Jack Prather, Thomas Danbury, and the writer were conducting a study for a television station which expected a new competitor within a few months. Among other things they were trying to determine how time buyers and others felt about the station and its personnel. In this situation it was important to study the client thoroughly. Many discussions were held, and many questions raised with station personnel. The study moved to a somewhat more systematic level: "focused interviews" with appropriate respondents. The focused interview is designed for such exploratory tasks and permits the respondent more latitude in question wording and question order than does the usual interview schedule.[4] The next stage was to be a full-scale survey.

Variable-Oriented Research

Usually studies which focus on variables rather than practical problems can be more readily and fully planned. Such studies often develop a sequence permitting use of essentially the same methods time after time. The variable-oriented researcher usually draws on a particular theory, while the man with the more global problem tends to be more eclectic in his choice of theory. To some extent theories determine the methods used. The problem-oriented study is more flexible, but this very flexibility can become a liability, since it often encourages researchers to "throw everything into the hopper." In either case, unless the researcher has a clear objective and some sort of plan, the sheer volume of the data he collects may become a frustration. (In the chapter which concludes this book Westley continues the discussion of the relationship between theory and measurement at various stages of research.)

Levels of Communication Research

The amount of planning a particular research project requires depends on the level of research appropriate at each stage. At one stage a researcher may be probing, using projective techniques or focused interviews to get relatively few people to express themselves as fully as possible on some subject. Such interviews may provide not only clues on what things may be important for his future study but may also provide rich materials useful in themselves. "Motivational research" functions largely at this level.[5]

At another stage the researcher may be using statements gleaned from the first study to get a systematic picture of the variety of ways in which people orient themselves to aspects of the world around them. Typical of work at this stage is the use of "Q methodology" to develop a typology of persons as to their news reading interests.[6] Subsequently, the researcher might want to focus on one or more of the variables developed at the typology stage in order to conduct experiments to determine how one variable affects another under controlled conditions, as in the case of the Yale studies of communication effects.[7] On the other hand, the next step might be to develop a rather precise description of characteristics of an audience, for example the readers of a particular newspaper. That would call for a survey of a large and representative sample. At another time the researcher might be interested in how people change in certain respects over a relatively long period—months or even years. This would lead him into a longitudinal or "panel" kind of study in which the repeated interviews are conducted with the same persons, as in the research on voting that Bernard Berelson, Paul Lazarsfeld and their colleagues have conducted.[8] Such studies are among the hardest to plan and carry out successfully, yet many of our broad, socially important communication problems (for example the effects of the mass media on conformity) require this kind of work.

At yet another stage the researcher might conduct a field experiment. For example, Donald Murphy's research on *Wallace's Farmer* used "split runs" to test how variations in treatment affect readership.[9] Here failure to plan adequately can be tragic. Numerous studies done under the National Defense Education Act's Title VII attempted to treat variables that were so complex and so ill-defined that it is impossible to draw usable principles from the research.[10]

Instead of probing an organization or institution, the researcher might study a single case, just one person, very intensively.[11] David Manning White's study of the "gatekeeping" decisions of one editor has become a classic, partly because it has stimulated more systematic "gatekeeper" research by Walter Gieber and others.[12]

Countless additional examples might be cited to show something of the range in type and level of communication research. In some of them careful planning is essential to success; in others too rigid planning could have restricted the research unreasonably, with relatively sterile results. Yet nearly every study can be helped by planning, at least planning broad strategy. This is especially true of the instruments and techniques for observation and data collection, sampling, and statistical analyses.

Guidelines for Research Planning

Here, then, are some things to consider in planning research:

Analyze the Problem

Thinking through and analyzing the problem you are studying will simplify planning. It is hard to set your course unless you know where you are going. On the other hand, if you are on an exploratory trip, do not be ashamed to admit that you do not know exactly where you are going. Do not state hypotheses just because you have heard that they are good things to have. But if you do have some good reasons grounded in theory for saying that one thing should lead to another or that you expect Variable X will be directly related to Variable Y, say so and explain why. Ask yourself, the experts around you, the books and journals how far you can go with present knowledge to answer the research questions you are asking. That is the purpose of your "review of related research."

Devise (or Borrow) Your Tools

Words and pictures do not *have* meanings; rather they *elicit* meanings in persons who perceive them. When you are planning your data collection, think of it as a communication situation which you are helping to stage. What kind of situation with what kinds of stimuli (introduced by you) will best elicit responses which will help you to measure the things you want to measure? Sometimes a direct question will do the job. For another purpose, handing the respondent a newspaper and asking him to show you how he goes about reading it might be appropriate. In still another situation you might have a confederate act pleased or displeased by what the respondent has said. Use your imagination.

Make use of already available instruments where you cannot construct something better. When you invent your own, you will have to provide some evidence that your data have reasonably high reliability and validity. (Do they consistently come up with the answer? Do they really measure the thing you are trying to measure? These issues are discussed more fully in Deutschmann's chapter.) Usually measures already developed at least have the advantage of previously tested reliability and validity.

Keep a Flow Chart

For anything but the simplest study it may be helpful to develop a kind of analytic flow chart. Often you can state in advance what tables your finished report will contain. Especially where you have specific hypotheses, it may be useful to indicate these by preparing the tables into which you will put the figures resulting from your research. Analysis sometimes becomes very complicated, and such "dummy tables" will permit you to see what steps must be taken between the data gathering step and the analysis. For example, it may be necessary to convert information items into some sort of scale. Your planning will then take into account how you get from the separate items to a position on a scale.

Describe the Analytical Scheme

Your problem itself will probably suggest an analytic model. Every type of analysis has its advantages and limitations. Much depends on the kinds of statements you want to be able to make when you have finished. If you want to test effects—that is, to be able to say that this factor produced that result under these conditions—an experimental design is probably called for (see Tannenbaum's chapter), and the analytical scheme may call for "analysis of variance." If, however, you want to assess the degree of relationship among a number of variables as they occur in a natural environment, your best bet may be a field survey (see Carter's chapter), in which case the appropriate analytical scheme may be correlation or factor analysis. The field survey may be especially useful if you want simply to describe how a particular population is distributed in various qualitative and quantitative variables. A single study often combines a number of analytic tools into an over-all scheme. Before you decide, you ought to know what types of analyses are available and what each can and cannot do for you. (Alman's and White's chapter gives an idea of some of the available statistical analytic tools.)

Develop the Sample

Few studies are conducted on complete populations, whether these are populations of people or newspaper items or whatever. Certain rules are followed to insure that a sample has as little bias as possible. For your particular problem you may find that you can sample most efficiently through a complex, multistage approach. Or, if you do a controlled experiment, you may have the much simpler problem of random assignment of your experimental subjects to the varied treatments. You may want to pretest the sampling approach, that is, to determine whether your sampling method yields a sample appropriate to your problem. In any case you must know your population, know the sampling possibilities, and know the precision you need before determining how the sample will be drawn. (The chapters by Alman and White, Tannenbaum, and Carter deal with various aspects of sampling.)

Plan Coding and Tabulation

Here is an area where it is easy to go astray, especially in a big project. In a well-planned study of some scope, item responses flow smoothly from completed interview schedules through an IBM puncher onto cards, through electronic machines onto summary cards, through more machines into printed tables which can be copied directly into the research report. If you have such a study, you must plan this flow on the basis of your analytical scheme, your measurements, and the sampling plan. You may also work in tests for statistical reliability. Much is being learned about how to set up programs to handle rapidly even some of the most complex analyses. As soon as you have completed the early stages of your design for this kind of study, take it to a computer expert. You and he will have to learn to speak the same language. But together you may arrive at a method of data reduction which will take a few minutes for a task which might require years to do by hand methods. Not every problem, however, must involve machines. Some can still be done more efficiently by three people with scratch pads. It is part of the planning stage of any study to determine when to use what computer programs and when to do the job by hand.

It is integral to this stage in the design of a study to draw up the "dummy tables" referred to above. These actually amount to a way of stating hypotheses in graphic form. Dummy tables tell you how your data will test the hypotheses you are interested in. They tell you what form your data must take, if the hypothesis is to be tested. They tend to eliminate early the inane hypotheses. They are invaluable in clarifying the picture of your objectives. Making them may suggest new angles, new hypotheses, vital questions which you otherwise might miss.

Make Arrangements for Handling People

Most studies involve doing things with people. The foregoing directions mainly involve asking people to do certain things at certain times. But much is not included about the interrelationships of people in the dynamic process of a study. Instructions for and general training of interviewers and coders, as well as their hiring and supervision, may be an important part of your study. Here again, a little pretesting effort may save a great deal of effort. Space in which people can work may need to be procured ahead of time. An experimenter will need to describe exactly the conditions under which he will treat his experimental subjects and how they are to be handled. Clearly defined responsibilities for staff members or for assistants in a less formal arrangement may contribute to the success of a project.

There usually are other elements you need to consider. Each new research experience will provide clues to what they are. One of the best ways to learn from those research experiences is to keep a study workbook. Whereas the design is a set of directions for what should be done, the workbook is a detailed report or, more exactly, a file of what was done. It includes every phase of research action from beginning to end—from notes on the first conferences with the research clients, if there are some, to the last bill for getting the research report published. So, make notes and keep them.

Carrying Out the Study Plan

An extended illustration may help to clarify the planning procedure. Let us describe the planning of a study which has since been published.

Choosing and Defining a Problem

Richard F. Carter pointed out in his study of the structure of controversial news stories that newspaper men have tried to write objectively of controversial issues.[13] But *intent* does not assure *effect.* Thus he was interested in finding out the effects of several alternative methods of structuring controversial news story elements.

A concept from perception theory led him to hypothesize different structural forms. Psychologists have recognized the effect of "set" in perception. For instance, studies have shown that a person who has decided his position or attitude will tend perceptually to reject elements in disagreement with this set. This set may be attained as follows: The reader recognizes from the first few words of the story what his position is with respect to the controversial issue. If the first paragraph cites someone as expressing his opinion on the issue, the reader recognizes his agreement or disagreement with the stated position—or authority—and may selectively read and comprehend the remainder of the story accordingly. (The reader may not recognize a common position, but he may form an opinion on the basis of the first few words and then selectively read and comprehend what follows.)

Identifying Key Concepts

Carter stipulated three important elements in the controversial news story: the issues, arguments related to the issues, and names associated with the issues.

The comprehension of these elements might be affected by two factors in news story structure as it is commonly practiced. Sets might be produced or elicited in these ways: First, the ordering of elements might bring about a set in the reader—if one side were presented before the other side of the issue. Second, if the elements were presented together as, for example, "Senator ——— said . . .," the influence of the authority for the position might bring about a set in the reader.

Carter's hypotheses, then, were these:

1. There is an effect on the comprehension of story elements as a consequence of the order of presentation for two sides of a controversial issue.

2. There is an effect on the comprehension of issues as a consequence of their congruent position with names associated with them in the controversial news story.

Carter concluded that several additional factors might influence these possible relationships. The familiarity of the reader with the issues could affect not only the *level* of comprehension but also the *relationship* between comprehension and story structure. And the familiarity of the reader with the structuring methods might also have some effect—that is, the reader familiar with current practices of reporting controversy might discount opening statements and alert himself throughout his reading. It would therefore be necessary to gather data on these characteristics of the reading audience sample.

Devising Measures

Measures were needed on these characteristics:

1. The independent variables—the structural forms. The measures here are qualitive. A news story was said to have (or not to have) certain structural characteristics. The independent variable was given three forms, which are shown below in a table from Carter's *Journalism Quarterly* article.[14]

2. The dependent variables—the story elements. He again used a qualitative measure, whether or not the experimental subjects could recall the issues, arguments related to the issues, and the names associated with the issues. Two items were to be recalled for each story element. For example, to measure comprehension of the elements in a story on farm price support levels, he asked his subjects:

a. What methods were advanced to give farmers higher prices:
   (1) (Flexible, lowered) price guarantees;
   (2) (Fixed, high) price guarantees.

b. What argument is given for each side:
   (1) would encourage higher (consumption) of farmers' produce;
   (2) production (costs) of farmers are higher.

c Who is associated with each plan:
   (1) Sec. of Agriculture (Benson) ;
   (2) Senator (Wiley) , Wis.

Given six stories, the experimental subject would have to recall, if possible, twelve issues, twelve related arguments, and twelve names.

3. Mediating variables—familiarity with story content and familiarity with structural forms. The "familiarity with story content" measure began as a qualitative measure, but through Guttman scale analysis it was converted to a quantitative measure. That is, the experimental subjects could be given a numerical score for their familiarity with the story content. The question used to get at story content familiarity is given below:

Under each of these subjects mark *all* the responses which describe your previous relation to it:

—— heard about it;
—— read about it;
—— talked about it;
—— written on it.

The question was asked for each of the six subject matters used in the structured stories.

To determine the familiarity of the experimental subjects with commonly used structural form, the following question was asked:

How much do you read newspapers for public affairs (politics, economic news, etc.):

—— not at all; —— occasionally; —— usually;
—— often; —— always.

The assumption was that exposure to newspapers for public affairs news is indicative of (i.e., related to) familiarity with their story structures. This too is a qualitative measure. These questions were then pretested to see if they would discriminate among experimental subjects, for if there is no variance among the measures, the questions

TABLE 1

STRUCTURE TYPES—A SCHEMATIC DIAGRAM

Paragraph	*Structure Type*	
Type I	*Type II*	*Type III*
1. One side is presented with its associated name; other side is excluded	Controversy is presented, but neither side of controversy	Controversy is presented, but neither side of controversy
2. Follow-up to 1st paragraph still on one side; mention of related arguments	One side of issue is presented with associated name	Two sides of issue are presented without associated names
3. Transition to other side of issue with associated name	Arguments related to side in 2nd paragraph are presented	Arguments related to one side of issue presented with name
4. Follow-up to 3rd paragraph on other side; mention of related arguments	Other side of issue presented with associated name	Arguments related to other side of issue presented with name
5.	Arguments related to side in 4th paragraph are presented	

are useless. (It is good procedure, of course, to submit your questions to experts for their suggestions before pretesting.)

Decisions on measures greatly affect analysis procedures and consequent results. If you convert a qualitative measure to a quantitative measure, then you must show cause. (This is discussed further in the next section.)

Not only must we consider factors which affect our principal hypotheses (as the mediating variables cited above), but we must also carefully watch for factors which might affect our measures of the variables in our hypotheses. One such problem is the order of questions: does the response to one question dispose the experimental subject to a particular response for a succeeding question?

Devising the Analytical Scheme

Analysis concerns itself with two problems: *What* do we analyze, and *how* do we analyze? Let us look first at *what* Carter was analyzing. Here we go back to measurement to see what measures he had to work with. His questions were designed to evoke qualitative answers. However, his analysis specified the use of quantitative measures for comprehension of story elements and familiarity with the story content.

He used the technique of analysis of variance for the analysis of differences in the comprehension of the story elements. This technique necessitates normal distribution of measures on the variable studied and is also to be used when the distance between measure intervals is equal (e. g., the distance from 1 to 2 is the same as from 0 to 1). He had to assume that his qualitative measures met these criteria. Further, the possible score on any element for a given score was 2. This reduces drastically the amount of variance possible and might affect the results.

When he made the transition from qualitative to quantitative for scores on familiarity with subject matter, he was on sounder ground. A Guttman scale analysis showed reproducibility of over .90. This means that the responses to this question were indeed measuring the same area of meaning, but in addition, it gives us some justification for assigning numerical values to the responses. (Again, let us emphasize the benefits to be gained in this area from reading the chapter by Deutschmann and the sources referred to therein.)

Now let us turn to the *how* of Carter's analysis scheme. The two major hypotheses stated above stipulated relationships of structure types to story elements. These hypotheses can be stated as "null hypotheses." That is, he tested them to see if chance could or could not account for the observed results. There are two ways to test for chance variation: significant differences and significant correlation. (They are, however, two sides of the same coin; for when we say there exist significant *differences* in the observed results, we are saying that the independent variable is *correlated* with the dependent variable.)

The test of significant differences was applied to the relationship of structure types to comprehended story elements. Carter used Fisher's analysis of variance technique in making his analytical design. He proceeded as follows: Each experimental subject read six stories, representing two repetitions of each structural type. His possible comprehension score was 2 for any story element for a given story. Thus an experimental subject's score could vary from 0 to 2. A score was also assigned each structure type, according to the number of elements correctly comprehended from stories containing a given structure. The analysis of variance technique compares the variance among the structure type scores with that among the experimental subjects' comprehension scores for a given element.

Perhaps we can see more clearly what is going on if we inspect the design.

STORY:

I	II	III	IV	V	VI
A	B	C	A	B	C
B	C	A	B	C	A
C	A	B	C	A	B

Where: A, B, C are the structure types. The six stories were presented in different orders (three), but the essential feature of the design is the alternate ordering of the structure types, without repeating any structure type with any story. Because no structure type occurs more than once with any story, it is possible to isolate the variance among stories (in terms of the dependent variable, story element comprehension). In this way a purer test of the effects of story structure was provided.

Tannenbaum's chapter goes more deeply into the problem of controls, but we see above one instance of *control by analysis*. It was possible to ascertain, and remove, the effect of story differences while studying the relationships specified in our hypotheses. (Another form of control is *direct control,* where possible factors are removed or equalized before analysis. Carter equalized the difficulty of his stories by equating them on readability as defined by Flesch. This was necessary because story difficulty could be encouraged or discouraged as the result of imposing structural differences.)

Ordering the structure types and stories in different sequences is also a form of control. But it is *assumed* control, in that the author expects any effect or ordering to be randomized by the different order sequences.

The analytical design is one of basic simplicity, with the simplicity achieved by numerous controls. The design for the analysis asks the question: Does the variance in comprehension scores for the story elements differ from chance variation when we go from one story structure type to another? And chance variation is estimated on the basis of variance among the experimental subjects' comprehension scores, from which effects of story and structure type had been separated by analysis.

The analytical design, however, had to go further yet. The mediating variables may alter the relationships stated in the hypotheses. The effect of familiarity with structure types was analyzed by going on with the analysis of variance technique. Such analyses were made for two subgroups of experimental subjects who possessed the qualitative characteristics of reading newspapers for public affairs news either "occasionally" or "always."

Significant differences were found to exist among structure types in relation to comprehended issues. The subsequent analysis of subgroups showed this relationship to be most evident among persons who said they read newspapers for public affairs news only "occasionally."

Analysis of the possible effects of familiarity with story content on the hypothesized relationships was not carried out. Rather, it was assumed that any effect would be random. The measure of this familiarity was correlated, however, with the comprehension scores alone. No significant correlations were found, and this would tend to give credence to the assumption. (A design similar to that used in connection with familiarity with structural types might have been used, or a covariance design to accomplish the same purpose.)

The hypotheses were stated generally; that is, there was no distinct hypothesis for each story element. But this is implied, and the analysis included separate studies of each element. The analysis plan would, of course, be the same for each element.

Earlier, the two hypotheses were stated separately, which would account for differences in the comprehended elements as a function of structure type. In the analytical design, however, they were not separated, and the results accordingly show the effect of order and names-divorced-from-issues acting in conjunction. More explicit consideration of the relation between the hypotheses and the analytical scheme might have prevented this confusion.

Developing the Sample

The study was made on fifty-nine persons, divided into three groups: high school seniors in social science; male college dormitory residents; and members of the League of Women Voters. Each of these groups was in turn divided into three groups so that any group did not read any of the three sequences of stories out of equal proportion. This did not prevent the reconstituting of the three original groups for analysis purposes, however.

But in order to combine all the groups for the analysis, it had to be shown that they were all from the same population—that is, that they were homogeneous with respect to the dependent variables being studied. M. S. Bartlett provides a test for this which fits in easily with the analysis of variance techniques.[15]

Why did it have to be shown that they were all from the same population? Because Carter wanted his results to be applicable for a larger population than the fifty-nine persons studied. In sampling for experimental or survey studies we need to know that our sample does come from the larger population we want to know more about.

The methods differ for selecting samples according to whether we want to ascertain the existence of a relationship or the extent of a relationship in a population. In this study the research man wanted to see if the hypothesized relationships existed. Thus, he made a first assumption that all members of a population would evince this relationship to some extent. Any sample of sufficient size, therefore, should indicate the existence of this relationship beyond chance occurrence.

If he wanted to know the extent that this relationship existed in that population, he would have to draw a strict probability sample to find out the information.

There are many decisions to be made in sampling, and the chapters by Tannenbaum, Carter, and Alman and White will help considerably with these problems.

Planning the Coding and Tabulation

The coding in Carter's study is limited to the assignment of numerical values to qualitative data, which we have already discussed. Working with relatively few variables and experimental subjects, he did not punch his codes into IBM cards for the analysis but entered them directly into tables.

The tabulation procedure follows from our statements of the hypotheses and analysis procedures. The table below, taken from Carter's *Journalism Quarterly* article,[16] shows how the variables from the hypotheses emerge finally at the tabulation stage.

TABLE 2

TOTAL ISSUES CORRECT BY STRUCTURE TYPES AND GROUPS

Groups	*No. in Group*	*I*	*II*	*III*	*Totals*
High School	14	26	31	37	94
College	22	49	54	62	165
League	23	60	59	62	181
Totals	59	135	144	161	440

Working Out the Logistics

Even a relatively small experimental study like this one has many operational problems. For instance, time and personnel had to be budgeted against available resources. In his study Carter coded, tabulated, and analyzed his own data. A larger study would necessitate instructions and arrangements for hired coders, analysts, and perhaps even project assistants to oversee the experimental situations in the absence of the director.

If the coded material had been punched in cards, arrangements would have to be made for machine time and machine operators. Machine tabulations would perhaps have to be converted for analysis purposes.

For all studies there are problems of arranging to have subjects available for testing—or interviewing—at times convenient to investigator and subjects. A report must be written, with concurrent arrangements for illustrations and tables for inclusion, etc. The details of research are multifold.

In Summary

In summary, it pays to plan. You may have noticed in the above example that there are, already written or at least outlined in detail, some vital parts of the final research report. They can be revised, where necessary, as we move along through the project. It is better to plan carefully and early and to revise later than to do little planning and to face weak or unintelligible results later. Also, if you are submitting your research proposal to somebody for funds, this early detailed planning will help to make your budget estimates more realistic than they might otherwise be. It is too easy, when one looks vaguely into a future study, to forget or ignore some of the costly little needs that will emerge later.

On the other hand, effective planning need not lead to inflexibility. Sometimes it is important to get a start even when you do not know where an idea will lead. Sometimes a surprising result will suggest wholly new directions, and old plans will have to be scrapped. Nevertheless, research is a complex task in which every step is related to every other step from literature search to final report. It takes effective planning to tie them all together into a significant contribution to knowledge.

REFERENCES

1. William Stephenson, *The Study of Behavior* (Chicago: University of Chicago Press, 1955).
2. Charles E. Osgood and Percy H. Tannenbaum, "The Principle of Congruity in the Prediction of Attitude Change," *Psychological Review*, 62 (1955), 42–55; "Attitude Change and the Principle of Congruity" in Wilbur Schramm (ed.), *The Process and Effects of Mass Communication* (Urbana: University of Illinois Press, 1955), 251–60.
3. Robert K. Merton, "Patterns of Influence: A Study of Interpersonal Influence and of Communications Behavior in a Local Community," in Paul F. Lazarsfeld and Frank Stanton, *Communications Research, 1948–49* (New York: Harper, 1949).
4. Robert Merton, Marjorie Fiske, and Patricia Kendall, *The Focused Interview* (Glencoe, Ill.: The Free Press, 1956).
5. Ernest Dichter, *The Strategy of Desire* (Garden City, N. Y.: Doubleday, 1960). Pierre Martineau, *Motivation in Advertising* (New York: McGraw-Hill, 1957).
6. Thomas Danbury and William Stephenson, "Typology of Newspaper

Readers." Paper read at the August, 1960, meeting of the Association for Education in Journalism at Pennsylvania State University.

7. Carl I. Hovland, *et al.*, *Yale Studies in Attitude and Communication* (Vol. 1: *The Order of Presentation in Persuasion*; Vol. 2: *Personality and Persuasibility* [New Haven: Yale University Press, 1957, 1959]).
8. Bernard Berelson, Hazel Gaudet, and Paul F. Lazarsfeld, *The People's Choice* (New York: Columbia University Press, 1948). Angus Campbell, Gerald Gurin, and Warren E. Miller, *The Voter Decides* (New York: Row, Peterson & Co., 1954).
9. Donald R. Murphy, *What Farmers Read and Like* (Ames, Iowa: Iowa State University Press, 1962).
10. Malcolm S. MacLean, Jr., " Critical Analysis of 12 Recent Title VII Research Reports," *Audio-Visual Communication Review*, 10 (May-June, 1962), Installment 4, A102–A114.
11. David M. White, " The ' Gatekeeper,' A Case Study in the Selection of News," *Journalism Quarterly*, 27 (1950), 383–90.
12. Walter Gieber, "Across the Desk: A Study of 16 Telegraph Editors," *Journalism Quarterly*, 33 (1956), 423–32; " How the ' Gatekeepers ' View Local Civil Liberties News," *Journalism Quarterly*, 37 (1960), 199–205; " The ' Lovelorn ' Columnist and Her Social Role," *Journalism Quarterly*, 37 (1960), 499–514. Walter Gieber and Walter Johnson, " The City Hall ' Beat ': A Study of Reporter and Source Roles," *Journalism Quarterly*, 38 (1961), 289–97.
13. Richard F. Carter, " Writing Controversial Stories for Comprehension," *Journalism Quarterly*, 32 (1955), 319–28.
14. *Ibid.*
15. Many statistics textbooks give this test. See, e. g., George W. Snedecor, *Statistical Methods* (5th ed.; Ames: Iowa State University Press, 1956), 96–97, 285–89.
16. Note 12 *supra*.

3

Experimental Method in Communication Research

PERCY H. TANNENBAUM

As a procedure of scientific inquiry, experimentation has not enjoyed particularly widespread use or success in journalism and communication research. The research literature in this field contains only a handful of reports of experimental undertakings. Nor can it be said that the focus and caliber of such undertakings have been such as to lead to striking theoretical developments or practical innovations.

But if communication is to achieve any status at all as a science —and this, presumably, is its *raison d'être* as an academic discipline —it must largely be founded upon, though not necessarily limited to, the experimental method. Speculation and conjecture, intuition and insight, classification and correlation—all these have their place in any scientific system; they are the raw materials from which theory is built. But scientifically considered, any theory, however elegant and ingenious it may be, is sterile unless it eventually lends itself to demonstration and verification. Within the scientific method of inquiry, experimentation is one of the principal procedures for determining such verification—a specialized procedure that attempts to reduce the degree of external contamination and internal ambiguity of the results of the inquiry.

This is not to suggest that verification is the only criterion for the acceptance of a theory. Nor does this imply that experimentation is the only method of scientific verification. It is *a* scientific procedure, but not *the* scientific procedure. Also, it is a means and not an end; it is part of the warp and woof of science but should not be confused with science itself. If it possesses certain properties which are customarily labeled as "scientific," there are other procedures which, although they do not share these same properties, also are legitimately within the scientific domain. In short, experimentation might be a condition necessary for the development of a science, but it is not the sufficient condition.

In this chapter, we shall attempt to explore some of the bases for that particular system of inquiry we call experimentation, to consider its chief ingredients, and to consider, too, some of its shortcomings. A particular focus throughout will be the role of experimentation in the fledgling field of communication research. This will not be, however, a how-to-do-it exposition, largely for the reason that no one experimental procedure exists for all given problems. But there are certain characteristics that any experimental undertaking should possess, the *modus operandi* of experimentation, so to speak, and these will be considered.

The Setting for Experimentation

The Motivation of Research

In this age of technological advancement it has become fashionable to think of science as being all clearness and light. To be sure, there is a real and important sense in which science does stand for law and certainty. But enter the portals of an experimental scientist's laboratory—be it a nuclear physicist's, a biologist's, a laboratory psychologist's, or even a communication researcher's—and the impression you get is more likely to be one of confusion than of the order he allegedly yearns for. This impression applies not only to the disarray of his gear and gadgetry but to his thinking and tinkering as well. He usually bears as little resemblance to the deep-eyed, furrow-browed Searcher for Truth as he does to the caricature of the mad scientist frenetically engaged in mystical alchemy. If he does exhibit some zeal and anxiety, it is as likely to be a function of his preoccupation with apparent trivia as of his being on the threshold of great discovery: scurrying around in quest of subjects for his experiments; trying to get some piece of apparatus to work; trying to measure something more exactly, and the like.

Only in moments of retrospective thought is he consciously aware of engaging in genuine science. As B. F. Skinner,[1] among others, has indicated, he need not enter the scientific arena to do battle with the Great Unknown, armed with a Hypothesis and with an Experimental Design. Nor is it necessary for him to tote along a Model, mathematical or otherwise, of the phenomenon he is studying. His Basic Assumptions are many but are rarely derived from a Deductive Theory. If he proceeds by Logic, as he must, it is often less relentless and rigorous than he might hope for. To be a good researcher he need not be consciously aware of all of these elements of scientific procedure—at least not in the sense that the capitalization of these terms implies.

If there is any one thing that characterizes experimental research, it is a type of trial-and-error probing; one might almost say groping. This is not to say that the researcher operates in a vacuum. On the contrary, there is often a body of knowledge that precedes his particular investigations, along with a more or less defined methodology for conducting them. But it is largely a chance proposition, and he is never quite certain what the outcome will be.

Paradoxically, it is this very uncertainty that accounts for the motivation of research as well as for its disenchantments. For experimental research is almost always a by-product of that curious mixture of doubt and certainty, of curiosity and faith, that separates the empiricist from the strictly rational pure theorist. A singular characteristic of scientific inquiry, then, is that it encourages doubt instead of suppressing it. From such a faith in doubt, as it were, is generated the motivation for conducting a particular piece of research.

Being a "doubting Thomas," the researcher is never fully sure nor satisfied. The exhilaration he may experience on completing an individual experiment is almost always blunted by the very uncertainty which initiates it. So he investigates and reinvestigates, checks and rechecks, always searching for something new.

Why all this relentless activity? It has, of course, a reason and an end purpose. This ultimate goal is difficult to pin down, but if one were pressed to do so, the issue might well resolve itself into the principle of *parsimony*: to describe accurately and predict a maximum number of events from a minimum number of postulates. So that while he may be largely motivated by an ever-present doubt, the experimentalist also has an unvarying faith—faith in the existence of an underlying *order*, if not in a basic lawfulness. His activity is almost always predicated on the belief that a basic set of principles does in fact exist to explain a particular phenomenon. And this search for parsimony is not merely a matter of elegance or economy. It is a matter of uncovering order and of understanding that order. From such understanding comes prediction and possibly control.

The experimentalist, of course, is usually a more modest and unassuming soul than such a lofty goal would imply. In a real sense, his motivation is not unlike that of the mountain climber who, when asked why he attempted to scale the world's highest peak, replied simply and honestly: "Because it is there." So, too, with the research scientist. Ask him why he pursues a particular line of inquiry, and he is liable to reply, "It interests me," or words to that effect. But underlying both his activity and that of the mountain climber—or the butterfly collector, for that matter—is an intense curiosity and a particular, even peculiar, faith. Like all faiths, science has its rituals and its procedures.

Establishing Functional Relationships

The procedures of science are outlined elsewhere in this book. These characterize the body of knowledge and experience that comprises the so-called scientific method—the way in which science progresses from doubt to certainty.

The scientific method aims at precision and exactness. This is why it relies so heavily on the use of rigorous logic and equally rigorous procedures for verification. By use of logic, it seeks to establish relationships that assume the form of *functions.* Although such relationships do not have to be expressed in mathematical terminology, they should, ideally, have the characteristics of mathematical functions.

There are three such characteristics to consider in defining any function: There must be a *domain* of one variable, a *range* of the second variable, and a *rule* or function that associates every element in the domain with some element in the range. It is then possible to chart any value of the domain into a value of the range via the prescribed rule.

In science we usually seek to establish such functions between two sets of variables—moreover, functions which imply *causal* relationships. The factors of causation that belong to the domain are called the *independent variables*; the factors of effect that belong to the range are called the *dependent variables.* We usually can specify the dependent variables quite readily; i. e., we know what effects we are interested in studying. But we are often in the dark regarding the crucial independent variables: we are not certain which factors cause these effects. On the basis of theory or hunch, or both, we can often surmise such causal relationships, but science also demands that we prove these suspicions. One role of experimentation, then, is at this more or less exploratory stage to test whether or not the presence of a particular independent variable does have a significant effect on some dependent variable.

But this is not enough. To have a well-defined function we must be able to go beyond just indicating that two variables are related. To say that variable A "leads to" variable B, or that B "is a function of" A, or that A and B "are correlated," indicates only the *what* of the relationship and not the *how*—i. e., we also must be able to specify the rule if the information is to be scientifically useful. Again, theory may provide some clues, but usually we have to plod along in tedious fashion to determine this rule: We induce different levels of independent variable A and get different measures of dependent variable B, and try to deduce the rule from these two sets of data. And this is a second role of experimentation.

In the last analysis science calls for the demonstration of such functional relationships beyond their logical development; it demands *verification.* A central criterion of a science, then, lies in its method of verification. Experimentation is an integral feature of the scientific method in that it provides for such verification under exact and exacting conditions. In a sense it is the acid test for any scientific hunch, hence for any scientific theory.

The Focus for Experimentation in Communication

How and where does experimentation specifically fit into the field of communication? To examine this question we must first take a brief look at the communication process itself.

For our purposes here the communication process may be considered simply as one in which a source transmits some information or meaning to a receiver. To elaborate somewhat, the *source* (which may be an individual person or a complex social institution such as a newspaper, etc.) is motivated to convey some intentions, which it translates into some convenient set of symbols (e.g., written or spoken language, pictures, combinations of musical notes, etc.). We refer to this process of translation of intentions into symbols as *encoding*, and the resulting set of symbols is called the *message*.

The communications process does not stop here. The message, in turn, provides a distinctive source of stimulation for whoever is exposed to it, the *receiver*. But for communication, as such, to take place, it is not sufficient that mere exposure take place. The message also must have some meaning for the receiver: i.e., he must be able to retranslate, or *decode*, the symbols into significances of his own, which may or may not agree with the intentions of the source. This decoding activity is at once the awareness of the significance of the message and a necessary prior condition if the decoder is to do anything as a result of the message.

It is obvious from this too brief representation of the communication process (cf. Wilbur Schramm [2] for a more thorough presentation) that the critical activities are the encoding and decoding behaviors of the source and receiver respectively. The other elements of the process are either necessary products for initiating such behaviors (there must be a source if encoding is to occur, and a message for decoding to occur) or specific products resulting from such behaviors. But both encoding and decoding are learned and implicit processes. They reside within the individual organism and are not directly observable. As a result, we are forced to make *inferences* of these implied processes from their observable consequences. The consequence of encoding is the set of symbols we call the message, and that of decoding is the set of instrumental acts we call the response. These two sets of observable data indicate the two main approaches to communication research and provide the subject matter for that research.

The first or "content-oriented" approach to communication research is best illustrated by studies of content analysis. Here the units for investigation are the characteristics of content and/or structure of the message as such. The analysis of such data allows for inferences of the intentions of the source and of his resulting encoding behavior, and sometimes for inferences of the effects it may produce. Experimentation has been used very little, if at all, in this area of research. Its most significant contribution would be more in bolstering the methodology of content-oriented research than in the formal testing of hypotheses. For example, in the study of daily newspaper performance in the 1956 presidential election proposed by the Association for Education in Journalism's Council on Communication Research,[3] experimental research would have been used in establishing more meaningful categories for content analysis. The proposal was that different suspected message characteristics (e.g., size of story, location of story, headline treatment) would be tested to determine whether they constituted biased news treatment.

The second or "effects-oriented" approach is concerned more directly with communication effects per se. Here the inquiry is directed at establishing and demonstrating functional relationships of the kinds indicated above, and this type of research provides the main focus for experimentation in communication.

The causal or independent variables in this research are usually of two kinds: factors of the message (e.g., the studies on the "indexing process" reported by Percy Tannenbaum) [4] and the factors of the receivers (e.g., the studies of the effect of various social and personality characteristics on susceptibility to persuasion through communication reported by C. I. Hovland, I. L. Janis, and H. H. Kelley).[5] This is why content analysis and audience research are so important for the development of a theory of communication behavior; among other things, they help specify the critical variables that may be operative in determining the why and wherefore of communication effects. The dependent variables in this research are the changes in the kind of decoding activity elicited in the receivers and in the resulting overt behavior. Here we typically focus on the more apparent changes: acquisition of new information and skills; attitude change; etc. Often, however, we are concerned with more remote consequences: e.g., sales fluctuations in studies of advertising effects; voting behavior; and the like.

Where do the specific problems—i.e., the specific cause-effect relationships to be investigated—come from for experimental research in communication? One source has already been hinted at—the results of other inquiry, e.g., from previous content analysis or audience research, and so on. To cite but one possible case: If a content analysis shows a high proportion of violence in television content, and if an audience survey shows a larger number of juvenile viewers of such content, experimentation may be used to test the notion (we can, if we wish, dignify it by calling it an *hypothesis*) that the amount of juvenile delinquency is positively related to the amount of TV violence. Similarly, a review of the research literature such as Schramm's[6] often produces research problems; it both summarizes the findings of earlier research and provides many tantalizing hypotheses for new research.

Another source of problems is established theory. A comprehensive theory will not only be based on the findings of research but should itself lead to detailed predictions of effects. If these predictions stand up under rigorous experimental scrutiny, then the theory becomes accepted. If experimental research fails to substantiate such predictions, then the theory is suspect and must either be revised or rejected. In the field of communication no such established theory exists at the present. But we do have a whole host of hunches, guesses, rules of thumb, and the like, and from such speculation and conjecture stem many of the hypotheses and problems for experimental research.

The Fundamentals of Experimentation

What is meant by "experimentation"? We have used the term rather extensively but have yet to define it. This is not a simple matter, largely because there is no single experimental procedure, and, like so many other concepts, it may have different implications in different contexts. One could attempt a direct frontal approach by encompassing the characteristics that are common to all experiments in a single definition; but, like most attempts at finding a common denominator, this would probably be too trite and sterile for our purposes. Or one could try a back-door approach by blueprinting a model experiment. This, too, would probably be too pristine and unrealistic to be of much use. Perhaps the best procedure would be a rather oblique approach—to start with the most obvious and fundamental characteristics of experiments and proceed from there.

Experimentation is a type of activity we call inquiry, and it deals with observations. This is not to say, of course, that all inquiry and observation are experiments. But the converse is true: all experiments are inquiries and rest on observation. One way to understand more clearly what we mean by experimentation, then, is to establish a dichotomy between experimental and nonexperimental inquiry and to differentiate between them. R. L. Ackoff,[7] following historical precedence, has suggested two dimensions for such differentiation: the problems that are investigated (i. e., the subject matter); and how these problems are investigated (i. e., the methodology).

The Subject Matter of Experiments

All inquiry and research, experimental or otherwise, has a particular problem as its point of initiation. As John Dewey[8] has suggested, people are confronted with a perplexity and from this they isolate a specific problem. As far as the researcher is concerned, it should be noted that such states of perplexity can be aroused while he is considering the work of other people or while he is observing nature first hand. Similarly, the manifestation of the perplexity—i. e., the actual problem he focuses on—can stem from a variety of sources. In any event the researcher must have the mental acuity and alertness to recognize a genuine problem.

But what constitutes a genuine problem? A common criticism of experimentation is that it deals with less pressing and less utilitarian problems than are warranted by the required effort. On the other hand, nonexperimental inquiry is often said to deal with problems of more immediate and practical significance. The history of science, however, contains abundant evidence for the utility of the long-range view and demonstrates that what are seemingly trivial problems may, in the long run, prove to be important ones. From the small acorns of plodding research on atomic structures have grown the big oaks of atomic and hydrogen bombs; from countless, relatively minute experiments there emerged a polio vaccine.

Likewise, not all nonexperimental inquiry deals with problems of the moment. Historical research, for example, is replete with instances of painstaking examination dealing with generalized, long-range problems—e. g., A. J. Toynbee's[9] exhaustive work on the uniformity of historical development, or within the communication field itself, F. S. Siebert's[10] effort to trace the development of press freedom in relation to changing political and social conditions. The distinguishing characteristic between experimental and nonexperimental inquiry does not lie in their respective subject matters.

Before proceeding with this comparison, one might well consider in further detail this charge of triviality of experimentation within the communication area. It is in the behavioral sciences, in general, and communication, in particular, that this criticism appears to be more widsepread and, at least at first glance, more valid. Few, if any, examples of the type cited above from the natural sciences exist in the social sciences to support the notion that experimentation will ultimately pay off, and the communication researcher is often berated for investigating trifling issues or "just trying to prove the obvious."

Much of this criticism is obviously warranted. Many of the critical problems in communication have been side-stepped in research to date, and much of the research has been redundant. There are reasons for this, of course. For one thing, there is a pronounced lack of appropriate measuring devices for many of the presumably critical variables, and without an adequate way of indexing something, it is impossible to study it properly. For another thing, the lack of a systematic theory has forced communication research—which, like most other forms of inquiry, follows a first-things-first procedure —to focus on the multitude of hunches and rules of thumb for problems. The field of communication abounds in such conjecture and speculation, largely because it developed as an academic discipline *after* a considerable period of applied practice. As a consequence, practices and procedures have been adopted without the prior benefit of research and theory. In time they became so established that they are now accepted as fact. When research techniques and measuring instruments are finally developed, it will behoove the researcher to put some of these hunches to test.

This is not to belittle the role that intuition and conjecture play in scientific theory-building. Indeed, every science, even the highly advanced ones, starts from a series of brilliant hunches and usually is dependent on keen intuition and insight for its advancement. But in the final analysis every hunch and every product of inductive or deductive logic must be tested and demonstrated if it is to belong to the body of scientific fact. It follows that the more a particular field relies on such speculation at a given time, the greater is the need for eventual rigorous research; and the area of communication is no exception.

The Methodology of Experimentation

We turn now to the second criterion for distinguishing between experimental and nonexperimental inquiry: how the problem, once it is isolated, is investigated. The difference here is largely a matter of the *degree of control* of the inquiry. In his quest for precision in the solution of a problem the experimentalist exercises a freedom of choice in directing his inquiry so that he relies progressively less on common sense and progressively more on objective control. There are three main characteristics of experimental inquiry that account for this difference: (1) The observations are more objective in experimental inquiry. (2) Possible contamination of the inquiry by outside variables is controlled. (3) There usually is involved a systematic manipulation of the specific variables under observation. Let us examine each of these characteristics in more detail.

Objective observation. In much but not all nonexperimental inquiry, the observations made are subjective ones—i. e., they are dependent on the personal judgments of the individual investigator and are thus subject to his biases and predispositions. This is most apparent perhaps in historical research where the conclusions reached are based on a person's own interpretation of available data. It is apparent, too, in studies of content analysis. For example, two investigators may use somewhat different sets of categories to analyze the same message and hence yield different findings, or two investigators may even use the same categories and yet come out with somewhat different relative frequencies of certain content types.

While scientific research generally aims at reducing such subjectivity, experimental research demands such reduction. This does not mean that experimental research must deal only with cold, hard, impersonal data. If this were true it would have only a limited application in communication research, where many of the problems involve attributes and judgments of human beings. Rather, objective observation means that the data generated must be unadulterated by the personal influence of the investigator; he must maintain a certain aloofness from his data and not allow his own biases to enter in the data-gathering and treatment. Many otherwise well-designed experiments suffer from this lack of objectivity, and hence their findings are suspect. It is equally true, however, that many of the crucial variables in communications are not amenable to objective observation, at least not today, and thus cannot be studied except by subjective judgment.

Another criterion of objectivity often cited is that the observations should yield *quantitative* data. This is actually more a matter of convenience and precision than of objectivity as such. It is true that quantitative data do lend themselves to various statistical treatments that often allow for an objective evaluation of the results of the inquiry, but quantitative data are not objective data in and of themselves. For example, the data from a content analysis may be expressed in quantitative terms but may still be derived from highly subjective judgment.

Controlled conditions. The keystone of the experimental method is the element of control—more specifically, as we shall use the term here, control of all variables other than those under investigation. Many of the dependent variables which a communication researcher is apt to study are susceptible to influence by a wide variety of independent variables. In an experiment we focus our attention on one or more of these independent variables and attempt to control the influence of all the others. The effects of uncontrolled variables may obscure the true nature of the relationships under investigation, or they may lead to fallacious interpretation of the results of the investigation. It is often impossible, particularly in communication, to exercise such control over all possible sources of influence. This is why replication of an experiment is such a desired procedure and not merely a matter of research redundancy. If the results of experimental investigations under a variety of conditions are consistent, then and only then can the demonstrated functional relationship be accepted as fact. If reproducibility of results is not apparent, then the relationship still cannot be regarded as tenable.

As a simple illustration of the pitfalls that are possible under inadequately controlled conditions, consider the following example: An experiment is conducted to measure the difference in learning material presented to two groups, one via television, the other in a standard classroom situation. Analysis of the data shows that the TV group makes a superior score. But unless the two groups were matched for intelligence, initial (pre-exposure) knowledge of the subject matter, and so on, we could not say that TV was the superior form of instruction. In this instance, matching the groups with respect to previous knowledge, IQ, etc., is equivalent to controlling for the influence of these variables.

Or consider another example, this one a little less obvious: There have been literally dozens of studies demonstrating attitude change as a function of an intervening communication. While most of these studies showed significant change, there were several where no significant change occurred, or where the changes were in a direction opposite to that implied in the message. However, when the data from some of these latter studies were reanalyzed, it was found that the pre-exposure attitudes were already very intense and hence not readily amenable to change. When this "external" variable of intensity of original attitude was controlled, we had one explanation for this seeming impasse.

Generally speaking, there are three ways of providing for control:

1. Isolation of effect. If, for one reason or another, a particular variable is considered to be relevant to the behavior in question, one obvious way of controlling its effects is to treat it as an experimental variable itself—i. e., subject it to experimental manipulation and observe its effects. As we shall see later, the current availability of more powerful statistical techniques permits the simultaneous experimental treatment of several independent variables. Under such conditions, it becomes possible to isolate as it were, the respective (and, incidentally, interactive) effects of the various variables under treatment. However, for reasons of economy and elegance of design, it is usually undesirable if not impossible to treat all such potential variables at the same time. The experimentalist then directs his attention to what, on a priori grounds, he figures to be the few most critical variables and attempts to control the remaining variables in some other way.

2. Constancy of effect. In experimental research we usually have several groups of subjects exposed to somewhat different treatments—e. g., we may have an experimental group which receives a communication and a control group which does not receive it, and then we compare the two groups with respect to some dependent variable. One way of controlling the influence of variables other than the experimental one (the absence or presence of the communication message, in this case) is to keep such other variables at a constant level in both groups. Whatever effect is exercised by the experimental variables is then a real one beyond the contaminating influence of the external factors.

There are, in turn, two ways generally available for providing for such constancy of effect: We can *remove* a contaminating variable from the experimental situation and thereby give that variable a constancy level of zero, or we can *induce the same level* of that variable in all our treatment groups. Removal of a variable is probably the more exact procedure, but it is usually the more difficult to accomplish. This is particularly true in communication research where the variables often are properties of the individual that cannot be turned on or off at will. Under some conditions, however, it is possible to remove the variable. For example, if one were studying the information and attitude change resulting from a bona fide magazine article, it is conceivable that knowledge of the magazine from which the article was taken might be a contaminating factor. By hiding the source of the article from all subjects, this variable could be controlled. There are times when we must go to somewhat greater lengths to insure such control. In studies of attitude change it is believed that subjects may react differentially and not give honest responses if they know the purpose of the study. For this reason we often attempt to disguise the purpose of the study in such a manner that the subjects are unaware that their change in attitude is being measured. Tannenbaum [11] even introduced an entirely extraneous test into the experiment to provide for such control.

Inducing a common level of the contaminating variable is usually a much easier and more commonly used procedure. For example, in almost all communication-effects experiments it is assumed that the effect will vary with the degree of attention to the message; we thus try to insure—via instructions and the like—equal exposure and motivation to attend in all subjects. In Tannenbaum's [12] study of the effect of headlines on news story interpretation, the potential contaminating factors of content and size of the story were controlled by having all subjects read the identical stories with only the headline being varied. Similarly, in C. E. Swanson's [13] investigation of readership as a function of readability, two versions of the same content were used as the test material. And there are numerous other examples.

3. Randomization of effect. The above procedures may be used to control those variables which we suspect may contaminate the experimental findings. We specify and isolate such variables and go to some pains to keep their effects constant or at least known. But what about those variables which we do not suspect or which, though we may be suspicious of their influence, we cannot keep constant for one reason or another?

In communication research we deal with many different sources of variation, several of which reside within the individual. Theory has simply not progressed to the stage where many of these variables can be specified—e. g., we suspect that there are factors within the personality of an individual which can influence communication effects, but we cannot identify these factors specifically. The few that can be specified are often not amenable to control either because they cannot—on ethical grounds, if for no other reason—be manipulated at will, or they cannot be indexed adequately with available techniques. As an example of the former we suspect that attitudes derived from family and friends are factors in the development of communication behavior in children, but we cannot legitimately raise a group of children in complete isolation to use as a true control group. As an example of the latter susceptibility to external influence is regarded as a vital personality factor in any communication effects study, but there is no generally accepted way of measuring this variable.

To accommodate for the influence of such vague and generalized factors, we usually make a tacit assumption. We accept the principle of homogeneous distribution of such variables and assume that they are randomly distributed in our various treatment groups. This assumption is not made blindly, of course. We try to select our groups and control our experimental conditions in such a manner that this becomes at least a tenable assumption for that particular experiment. This is why we select our experimental and control groups so that they are not too divergent in basic attributes—intelligence, motivation, etc.—prior to the experimental treatment. For example, if we are forced to use college undergraduates as our subjects, as we often are, we usually select two or more sections from the same course to serve as our treatment group. Or if we are focusing on the general population, we try to use adequate sampling procedures so that many of these factors will be controlled through random distribution.

Another manifestation of this assumption of homogeneous distribution is the use of larger sized samples than might otherwise be necessary. By increasing the number of his observations the researcher has a more reasonable basis for his assumption of randomization, and the larger the sample size the more stable and more representative are his data. Such procedures may not guarantee complete control, but they are steps in approaching it.

Manipulation of experimental variable. The prototype of an ideal experiment is one in which all causal factors but one are kept constant, and that one (the experimental variable) is allowed to vary in a systematic manner while observations of concomitant or successive changes in the dependent variable are made. We have used the term "control" to refer to keeping the nonexperimental variables constant. The term "manipulation" is used to refer to the controlling of the experimental variable by systematic manipulation.

Many times, particularly in so-called "laboratory" experiments, the manipulation is deliberate and intentional. Under such conditions the investigator intervenes to influence the events to be observed and exercises almost complete control over the experimental variables. For example, when Jean Kerrick [14] was interested in investigating the effects of captions on the interpretation of ambiguous pictures, she kept the pictures constant and inserted her own, deliberately manufactured captions. Similarly, C. Hovland and W. Weiss [15] purposely assigned specific sources to the same stories in their study of the effect of source credibility.

But not all experiments must have this element of forced manipulation. The astronomer cannot manipulate the stars and planets of the solar system, yet he can effectively conduct controlled inquiries into their movements and relationships. The social scientist likewise cannot vary the groups of people he studies, but this does not stop him from conducting experiments with groups.

In the field of journalism and communication there are times when conditions are such that deliberate manipulation is not necessary to conduct efficient experiments. When former President Truman spoke in Minneapolis some years ago, C. E. Swanson, J. Jenkins, and R. L. Jones [16] were able to capitalize on the situation and conduct a controlled study. Similarly, Tannenbaum [17] used a live situation in studying the effects of a TV coverage of a congressional subcommittee hearing. More dramatic perhaps was the good fortune of I. L. Janis, A. A. Lumsdaine, and A. I. Gladstone.[18] In June, 1949, they had started a study in which opinion measures were obtained before and after exposure to an "optimistic" message that claimed

Russia could not produce atomic bombs for some time to come. Less than three months later the unexpected announcement was made that the Soviets had exploded such a bomb, and the investigators were able to use this situation to study the effect of preparatory communication on reactions to the news event.

The identification of deliberate manipulation with control has a historical basis in terms of the ideal experiment indicated before. Here, one independent variable is allowed to vary while all others are controlled or held constant, and its effect on the dependent variable is measured. But today the dependence of the dependent variable on any number of independent ones can be determined by modern statistical analysis. Consequently deliberate manipulation is no longer necessary to the same degree as before. It also permits the experimentalist greater freedom; he is no longer confined to the laboratory but can study many relevant problems where they actually occur.

We can now return to our original question: What do we mean by experimentation? A definition may go something like this: Experimental research is research in which one or more independent variables that are assumed to be relevant are systematically manipulated, and their effects, both independent and interactive, on some dependent variables are observed under objective conditions with the possible contaminating effect of other independent variables held constant. This is admittedly a rather lengthy definition, but as we have seen, each element is important.

The Design and Procedure of Experiments

Experimentation is but one form of research activity, and, as such, shares many of the characteristics of design and procedure that any research undertaking assumes. Most of these will be indicated in some detail in another chapter. However, at the risk of redundancy many of these points may profitably be repeated within the context of experimental research. Instead of amplifying these points by resorting to generalized statements of experimental procedure, the author has selected the case-history approach, a step-by-step presentation of one of his own studies. This is not the most representative study in communication nor is it the most significant, but what it lacks in importance is offset to a degree by the accessibility and intimacy of detail.

A Typical Communication Experiment

The experiment to be reported was conducted some years ago at the University of Illinois with a minimum of expense (estimated cost: $200) and was reported in the literature.[19] For this reason many of the smaller details (e.g., the exact nature of the test material, the specific findings, etc.) may be omitted here. We shall attempt merely a survey of what motivated the study and how it was designed and conducted, with reference to the usual steps through which most experiments proceed.

Isolation of the problem. The particular problem for this study stemmed from the author's experience on the news desk of a metropolitan daily newspaper. In the course of his duties he became aware that often radically different headlines decked the same wire-service news story in different papers. He wondered if these different headlines really had different effects on persons exposed to them. This suggested to him an interesting intellectual exercise, but it was not until he arrived at Illinois as a graduate student that the opportunity to test this experimentally was available.

Review of the literature. The first step was to see if anyone else had been titillated by the same problem, and a survey of the available literature was undertaken. He uncovered a number of studies that had investigated the problem to a degree, but none of them had attacked it directly, and the decision was made to proceed with an experimental study.

Formulation of hypotheses. This may not be an essential step in all experimental undertakings, but (especially for the novice) it is more than mere elegance. Experiments are rarely conducted to "explore" a problem. They usually test a possible solution to the problem. We call such possible solutions hypotheses, and if we can state them in concise and precise nomenclature, they often help focus the entire investigation and reduce extraneous detail.

So it was in this case. I had rather vague ideas of what it was I wanted to measure, but under prodding from my mentors, I narrowed the problem down to two hypotheses: (1) Different headlines presented with the same material give rise to different impressions of the content. (2) This effect of the headline is in inverse proportion to the extent to which the story was read. We now had isolated the variables: For the first hypothesis the independent variable was "the headline," and the dependent variable the "impression of the total story"; for the second hypothesis the independent variable was the "extent of reading," and the dependent variable the "effect of the headline."

Operational indices. The next step was defining, in terms of the actual measurement operations to be employed, just what was meant by the concepts indicated in quotation marks above. This is an important step that is often by-passed in research, as it first was in the present study. It was not until after a good deal of time and effort had been put into the planning of the study that these important questions were raised: What do these things mean? How are you going to measure them?

Many of the variables in communication research can be measured with available techniques. Far more cannot be measured—in the sense of using scales with properties of the number system—at present. Yet, if we are to study a variable, we must be able to index it in some way.

Identifying the headline was not too difficult. It was finally decided that here the interest should be in the gross content of the headline as it reflects a particular point of view on a controversial issue. Thus, given a story about a trial, three headlines—one indicating guilt of the defendant, one indicating innocence, and one being noncommittal—would allow for testing the effect of this independent variable. Identifying the dependent variables—impression of the total story—was another matter. After some consideration it was decided to index this variable by a simple opinion question regarding belief in the guilt or innocence of the defendant. Similarly, for the second hypothesis "the extent to which the story is read" was indexed by a simple—and probably inadequate—question asking the respondents to indicate in one of four categories their own extent of reading the particular story. As an index of the dependent variable a simple dichotomy of replies on the first question into those in line with the headline and those discordant with the headline's intention was employed. These were probably not the most sensitive measures, and if we were to repeat the study today, we might employ somewhat more sophisticated ones.

Experimental design. Having an experimental design is usually desirable but not always possible. This refers to setting down a schematic representation of the treatment groups, which offers the advantage of pointing to a proper design for analysis of the data—i. e., which statistical procedure to use. In the present instance this was relatively straightforward. (In other instances the researcher often has to gather his data and then see how he can best handle and analyze it.) At any rate, for the first hypothesis the experimental design looked something like the chart below; and a similar one was available for the second hypothesis. After the appropriate numbers were placed in each cell of the grid, a Chi-square analysis was

Treatment Group	Number of Replies		
	Guilty	*Innocent*	*No Opinion*
Guilty-headline Group			
Innocent-headline Group			
Neutral-headline Group			

rendered (since the data would be expressed in frequencies) to see if there was any significant difference between the three groups in their distribution of replies. Of course, this was easier said than done. We first had to administer the material, get the replies, etc. before we could fill in those magic numbers.

Test material. We had decided at the very outset that we would try to make this study as realistic as possible. Countless different procedures to insure reality presented themselves and were quickly discarded because they were impractical in view of the money and time available. (Most experimental procedures were usually results of such compromise between the ideal and the practical.) For the test material we decided to use news stories written in regular newspaper style and presented on a regular front page. Fate was not too kind, however, and no such realistic situations presented themselves. It was decided to make one up. We selected a plausible though hypothetical topic—an account of a murder trial. The story was written in standard Associated Press style, and three adequate and plausible headlines were prepared. Then, a back copy of the student paper at the University of Iowa was borrowed, and one story that seemed to fit was deleted. In its place the planted story was set up in the same type as used by the *Daily Iowan.* The three altered front pages—one for each headline—were then duplicated by offset printing.

We also had done the same for another story, one dealing with alternate forms of accelerated college programs. This required at least three additional front pages to be run off. For one reason or another it was surmised that there might be some interaction between the two stories, so we arranged for nine front pages to be run off, representing all possible combinations of the two stories and their respective headlines. This was probably unnecessary and more than doubled the printing costs.

Subjects. It was decided, for reasons of economy and availability, to use college undergraduates as subjects in the experiment. But we wanted to have all groups (remember, we had nine by now) matched. For this reason, nine different quiz sections of a Psychology 100 course were selected as subjects (and we would hate to relate the hours spent writing memoranda and holding conferences until this hurdle was cleared).

Questionnaire and instructions. Running off the questionnaire was a fairly simple matter. We knew by now which key questions we wanted to ask, but in order to disguise the aim of the experiment somewhat, these questions were embedded among a larger number. Subjects were told that this was a study of "newspaper reading behavior of a college population" and that they should read the page as they would read it ordinarily. Their attention was also called to the two test stories, along with several others, as typical stories that might interest the average college student.

Was everything under control? We were all set to go at this stage. The test material was ready, so was the questionnaire, and arrangements had been made for subjects. This perhaps is the most crucial moment in any experimental undertaking. One must pause at this point and check every detail to see that none has been overlooked.

Everything looked ship-shape. The test material was such that all groups had the same material except for the particular headlines, the main independent variable. The groups seemed as matched as we could make them. The experimental situation was still of the laboratory type, but it was the closest we could get to a realistic situation under the circumstances.

Collection and analysis of data. The data collection went fairly smoothly. The subjects seemed to co-operate quite readily and appeared reasonably motivated with the task. They read the pages, filled in the questionnaire, and we had our data. Not every study proceeds quite as smoothly, of course. Often, subjects do not co-operate, or something else goes wrong, and the experimenter has to repeat the entire procedure.

For this study the data treatment was also quite simple. We merely counted the number of replies in each category for the different groups, plugged these frequencies into the analysis designs, and ran the Chi-squares. Again, not all analysis proceeds as simply as this. Most studies require many hours of poring over data and often the use of electric computers.

The study was now completed. In writing it up, we merely reported what was done and tried to interpret the findings, which were generally quite clear cut, within a meaningful framework.

This was one of the first experiments we conducted, which partially explains its simplicity. Since then we have been exposed to other, more advanced procedures, and if we were to repeat the study today it would probably be a little more complicated. For one thing, we would attempt to obtain more sensitive measures of "impression" and "extent of reading." For another, we would probably use an analysis of variance design and make one of the independent variables the content of the story. In this way one could pull out the effect of the interaction between headline and story content, which is probably the critical factor involved in this type of behavior. And we might try to get different types of subjects.

Did this study prove anything? As an isolated investigation it probably does not add up to very much. But it did set the stage for a number of other studies all focused on the central theme of an indexing process in communication effects.[20] Considered together, these studies do tell us a little more about how a message achieves its effects. And this is the way science develops: one study leads to another; methodology becomes sharpened; and before too long, a body of knowledge develops.

Other communication experiments differ from this illustrative one in various ways. But almost every one has to go through similar if not identical steps. A problem and a hypothesis must be formulated; a design of some kind must be set up; appropriate test material must be lined up if it is not already available, and so on. All along, the experimenter must pay careful attention to each little detail, because experience has shown him that often the little things turn out to be the big things. Even when the decks are finally cleared and he does embark on a systematic investigation, all well planned and laid out, the pitfalls are many. Apparatuses break down; side issues crop up unexpectedly; his findings may turn out to be unrelated to what he was looking for. But one of the charms of experimental research is that such pitfalls often have their rewards: from broken down apparatuses, newer and better ones are constructed; from an initially distracting side problem may emerge a major issue; he may not find what he set out to find, but what he does find may be more rewarding in the long run.

Experimentation in Communication—Past and Future

The scientific study of journalism and communication is still in its infancy, but there are signs of a growing maturity. Not the least of these omens has been a marked increase in the number and caliber of research undertakings, including experimental research. When C. L. Allen [21] wrote his summary of experimentation in communication less than a decade ago, there was only a handful of such studies to be cited. Today there are only several handfuls, but the rate of such undertakings is definitely on the upsurge. More important, the quality of the research has also improved.

One of the principal reasons for the paucity of research in the past has been the inherent difficulty in conducting experiments. With its demands for exactness, it is often too exacting. Or, as one wag put it: "If you insist too much on experimental rigor, you get rigor mortis in your findings." This is still true to an extent, and there are many authorities who believe that the hallowed role that experimentation has in the physical and natural sciences should not be carried over, lock, stock, and severity of method, to the behavioral sciences. The phenomena are different, they argue, and so should the methods be different. This is neither the time nor the place to speculate on this matter, which only time and experience will decide. In the meantime, it is probably just as well to proceed with what we have available.

But do we have enough available? We can borrow the method of experimentation, but can we apply it to meaningful situations within the field of communication? This points to another source of reasons for the relative lack of experimentation to date: We cannot measure what we would like to measure; we cannot manipulate what we would like to manipulate, and so on. Actually, this has been more true in the past than it is today and will probably be less true in the very near future. In the years since the end of World War II there has been a tremendous upsurge in social science research, and many of the resulting developments appear to be readily applicable to communication.

Foremost among these developments has been the emergence of valid measurement instruments. For example, we now have available a number of scientifically developed scales for the assessment of attitude. Even more promising has been the development of an instrument to measure certain aspects of meaning,[22] another most crucial variable in communication. This instrument, which has been dubbed the "semantic differential," provides a multidimensional measure—i. e., it measures across several different and mutually independent dimensions at once. There are other such instruments being developed at this writing. Together they hold great promise for communication research, because more and more we have been finding that the effects a communication message may have do not vary only in single ways but involve several different attributes at once. Indeed, many of the most striking applications of the semantic differential technique have been directly in the communication area, not only in straight effects studies,[23] but also in such critical yet unexplored areas as aesthetics and psycholinguistics.[24]

Along with this development of measuring instruments, there has been a corresponding—and in many ways, even more encouraging—evolution of new statistical designs and techniques. Most striking among these has been the improvement in sampling techniques, which cut down a good deal of the guesswork involved in drawing a sample and making inferences from that sample to the larger population. Similarly, the analysis of variance technique seems to be tailor-made for communication research. Not only does it allow for the assessment of the effects of a number of independent variables at once, but it also makes possible the identification and indexing of the effects of the interaction between these variables. We have paid considerable lip-service to this concept of interaction in communication, but we rarely have tried to demonstrate it experimentally or to measure its significance in particular situations.

The powerful statistical technique of factor analysis also bodes well for the future of communication research. While it is more an exploratory rather than a hypothesis-testing technique, and hence not directly involved in experimental research, it still can provide the impetus for experimentation. It provides a means for determining the basic dimensionality of large arrays of data and hence may be valuable in specifying the kinds of variables—independent and dependent—that experimentation should focus on. A prime example is M. S. MacLean's and W. R. Hazard's[25] study on news picture preferences. Another is the use of factor analysis in the development of categories for analysis of mental health content in the mass media and in the subsequent application of such findings in experimental situations.[26]

Given such new tools and techniques, it is only natural to expect that more and better experiments will be conducted in communication, along with a focusing on more immediate and practical problems. Lacking the resources to study some of these pressing problems, the communication researcher has had to occupy himself with less significant issues. Now, given the tools, he is in a better position to do the job.

There is still one risk, albeit a calculated one, that experimentation always faces. This is the matter of the derivation of general principles from the findings of single experiments. It is one thing to conduct a neatly designed and well-executed experiment, but it is another to interpret and convert the results of such experimentation into principle and law.

This involves two steps. The first is making logical inferences from the data of observation. Even if our observations are obtained under the most carefully controlled conditions, even greater caution must be exercised in their interpretation. The most common failing here is in assuming that because our data do not disprove the hypothesis, they necessarily demonstrate it to be true. Rigorous application of the principles of formal logic is what is required to prevent our going astray, and this point cannot be overemphasized. The man who conducted a large-scale survey and found that more people died in bed than anywhere else made a very accurate observation. But when he concludes from such data that beds are more dangerous than, say, foxholes, he fails to follow the principles of logical inference. In much the same manner attributing cause-and-effect relationships from correlation data has also led to fallacious and misleading interpretation.

Similarly, there is no substitute for formal logic in the next step of science; organizing these inferences into a generalization or law. In the field of communication we are still a long way from approaching this stage, but when the time comes, we must be sure to be on the alert. There seems to be an almost irresistible urge in the behavioral sciences to generalize the inferences drawn from a series of separate experiments into some short-hand formula or law. This is not necessarily bad, except that all too often it has been premature and has attempted to incorporate too much of behavior under one heading. The rule here is that the law must not attempt to go beyond the data presented and should not include classes of data which have not themselves been subjected to careful observation. This necessitates a lot of work and effort, but such are the ways of science. In the long run, cautious scientific statements may lead to final answers more readily than jumping to quick conclusions. To draw general conclusions from experimental findings is an obvious criterion for their acceptance, but we need not be carried away with it. Not every experiment has to be the key to our knowledge of the communication process. By the same token, the reporting of negative experimental findings—i. e., results which do not confirm the original hypotheses—is also vital in building a theory. There is no need to be apologetic about such findings; they should be presented in much the same manner as positive, tangible results. This will both serve to avoid unnecessary replication of experiments and also point the way to more crucial problems.

REFERENCES

1. B. F. Skinner, "A Case History in Scientific Method," *American Psychologist,* 11 (1956), 221–33.
2. W. Schramm, "How Communication Works," in W. Schramm (ed.), *The Process and Effects of Mass Communication* (Urbana: University of Illinois Press, 1954).
3. R. B. Nixon *et al.,* "A Proposal for the Study of the Role and Performance of the American Daily Newspaper in the 1956 Presidential

Election Campaign," Sigma Delta Chi Committee on Ethics and News Objectivity (1955, *mimeo.*).

4. P. H. Tannenbaum, "The Indexing Process in Communication," *Public Opinion Quarterly*, 19 (1955), 292–302.
5. C. I. Hovland, I. L. Janis, and H. H. Kelley, *Communication and Persuasion* (New Haven: Yale University Press, 1953).
6. W. Schramm, "The Effects of Mass Communications: A Review," *Journalism Quarterly*, 26 (1949), 397–409.
7. R. L. Ackoff, *The Design of Social Research* (Chicago: University of Chicago Press, 1953).
8. J. Dewey, *How We Think* (New York: Heath, 1933).
9. A. J. Toynbee, *A Study of History* (New York: Oxford University Press, 1947).
10. F. S. Siebert, *Freedom of the Press in England 1476–1776* (Urbana: University of Illinois Press, 1952).
11. P. H. Tannenbaum, "Initial Attitudes Toward Source and Concept as Factors in Attitude Change Through Communication," *Public Opinion Quarterly*, 20 (1956), 413–25.
12. P. H. Tannenbaum, "The Effect of Headlines on the Interpretation of News Stories," *Journalism Quarterly*, 30 (1953), 189–97.
13. C. E. Swanson, "Readability and Readership: A Controlled Experiment," *Journalism Quarterly*, 25 (1948), 339–43.
14. Jean S. Kerrick, "The Influence of Captions on Picture Interpretation," *Journalism Quarterly*, 32 (1955), 177–82.
15. C. I. Hovland and W. Weiss, "The Influence of Source Credibility on Communication Effectiveness," *Public Opinion Quarterly*, 15 (1951), 635–50.
16. C. E. Swanson, J. Jenkins, and R. L. Jones, "President Truman Speaks: A Study of Ideas vs. Media," *Journalism Quarterly*, 27 (1950), 251–62.
17. P. H. Tannenbaum, "What Effects When TV Covers a Congressional Hearing?" *Journalism Quarterly*, 32 (1955), 434–40.
18. I. L. Janis, A. A. Lumsdaine, and A. I. Gladstone, "Effects of Preparatory Communications on Reactions to a Subsequent News Event," *Public Opinion Quarterly*, 15 (1951), 487–518.
19. Note 12 *supra.*
20. Note 4 *supra.*
21. C. L. Allen, "The Experimental Method and Communications," in R. O. Nafziger and M. M. Wilkerson (eds.), *An Introduction to Journalism Research* (Baton Rouge: Louisiana State University Press, 1949).
22. C. E. Osgood, G. J. Suci, and P. H. Tannenbaum, *The Measurement of Meaning* (Urbana: University of Illinois Press, 1957).
23. See, e. g., note 17 *supra.*
24. Note 11 *supra.*
25. M. S. MacLean and W. R. Hazard, "Women's Interest in Pictures: the Badger Village Study," *Journalism Quarterly*, 30 (1953), 139-62.
26. C. E. Osgood, J. C. Nunnally *et al.*, *Communication of Mental Health Information; Phase I Report* (Urbana: Institute of Communication Research, University of Illinois, 1955, *mimeo.*).

4

Field Methods in Communication Research

ROY E. CARTER, JR.

FIELD RESEARCH has been variously defined in the social sciences in terms of locus, in terms of procedures used, and in terms of research approaches. In this chapter field research in mass communication is defined as research involving the study of media-related characteristics or behavior which takes the investigator outside the library and laboratory and "into the field" where he looks at *people.* The fact that the behavior or characteristics which are inquired into must be media-related in order for the investigation to qualify as communications research does not mean that the relationship must be that of medium and audience. The research may, for example, deal with initial communicators (e.g., news sources) or with content "gatekeepers" (editors, for example).[1] Furthermore, the mail questionnaire study is treated as a field procedure. Here the investigator's measuring instrument goes into the field and "observes."

Most journalism field studies have been audience inquiries; through the sample survey, an effort has been made to identify and describe the people who make up the audience for some media product (e.g., items in yesterday's newspaper). In general, differential descriptions and breakdowns have been obtained in terms of objective or demographic characteristics like sex, age, education, and rural/urban residence. Sometimes (by means of the panel method) audience behavior has been traced through time, and in a few studies integrated use has been made of content analysis and other research procedures along with the field study.

Distinguishing characteristics of experimental method and research models delineating the controlled experiment are presented in other chapters. Although research specialists usually make a distinction between "analytic" (or "explanatory") and "descriptive" surveys, the explanatory utility of surveys is limited, and even where a controlled experiment is approximated through refined cross-tabulation procedures, the researcher would do well to test his hypotheses further in experiments.

Field study of an audience does, however, yield kinds of data difficult to obtain in the laboratory—information on audience exposure to media content when the normal patterns of "self-selection," the tendencies of people to read or consume content which rewards them, are operative. Suppose controlled experiments with so-called captive audiences establish that editorial A is more persuasive than editorial B, at least for the kind of audience of which the subjects are a sample. The question then arises, how many audience members would select either version and be persuaded by it under more normal conditions? A field survey may show that editorial B has more interest-value for readers than editorial A, when readers are free to read or not read, as they choose. Thus the "weaker" of the two editorials, by attracting *more readers,* may actually prove to be the more persuasive, in terms of the net number of persons reached and influenced.

Ideally, then (1) laboratory findings concerning communication should be cross-validated by field studies, which permit more normal conditions of selection, exposure, and attention level; and (2) suggestive evidence of relationships obtained by surveys should be scrutinized further under the more rigorous control permitted by experiment.

This does not mean that the field researcher himself cannot carry out a controlled experiment. In fact, the split-run technique (the material is changed during the press run) enables him to do just that—he can vary the content of the communication and present it to equivalent audience subgroups by random allocation of the different versions. Samples of groups receiving each version can then be queried to find out how the two versions were differentially perceived, liked, interpreted, or acted upon. Limited use has been made of split-run procedures in communications research, apart from pretesting of advertisements (e.g., via the differential response pull of the same coupon offer contained in two ads for the same product).

Operationally, field research in mass communication generally takes one of the following forms: (1) direct observation of behavior; (2) the interview; (3) the self-administered questionnaire; or (4) some combination of the foregoing procedures.

The first of these procedures is the least frequently used, and the second is the one most frequently encountered in mass media research. Observation may be "participant" or "nonparticipant," "controlled" or "uncontrolled." The self-administered questionnaire may be filled out in a group situation (such as a classroom) or may be left with the respondent to be picked up later. Again, it may travel one or both ways by mail.

The interview may be loosely or highly structured; the respondent may be asked to answer within a framework of response options or may be queried via "open" questions and prodded by "probe" questions. Answers to "open" questions may be coded (classified) by the interviewer or in the survey office.

Emphasis in the following discussion is a function of three interrelated factors: (1) adequacy of existing literature; (2) probable utility of a given procedure to a relatively inexperienced researcher with limited funds; and (3) usefulness of a procedure in the light of current trends in communications research. The focus of the present chapter is on the use of different field procedures in a mass communications research setting. Illustrations from past research and suggestions regarding future research are drawn from the mass media field, but no attempt has been made to outline in detail the steps in conducting, say, a recognition-type survey of newspaper readership. An adequate manual for this somewhat standardized procedure, though needed, would of necessity be longer than this entire chapter.

The mail questionnaire is discussed fully because of its misuse in the past, its potential usefulness in studies of scattered communicators and "gatekeepers," and its popularity with master's degree candidates who may use it unwisely. The discussion of sampling is nontechnical and aims primarily at introducing the student to some of the logical problems involved in drawing samples and in projecting findings to populations. Attention is directed to observation methods because of (1) their neglect in the past and (2) their probable importance in future studies of communication enterprises and of group influences on media-related behavior.

Observation: A Tool in Communication Research

Most knowledge that people have about the behavior of others comes from observation. Sometimes such knowledge is accurate, and at other times it is marked by a great deal of error. If such knowledge were not reasonably dependable, we could not become socialized into group life and could not acquire enough understanding of other persons to see us through even the most rudimentary interpersonal relations. Observation qualifies as a scientific procedure, however, only when it is carried out systematically and yields results which hold up under scrutiny as to their reliability and validity.

For a long while anthropologists have made wide use of participant observation in the study of primitive societies, and sociologists and anthropologists have used variants of this procedure in the study of communities, work groups, informal social organizations, the professions, and such "special" social strata as dance band musicians and prison populations. More recently social psychologists have developed systematic procedures and devices for the observation of interaction in small groups, and a few investigators have used observation in the study of media-related behavior.

It is easier to delimit nonparticipant observation than it is to define participation. Obviously the researcher who observes and records small-group interaction from behind a one-way screen (the observer sees the group but the group sees a mirror) is a non-participant, provided he does not interact with the group, and the same point can be made concerning much scientific observation of children's play groups.

Where the observer interacts with those he studies, there will be varying degrees of participation. Thus William Foote Whyte, introduced to a slum area group as a local historian, was accepted by the group, yet did not always conform to group norms.[2] In retrospect, Whyte has suggested that "total immersion" rarely is practicable; moreover, he points out, participation can lead to a tendency to take for granted (and thus fail to record) behavior which the group takes for granted. Others have suggested that the emotional overtones of participation may reduce the observer's objectivity.[3]

The observer in a social group, then, may have several roles, any or all of which may be operative within a given study: He may be a participant, a learner, or an attentive listener. Many participant observers have been concerned with obtaining a "holistic" description of group structure and group process, rather than with testing specific hypotheses. The range and volume of behavior which is observed, however, makes the recording task a formidable one unless the researcher is armed with fairly clear-cut definitions of what he is looking for.

A usual procedure in participant observation is to obtain, early in the study, the support and approval of leaders in the group or community being studied. A second common practice is the early enlistment of informal collaborators or informants who are at least partially aware of the scope and purpose of the research and have a broad knowledge of the group being studied. Where more than one observer has gathered the data, problems of reliability and bias can be threshed out in group and individual conferences, a procedure which Whyte has called "the heart of the formal training" in such methods. Howard S. Becker has made a general plea for increased formalization and systematization of the techniques used in participant observation. He also describes new *reporting* techniques which give the reader "greater access to the data and procedures on which conclusions are based."[4]

That participant observation and the use of informants can yield results comparable to those obtained by other methods is pointed up by two studies. In the first,[5] informants (Navy enlisted men) ranked the crews of ten ships in a submarine squadron on morale. Rankings correlated .90 with the results obtained by use of a thirty-item morale scale. This finding led the investigator to conclude that "the use of informants in quantitative studies may be successfully carried out and may produce findings of validity and generality." In the second study,[6] two researchers used (1) ratings by an anthropologist field worker and (2) sociometric techniques to measure prestige in a small rural community. The field worker rated, on the basis of their prestige "in the eyes of the community," the two-thirds of the population he had come to know during a year of intensive work. The 547 respondents in the sample survey were asked to name persons exerting leadership or having influence in the community. There was close correspondence between the results obtained by the two methods.

Participant observation requires highly developed research skills and ability to change roles readily and rapidly. Such flexibility and adaptability is not easily acquired, and the problem is complicated further by the fact that, if there is to be any assessment of the reliability of observation, a study will require more than one observer. Although mass media researchers have made little use of participant observation, the technique might be well suited to studies (conspicuously absent from the literature) of power structure, of patterns of influence, and of interaction processes in such a milieu as the newsroom or the editorial conference.

Measurement of exposure to mass media content poses serious validity problems. Respondents may "recall" or "recognize" content to which they have not been exposed, or they may fail to remember content which they have seen or heard. The "actual behavior" measurement procedures which have been used (e.g., "coincidental" phone call, Nielsen Audimeter) are in a sense observation techniques, and the same point may be made with respect to devices like the eye camera and the program analyzer,[7] which in effect are mechanical-electronic observers of audience responses to specific stimuli. Recently, Leo Bogart used an eye-camera technique to obtain records of the advertising which experimental subjects actually *scanned* in a newspaper (as measured by eye fixations). These records were then compared with what was *remembered* in a conventional recognition-type readership survey.[8]

Observation of media exposure has been part of other research designs. Walter Steigleman made a study[9] of headlines and newsstand sales in which he used an observer technique. Lloyd Warner and Paul Lunt, in their "Yankee City" study of social class,[10] stationed helpers at a newsstand to keep tab on who bought what papers and magazines and also placed observers at a theater to chart movie attendance. Mildred Parten described a taxi company's participation in a study of radio listening. (Drivers kept a record of patrons' reactions to the radio's being on or off when they entered cabs.) Observation also has been employed as a research tool in other studies of radio audiences.[11]

H. C. Ludeke and R. A. Inglis once described a procedure in which subjects were given an eye-fatigue test to distract them from the real purpose of the experiment, after which they were seated in a reading room and handed an advance copy of a magazine to read. Observers recorded subjects' reading behavior while viewing them through one-way glass.[12]

Frank Stanton's observation of magazine readers in public places and D. B. Lucas' use of a concurrent-observation procedure to study reader attention to a publication given theater patrons[13] are other examples of communication studies involving observation of audience behavior.

Another aspect of communication research in which observation has been used is the study of news sources and news "gatekeepers." Walter Gieber and Walter Johnson combined observation methods with detailed interviews in a study of relationships between reporters and city-government news sources,[14] and one of Gieber's students employed a participant-observation approach in a study of newspaper reporters in a suburban community.[15]

Charles Swanson, James Jenkins, and Robert Jones, in an intensive study of a major communication event (a presidential address), stationed observers in an auditorium and also in "blue-collar" and "white-collar" bars to record audience responses to the live and telecast speech. One objective (in the case of the auditorium observation) was to check on the performance of *reporters* as observers who pass their observations on to others. In this study, integrated use was made of observation of an event, observation of audience groups, content analysis, a sample survey to determine what was learned and what was remembered, and intensive analysis of individual cases.[16]

One British research organization, Mass Observation, made extensive use of observation methods for a quarter of a century. Procedures included eavesdropping, recording of incidents and street scenes, analysis of wall drawings, sermons, and other verbal and nonverbal communication, and use of a national panel of voluntary observers.[17]

The mass media researcher who uses observation as a tool should set up a content-analysis scheme which will enable him to "keep books" adequately on the behavior he observes. Systems and devices for recording observed behavior have been developed by small-group researchers in social psychology. One of the best-known schemes is R. F. Bales's "interaction process analysis" coding scheme for describing acts which occur in problem-solving groups. Other investigators have produced category systems for the study of leadership in small groups and of "time" aspects of group interaction.[18] Along with these procedures, various mechanical and electronic devices have been used in recording observations. Sometimes, as in the case of the Bales-type analysis, recordings of verbal interaction plus descriptions of nonverbal behavior are used for recoding as a reliability check.

In some small-group studies, however, reliability either has not been reported or has been described in nonquantitative terms (e.g., as "adequate").

Systematic observation procedures must be developed and used in mass media research if future investigators are to deal adequately with the question of group influences on media behavior. Group standards and group norms presumably affect what is selected from the media and how it is perceived, and media content helps set the agenda for what group members talk about and provides some of the symbolic content of communication within groups. Further exploration of this problem area probably will require two kinds of observational procedure: (1) participant observation in formal and informal groups, and (2) systematic observation of contrived groups set up for experimental purposes.

The Sample Survey

Problem and Population

The survey researcher has to make certain crucial decisions early in each study. As in all research, the first task is that of defining the problem. If the study has a sponsor, several conferences may be necessary. Sometimes the researcher will have to "read between the lines" and tell the sponsor what is wanted. Almost always it will be wise to prepare a formal, written statement of the survey objectives.

As a scientist, the researcher will seek to relate his research problems to some body of theory and will try to structure his inquiries in such a way that his findings will have consequence in terms of the theory.

The newcomer to research sometimes asks, why worry about hypotheses? Why not "get the facts" and let them speak for themselves? The answer is that in the absence of hypotheses, the researcher will have no meaningful population of questions from which to draw a question sample. What sometimes happens, however, is that the researcher merely asks questions someone else has asked, without serious consideration of their relevance.

Occasionally such plan-free queries will produce helpful results (through the discovery of an unanticipated relationship), but the occurrence will be rare and the cost high. In general, every extraneous question complicates a survey and increases costs. There may be occasions, however, when the survey director will include one or more questions purely for motivational purposes (e. g., he may ask something about a subject which may be of interest to respondents if the basic problem is likely to be uninteresting to them).

A statement of the research problem will require a definition of the population to be studied, and this definition will have a bearing upon all subsequent phases of the study. It is important that the population consist of accessible elements in order to maximize the rigor with which a sampling design can be carried out. A study of subscribers to the St. Waukee *Bugle* might not be practicable at a given cost if the newspaper's circulation territory is large, whereas a study of subscribers in the city and its suburbs might be relatively easy to carry out.

If the researcher's objectives point toward explanation rather than description of phenomena or if he is interested in a detailed analysis of the characteristics of specific subgroups in the general population, a general-population sample may not meet his needs.

Suppose the investigator's hypothesis is essentially this: readers of a certain right-of-center magazine have "higher" scores on a personality scale measuring "authoritarianism" than do non-readers. He might, of course, draw a general-population sample and administer the scale to all persons within it, while also determining who were and who were not readers. If, however, the researcher were able to develop a simple question which would enable him to identify readers and nonreaders, he could save time and money by interviewing *all* readers and only a randomly selected subsample of the nonreaders. In other words, the reader probably would be rare in the general-population sample, and an extremely large sample might be required in order for reader breakdowns to yield statistically reliable data.

The procedure suggested above (interviewing all the readers and only some of the nonreaders) would still be expensive. Actually, the investigator very probably would seek subscription lists or other circulation data as an aid in drawing the sample of readers. This, however, would make it necessary to restate the hypothesis in terms of subscribers instead of readers. Such a restatement should be scrutinized and considered in terms of its tenability, as compared with the original version, and in terms of the theory from which it was derived.

The problem of defining a survey population is a complex one, especially when the researcher seeks explanation *and* description as products of the same study. With the former goal, the researcher will have in mind a model of groups of respondents *equated* in terms of every other relevant variable, but with measurements (in the present example) on authoritarianism and readership. Even if he carries out a refined analysis in which, for example, he holds constant such variables as socio-economic status (i. e., examines the relationship between authoritarianism and readership separately for different socio-economic levels) and thereby approaches the explanatory model, he will still feel insecure in his findings and will be beset with uncertainties about the direction of causation. (Do authoritarian folk select the magazine because of their pre-existing beliefs, attitudes, and values, or has the magazine content made them what they are, or are there uncontrolled external factors which account for both phenomena?) If, on the other hand, the researcher wants to *describe* the readers in terms of the social matrix in which they live, then he of course needs data on the general population in order to make such differential descriptions.

The researcher would do well to look into a work like Herbert Hyman's *Survey Design and Analysis,* an entire volume devoted to problems like the foregoing. One point which Hyman makes is that the researcher should not become obsessed with the search for a "first cause." He also shows the incompatibility, in a sense, of the sampling requirements in descriptive and explanatory surveys.[19]

Sampling

The reader has been introduced, presumably, to elementary sampling theory. He knows that the distinguishing characteristic of a probability sample is that every element (individual, household—whatever unit is sought) has a specifiable probability of selections. This known probability, in turn, makes it possible to estimate sampling error, set confidence limits, and test differences for significance.[20]

The quota sample, which prescribes representativeness on such variables as age, sex, education, urban/rural residence, and socio-economic status (as variously estimated) leaves choice of respondents (beyond these limits) pretty much up to the interviewer. Where quotas are controlled on factors other than occupation and education, quota samples tend to be biased upward with respect to these two characteristics. (Better educated people are sometimes easier to interview, and white-collar workers may be more willing than their working-class brethren to submit to interviewing.)

If age, sex, or other quotas are met within *small geographic areas* (e.g., block clusters), at least some of the opportunity to inject an upward socio-economic bias into the sample is reduced by the relative homogeneity of neighborhoods. However, a recent study by the author[21] indicates that, even under these circumstances, interviewers tend to select households which are perceived as having higher income. This problem could be reduced, presumably, by charting an interviewer's course through the area in such a way as to provide a random starting point and an interview attempt in every *n*th household. (A controlled, systematic method of selecting substitute households also should be provided—for example, the household to the right or left of the predesignated stop.)

A probability design, properly planned and carried out conscientiously, takes respondent selection out of the hands of the interviewer and places it completely under the control of the survey office. Furthermore, known probability of selection makes it possible to obtain an unbiased estimate of sampling error.

Sometimes the researcher will discover that his population is already catalogued, but more frequently he must draw his sample from a population which will require some catalogue work of his own. In the typical two-stage area sample in a small city, for example, he may number city blocks in serpentine order on a map, "cruise" or "block list" the blocks (i.e., catalogue the dwelling units), and then sample households within the selected blocks. Or if he is sampling newspaper subscribers, he may obtain lists of subscribers in the selected blocks and do his subsampling from the lists.

Obviously, there are many problems apart from the technical ones of making population estimates and estimates of sampling error. There are, for example, cost questions: What subsampling ratios should be used where? (Should the researcher take only a few blocks and sample heavily within them or should he take many blocks and sample thinly within them?) In general, it will behoove the field research newcomer to (1) immerse himself in the literature on sampling or (2) lean heavily on expert counsel. He probably will need the latter in modified form even if he relies on the former.

The adequacy of population catalogues, whether they consist of city or telephone directories, mailing or meter lists, or card files, depends primarily on two factors: (1) How accurately and completely does the catalogue list and locate the population it purports to include? (2) Is that population really the one in which the researcher is interested?

Many special populations (e. g., members of an organization) are fully and currently catalogued. In general, catalogues decrease in adequacy as one moves toward general-population samples. The telephone directory has some bias at both ends of the socio-economic ladder (there are those without phones and those with unlisted numbers), but it is issued frequently and is usually fairly complete. A random sample from the book will not give equal probability of selection to all telephone households, however, if some telephones and some individuals are listed more than once. A private branch exchange (a single number) may represent a sizable number of persons. City directories are issued infrequently, and in some cities they provide incomplete listings of such areas as back-alley slums.

Inadequacy of catalogues of the general population was one of the reasons for the development of area-sampling methods. In some European countries voting lists or other records are maintained which are sufficiently complete and accurate to permit drawing a general-population probability sample. In the United States a complete and up-to-date street-address city directory may make it unnecessary to list or "cruise" blocks. (The street-address directory would be used in a city to permit two-stage sampling and thus reduce interview expense by restricting interviews to selected blocks.)

Selection of interviewees from an alphabetical telephone directory results in high dispersion of interviews, but this is no disadvantage where interviewing is by telephone. A few years ago Stanley L. Payne delivered a convincing plea for a reconsideration of the telephone interview as a research procedure.[22] Apart from noting that nearly all homes in some communities had telephones, he pointed out other advantages: random selection, lessened need for substitutions, "reasonable privacy," availability of such personnel resources as phone-operators-turned-housewives, and unlimited call-backs. He added that "surveys now being made by telephone hold respondent interest through 25 questions or more." One warning: The interviewer should say "research study" rather than "survey" to avoid being perceived as a salesman.

When the population to be studied is a small, uncatalogued subgroup of the general population, a telephone survey may be an appropriate way to *locate* members of the population, particularly if (a) almost all homes have telephones and (b) there is no reason to believe that having a phone is correlated with the behavior or characteristics under study.

In 1961 the author made a detailed study of adult evening viewers of educational television in the Minneapolis-St. Paul area. Since it was known that regular evening viewers constituted only a small percentage of the over-all population, a telephone screening procedure was used. (Earlier research in the same community had shown that there was little or no chance of finding educational television viewers in nontelephone households.)

A three-stage probability (random-type) sample was selected by the following method: First, the author drew a random (geographically stratified) sample of small block-clusters. Next, he *listed* (from newly issued street-address phone directories) all telephone households in each selected area and drew a random sample from each cluster. Lastly, a procedure for random selection of an adult resident of each household was incorporated into the telephone interview procedure.

Through use of the telephone screening process it was possible to locate a sample of regular evening viewers of educational television who were then interviewed in detail in their homes. Only about one-ninth of the telephone respondents "qualified" for the personal interview. Cost of identifying such a sample by field interviews would have been prohibitive.

Precision of Results *

Whereas *representativeness* of a sample is a function mainly of sampling procedure, *precision* of results is largely a function of sample size. Here the researcher has a knotty problem which is apt also to mar any clear-cut distinction between descriptive and explanatory surveys. Most surveys call for the collection of data on several variables which themselves differ as to their dispersion in the population. The research man may ask one question of the "yes/no" type which (in the population tested) is distributed .60/.40. Another question may elicit responses which (in the population, not the *sample*,

* This subsection presupposes some familiarity with sampling statistics.

although it is the sample value which must be used in estimating the standard error), are distributed .80/.20. Clearly, the standard error $\sqrt{\frac{pq}{n}}$ of the first question will be larger than that of the second. Again, if scales or other measurement techniques which yield "scores" are used (and here the statistic will be the standard error of a measure of central tendency, usually the mean), some sets of scores will vary more than others, and the sampling errors of the different measures will vary.

Thus the researcher must decide how much sampling error (in absolute terms or, in the coefficient of variation, as a percentage) he is willing to tolerate in the most dispersed variable. As a result, he may sometimes find that a limited budget simply precludes his doing the survey. That is, he may discover that the precision he regards as minimal cannot be attained with the sample size he can afford.

Such a dilemma need not always result in abandonment of a survey plan. Sometimes what is needed is a modification of the sampling scheme. It should be noted, for example, that successful stratification (see below) will, for a given sample size, result in a reduction in sampling error. And there are other procedures (e. g., ratio estimates) which, by making use of already available information, increase obtainable precision with a given over-all sample size.

Variability, desired accuracy, and the kinds of breakdown needed— these are the three crucial factors in determining sample size, apart from the overarching question of budget. (Cross-tabulations enter into the picture in that the researcher will want reasonably reliable frequencies in the cross-tabulation cells.)

Volumes like Morris Hansen *et al.* include useful guides to decisions on minimum sample size needed.[23] The present author has found the following rule of thumb helpful in making preliminary estimates when the sample is to be small in comparison with population size (i. e., not larger than 25 per cent of the population), thus making it feasible to ignore the finite multiplier: Let B be the *over-all* width in percentage points of the confidence band sought. If the population "break" on a dichotomous variable is assumed to be as bad as possible in terms of sampling error size (i. e., 50–50), and if a slightly better than .95 level confidence band is sought, making it possible to round 1.96 standard errors to 2, the necessary sample size for simple random sampling is $n = \frac{40{,}000}{B^2}$. Thus, if we are willing to settle for a confidence band 20 percentage points wide ($B = 20$), the minimum sample size is 100. Or, if we are considering a given sample size—say, 400—the confidence limits are obtained quickly: $B^2 = \frac{40{,}000}{400} = 100$; $B = 10$; limits $= \pm 5$.

The estimate, as set up here, is based on simple random sampling, and the formula assumes a 50–50 split in the population (a conservative approach, given a dichotomous variable). For a continuous variable, the problem is different: The researcher will not be able to set up an estimate until he can make at least a fair guess concerning the dispersion of the variable in the population. His best single aid will be published reports of surveys on similar populations in which the same or similar variables were measured.

When the researcher departs from simple random sampling, he is likely to do so through stratification or through cluster sampling. These two procedures ordinarily have opposite effects on sampling error. In stratified sampling, the objective is to form, on the basis of one or more variables related to the variable studied, strata which are as homogeneous as possible. Where the same sampling fraction is used for all strata, there will always be a gain if the basis for stratification is correlated with the characteristic being measured. Sampling theory prescribes (for greater efficiency) heavier sampling in those strata with large variances, but such a procedure (disproportionate sampling) carries a risk factor: If strata variance differences turn out to be different from what was expected, over-all sampling variances may be increased.

In cluster sampling, with or without subsampling within clusters (e.g., city blocks), the objective is different. It is hoped, at least, that clusters are heterogeneous. To the degree that people within clusters tend to be more alike than people in the population generally, sampling error is increased. In fact, the difference in sampling error between a simple random sample and a cluster sample can be expressed as a function of intraclass correlation, a measure of the homogeneity or likeness of elements within clusters.

W. Edwards Deming, in a recent and readable book on sample design,[24] develops in some detail a procedure called "replicated sampling," a method which makes it possible to obtain simplified estimates of sampling error without recourse to the complicated formulas used with multistage sampling. Also introduced is the idea of regularized "audit" systems to evaluate the nonsampling errors which occur in surveys.

Interviewing and Interviewers

Once the field researcher has formulated his problem and designed his sampling procedure, he must develop a measurement instrument and take it into the field. This section deals with field work problems in surveys in which interviewers are used.

Types of Interview

Interviewing procedures vary in the degree to which the entire interview and/or individual questions are structured or standardized in advance. There are healthy differences of opinion about how structured most interviewing should be, but there is general agreement that the less standardized the questions and the interview procedure are, the more skillful (and better paid) the interviewer must be.

Many anthropologists and some sociologists have argued that the conversational interview, unstructured save for an "interview schedule" listing principal points to be covered, permits greater depth of inquiry and response than does an interview in which the same questions are always asked in the same way of each respondent. Such an approach probably has more merit in the hands of an anthropologist or a clinical psychologist than in the hands of an interviewer such as the media researcher is likely to use.

Farther along the standardized/unstandardized continuum is the relatively standardized interview with questions of the "open" type. The question is asked in a uniform way, but the respondent's answer (in his own words) is taken down by the field worker. Less interviewing skill is required in this approach. In many surveys use is made both of open questions and of standardized questions of the dichotomous ("yes/no," "agree/disagree") or multiple-choice type. If the completely standardized item is the only kind used, the interviewer's task consists principally of checking off answers on the schedule. (There is less than full agreement on the use of these terms, but "interview guide" is used frequently to describe the set of points or questions covered in relatively unstructured interviews; "schedule" is used to denote a form which lists questions in the way they are to be asked and leaves room for the interviewer to write or mark down the responses; and "questionnaire" is used to describe either an "interview schedule" or a form which the respondent himself fills out. Some survey organizations refer to their questionnaires as "ballots.")

Disagreement over the relative merit of standardized and unstandardized question form usually has hinged on the issue, which is more important: questions identical in wording but possibly different in meaning to different groups (e.g., the educated *vs.* the illiterate), or questions similar in meaning though varied in wording to fit the vocabulary and background of the individual? Actually, interviewers will differ among themselves in their ability to make appropriate "meaning" translations, and the survey director will rarely be able to assure himself that the questions, as asked, are really comparable in meaning for all respondents. It seems likely that studies of meaning by the "semantic differential" and related procedures (see Chapter 6) eventually may provide empirical answers to some problems of this type.[25]

Proponents of the open question in the standardized interview would structure the question uniformly for all respondents but allow answers to vary rather than fit them (or force them) into standardized categories. Questions are phrased in everyday language, and probe questions are used to amplify responses and to make them conform to the dimension of measurement sought.

Questions asked in a survey in its final form are likely to be more structured than those used in pretesting a questionnaire or in conducting a pilot study. Thus, the advocate of standardized multiple-choice questions will determine his response categories by asking the questions in open form in the preliminary study. Similarly, the user of open questions may make use of a relatively unstructured interview at the pretest stage. Sometimes the interviewer is provided with a set of instructions telling him, in specific terms, how he may reword certain questions if respondents do not seem to understand them. Where response categories are provided, interviewers may be instructed to write out asides, comments, or answers in which reservations are expressed.

Robert Merton's "focused interview" is another procedure which has been used in mass media research. It has the following characteristics: (1) Subjects are known to have been exposed to certain communication content or to have been involved in specific situations.

(2) The researcher has carried out a content or situational analysis of the experience and has derived from this a set of hypotheses and an interview guide. (3) Interview techniques are used to focus on the subjects' original responses to the communication content. (4) Insofar as possible, subjects themselves help structure the situation. In short, the content analysis provides a focus of inquiry which nevertheless permits a nondirective interviewing approach in which the subject himself contributes a great deal to the direction the interview content takes.[26] Although the focused interview has a number of advantages, particularly in helping to explain the observed effects of communication, it requires considerable interviewing skill.

Most of this chapter deals with the situation in which one respondent is interviewed at a time. The focused interview is adaptable to group interviewing, and market research specialists have experimented in recent years with other group interview procedures. A hazard in the group interview is the possibility of group influence on the individual, either through "bandwagon" response or as a result of his perceptions, expectations, or beliefs concerning other members of the group. One social scientist who has worked with the group interview concludes that it is "a valuable supplement to individual interviewing," even though individuals' opinions seem at times to be "modified or suppressed in the presence of the group."[27]

Some market research experiments with the group interview have involved verbatim recording of discussion content, which in turn has been interpreted by persons skilled in clinical psychology. Little data seems to be available, however, on the interexpert reliability of such judgments.

Interviewer Recruitment

Although some criteria usually regarded as appropriate in the selection of field staffs have not always discriminated between interviewers judged more and less successful by their employers, survey specialists have accumulated considerable practical information about staff selection. Paul Sheatsley mentions among other factors, health, interest, intelligence, and temperament.[28]

Intensely partisan interviewers are particularly inappropriate in opinion surveys. With informational items, some middle ground beyond naïveté but short of expertness probably is desirable. Experience is usually important, but some survey organizations with highly institutionalized procedures have found that prolonged experience with other agencies is more a handicap than an advantage.

The ideal interviewer probably is someone whose appearance will not attract undue attention to himself. He is friendly, self-assured, but not too garrulous or aggressive. There are other desirable interviewer qualities which may not occur to the researcher at first—the matter of legible handwriting, a requisite when open-end questions are used, or possession of a car when much travel is required to reach assigned households.

Where may the field research novice look for interviewers? He would do well to inquire into the availability of interviewers who have worked for established survey organizations, and he may even find it worthwhile to contract with such an agency for his field work. Advanced undergraduate and graduate students may be suitable for some types of interviewing, and women schoolteachers, women's club members, and other reasonably well-educated women often may be available for part- or full-time interviewing work. Many survey organizations have found that women interviewers are more satisfactory than men for most types of survey in the United States. Students often find it difficult to commit the time required in a major interviewing effort.

The researcher should hold orientation and training sessions in which he explains the purposes of the study and goes over the interview schedule with his interviewing crews. Practice interviews may be helpful, particularly if they are accompanied by role-playing in which the respondents provide examples of such problem reactions as refusals and extra-dimensional responses (not answering the question as asked). It may be possible to effect a further reduction in field errors by giving interviewers coding practice on questionnaires filled out to illustrate major types of interviewer error.[29]

Such preliminary rehearsals should increase interviewer morale and decrease interviewer cheating. Adequate pay (usually at an hourly rather than a per interview rate) is another strong deterrent to the temptation to fill in answers to questions which were not asked or to fake interviews. Further precautions include systematic post-card, telephone, or reinterview contacts with persons claimed as interviewees (e.g., every tenth case), and the use of legalistic pledges on each interview form. Some pollsters have used ingenious "internal" check questions as a detection device.

The researcher should select more interviewers than he predicts will be needed to complete interviewing during the time interval he specifies, since there is likely to be some attrition. The beginner's cost and time estimates (matters on which he should seek expert counsel) will more often understate than overstate the resources needed.

Access to Respondents

One essential interviewer skill is the ability to convince respondents of the importance of surveys and thus minimize the refusal rate. Interviewers for some national survey organizations average no more than one refusal in twenty contacts. Part of this success can be attributed to emphasizing the importance of the survey, but another factor may be the degree to which the interviewer seems to know what he is doing.

In almost all surveys interviewers should carry identification cards. Frequent use of a "survey" line by salesmen has led some survey researchers to make a practice of notifying the local Better Business Bureau prior to field work, so that the legitimacy of the study may be verified by respondents.

If a specific respondent (e.g., "head of household") is to be interviewed at each address, then the problem (not so easy as it may look!) is that of defining "head of household" adequately. If the survey calls for interviewing one "adult" at each address, the interviewer should have some technique for random or systematic selection of a respondent within each household. The household then becomes the last "cluster" in a multistage sample with intracluster sampling.[30]

The researcher must decide how many call-backs are to be made before interviewers give up on an address, and forms must be furnished on which to record the efforts made to reach each sample member. One frequently cited example of "not-at-home" bias arose in a survey about victory gardens during World War II. Being at home was related to digging in the garden, and fewer gardeners, proportionately, were yielded by each call-back. Similarly, the *media* exposure patterns of people may be intimately related to when and how long they are home.

When call-backs fail, the interviewer may be able to inquire about the persistent not-at-homes and thereby make it possible to compare these folk, on at least one or two variables, with people who are accessible. Where call-backs are too expensive or otherwise impractical, the researcher may wish to use a procedure developed by Alfred Politz and Willard Simmons,[31] whereby estimates are computed by weighting each respondent's answers by the reciprocal of the estimated proportion of the time he is at home. The refusal and not-at-home groups in a survey together may serve to restrict the range on one characteristic—age. Refusals tend to be relatively high among older folk, whereas the not-at-homes often include a disproportionate number of single persons and newly married couples without children.

Bias, Error, and the Interviewer Role

Considerable research has been carried out in recent years to assess the error introduced in surveys by interviewers.[32] The term "interviewer bias" has been used to describe a constant error in a given direction (e.g, the tendency of white interviewers to elicit more conservative opinion responses from Southern Negroes), whereas "error" is a more inclusive term that also describes individual errors which may tend to cancel out. Interviewer effects of even the latter type, however, make it more difficult than it would be otherwise to confirm the existence of relationships between variables. (The reader will recall that observed relationships, whether measured by a product-moment or other correlation coefficient or established by some simpler tabulation procedure, have a ceiling imposed by the reliability of the measures.)

Research findings indicate that interviewer bias is more frequently a function of an interviewer's expectations concerning a respondent than of his own opinions. As Hyman expresses it, "Idealogical bias is only of secondary significance as compared with expectational biases."[33] How does this happen? There are several possibilities. The interviewer may have certain general expectations concerning public opinion on a given issue, and he may either communicate his expectations unconsciously to respondents (and thus provide cues for the response he expects), or he may misconstrue and misrecord what respondents say. Again he may influence or misinterpret responses as a result of stereotyped expectations concerning the opinions likely to be held by a member of a given sex, age, or ethnic group. Research evidence indicates that interviewer effects may be maximized in relatively unstructured situations—the open question or field ratings of respondents on environmental characteristics (e.g., "condition of dwelling").[34]

Insufficient space is available here to summarize research findings concerning interviewer error, but it is important to note that the over-all error introduced by trained interviewers seems to be of modest magnitude—not large enough to bring into serious question the findings obtained in most surveys. The survey researcher should realize, however, that most studies of interviewer error have involved the experienced and well-trained interviewing staffs of national survey organizations. Inexperienced or ill-trained field workers may introduce a great deal of error into a survey. This possibility—plus the fact that greater interviewing skill is needed for open questions—biases the present author in favor of rather highly structured questions which have response categories based on pilot studies adequate to tap the range, though not the relative frequency, of various answers. With structured questions of this type, the result is essentially "respondent coding"; that is, the categories are provided the interviewee (rather than the interviewer), who makes a choice from them.

When open questions are asked, the author prefers office coding to field coding. In the latter procedure, answers are classified into predetermined categories by the interviewer. Here error can occur either through misclassification or through interviewer influence on the respondent, whereas a near-verbatim report of what the respondent said, coded later in the research office, is subject mainly to the latter type of error. The pressure that field coding imposes on the interviewer may lead him to force answers into ready-made categories, even though space is provided for "other" responses. (Similarly, the person who fills out a self-administered questionnaire may avoid use of "write-in" categories when he can more easily make only a check mark.)

Most handbooks on interviewing emphasize the establishment of "rapport" at the beginning of the interview, followed by an appearance of neutrality and detachment once the interview is in progress. In a theoretical appraisal of these two interview aspects in the light of Talcott Parsons' "pattern variables" treatment of social roles, Lawrence Podell has observed certain unfortunate consequences which may stem from this pairing of an initial friendliness with a non-committal and unresponsive role later on.[35] For one thing, the respondent may look for evidence of interviewer approval or disapproval.

Ideally, what should the interviewer-respondent relationship be? This will vary from survey to survey, but the present author favors placing less emphasis on the establishment of rapport than on assuring the respondent of the importance of the survey. (Needless to say, the interviewer himself must have been convinced of its importance, both through explanation of the purpose of the survey and through sympathetic treatment by the project director.)

A task-oriented atmosphere should help minimize the tendency of the interviewee to look for signs of approval or disapproval, agreement or disagreement, and so on; and the interviewer should try not to provide such cues. If the situation is impersonal and task-oriented, "deadpan" behavior on the interviewer's part is not likely to be interpreted as a sign of unfriendliness.

Open questions facilitate interviewer-respondent interaction, especially insofar as they necessitate (1) probe questions to insure a full answer to each question and (2) a "closing" move whereby the loquacious interviewee is led on to the next query. Structuring the interview somewhat fully, in contrast, reduces the interaction and tends to focus attention on the questions themselves (e.g., through consideration of response categories on a card).

There are other possible facilitators of successful interviewing. The interviewer should have a thorough knowledge of the purpose of each open question, if any are used, so that he will know what to probe for. He should, of course, arrange to interview the respondent alone, so that the latter will not be influenced by real or imagined pressures from, say, other members of his family. Modest dress and manner but a middle-class appearance probably will encourage willing responses from working-class people, inasmuch as there seems to be, in American society, a kind of pervasive desire to communicate upward in the social structure.[36] That responses actuated by such a tendency will be candid is less certain. Here, again, task orientation and a relatively "invisible" interviewer may be the most desirable combination.

In a small community it is important that interviewers who are hometown folk be assigned to districts other than the ones in which they live.

Question Design

Public opinion polls and social and market surveys have burgeoned in recent decades, and a great deal has been learned about asking questions. Sophistication in question design has been accompanied, however, by wariness—even the best designer of questions pretests them. The plain fact is that answers to questions depend on how they are asked—so much so that one social psychologist has argued that modern probability sampling may be no better than a "scalpel in a butcher shop" as long as sampling error is exceeded by the variability in response producible by different wordings.[37]

An excellent guide to question design is Stanley L. Payne's scholarly but entertaining little volume, *The Art of Asking Questions*,[38] which abounds in specific examples of bad questions and ambiguous words. For example, the words "any" and "country" are undesirable, the former because it may mean either a single case or every case (try "any reason" for size!), the latter because it may mean either a nation or a rural area. Only experience would teach the researcher that respondents may use "own" indiscriminately as a verb ("Yes, I 'own' a telephone") or that they may think, when "Who" is used to start a question, that the answer has to be one person, not a group.

Since minor changes in wording may effect major changes in response distributions, the survey researcher leans rather heavily on the relatively high internal comparability of findings. Three ways of asking people whether a newspaper is "fair" in its treatment of national political issues may lead to three quite different proportions answering "yes." Yet all three questions may show the same pattern of differences in response between, say, Republicans and Democrats. If you have used one form (which seems to be satisfactory) in survey A dealing with newspaper X, then a second researcher can make a meaningful comparison of public opinion concerning your paper and paper Y studied in survey B if he uses your question wording. If he changes it, the water is muddied.

Noteworthy examples of replication of questions from one communication study to another include Charles E. Swanson's "midcity" use of items which Leo Rosten and F. V. Prugger had asked newsmen in earlier studies; Edwin Braman's and Robert Jones' replicated study of television ownership and newspaper advertising reading; and

Raymond Nixon's report of surveys in which opinion questions about the media were put to samples in four cities in 1940 and 1953.[39] In the early 1960's the Inland Daily Press Association sponsored a series of "image" studies of daily newspapers which included a standardized questionnaire consisting of semantic-differential rating scales (see Chapter 6) and verbal attitude items from a series of scales developed at Stanford.[40] This was a forward step which could lead to the accumulation of a great deal of useful comparative and cumulative data.

There are many survey questions or items which have already been thoroughly researched. Experience tells us, for example, that a question about attained education elicits fewer erroneous responses if it is phrased in terms of the *last year* of school or college completed and if the name of the institution is asked, than if the respondent is merely asked how much education he has had. Many researchers, in *reporting* demographic data, have elected to use a set of "standard breakdowns" (categories) recommended and made available by the American Association of Advertising Agencies, American Marketing Association, and Association of National Advertisers. Advantages include compatibility with United States Census breakdowns.

Some Sources of Ambiguity

One kind of error in surveys is the result of misperception of the interviewer's words, either through confusion with another word or through the influence of context. A classic example is the story of the poller who asked Southern Negroes if they favored government control of profits. Sentiment was overwhelmingly negative, since it was obvious that "prophets" should be regulated only by the Lord. A North Carolina survey of TV-viewing disclosed surprising interest in "foreign news" among rural folk. Re-interviewing showed that the word "foreign" had been pronounced so that it was heard frequently as "farm."

Contextual influences on the perceived meaning of a question may stem from verbal habits which are fairly diffuse in the language community, or again they may come about as the result of the specialized vocabulary or special concerns of a given group. Both types of problem appeared in pilot-run materials used by the author in a study of relationships between the press and the medical profession. Doctors were asked to indicate agreement or disagreement with a series of statements about newspaper treatment of medical news. (Together, the statements constituted a Guttman-type attitude scale.) It seemed desirable to alternate between statements favorable and unfavorable to newspapers, and as a result the following statement was used: "In general, more *good* than *harm* is done by newspaper stories dealing with developments in the field of medicine." (Response categories were strongly agree, agree, disagree, strongly disagree.) "Good" and "harm" were underscored, but many physicians read the phrase as "more harm than good," the cliché with which people are most familiar. The author was able to detect the misfire, inasmuch as several respondents (in a "comment" space which was provided) wrote in remarks which were congruent only with an unfavorable answer.

A different type of contextual influence on responses was illustrated when, in a series of pilot interviews, the author asked doctors whether they agreed that medical schools should put more emphasis on "social aspects of medicine" in their curricula. Several respondents' replies showed that they heard the phrase as "socialized medicine." Here, preoccupation with a much talked-about issue led to an extreme instance of misperception.

Another perception problem arises when the interviewer stresses certain words. Ordinarily, the study director will provide visual indicators of stress (capitals, italics, etc.), when it is intended, and will try to construct his questions so that they will be read in much the same way by all interviewers.

Survey researchers may wish to avoid generalizations and broad, evaluational terms like "frequently," "regularly," "fair," and so on, simply because such words mean different things to different people.

One way to reduce ambiguity is to make questions specific. Thus, instead of asking a respondent what his religion is, the researcher may ask about religious preference or frequency of attendance at church. Or, he may go a step farther and ask merely whether the respondent went to church last Sunday. If interviews are spread out over several weeks or if there is no evidence that "last Sunday" was a "special" Sunday within any denomination, the "last Sunday" question may be more satisfactory simply because it is easily understood and minimizes memory strain.

The same principle can be applied to opinion questions. Rather than ask unionists whether management is "fair" to workers, the researcher may cite a number of specific practices (of varying degrees of "unfairness") and ask subjects whether they believe management actually engages in these behaviors.

Overburdening the Respondent

The researcher asks the respondent a question, ordinarily, either to obtain factual data or to elicit an opinion. Either kind of question may go awry because it requires too much of the person answering. He may express an opinion when he really does not have one, or he may give a factual answer when he does not really understand the question. If the burden imposed by a question is sufficiently intolerable, the weakness will show up in the form of respondent resistance in a pretest. It did not take very many interviews for a graduate student to realize he was asking too much when he said to people: "About how many cents per mile would you say it costs to operate your car, taking gas, oil, depreciation, insurance, and all other expenses into account?"

Vocabulary or syntax difficulties may foul a survey, especially if the researcher confines his pretest to college students or other people who are above average in literacy. A large daily newspaper spent a sizable sum in the mid-1950's for a survey of reader reaction to the use of colored illustrations on page one. Dissatisfaction in certain districts was hard to explain until it became apparent that many Negro respondents in colored residential sections meant what they said (but in a different frame of reference) when they complained that the paper was not printing enough "colored" pictures. The saddest aspect of this type of finding, of course, is that although the existence of such a bias in question interpretation may be confirmed, there is no inexpensive way to assess the *magnitude* of the error.

"Double-barreled" questions should be avoided. A single response to what is really two questions is always ambiguous. What did a 60 per cent "too many" response mean when people were asked the following? "Would you say the *Campus Bugle* prints too many student-contributed cartoons and letters, too few of them, or just about the right number?"

Avoiding Bias in Question Design

Survey people apply various principles in an effort to avoid slanting questions in favor of some specific mode of response. Thus the researcher usually will state both alternatives in an opinion question, not just one. ("Should the *Daily Bugle* continue to print the Drewson Pegark column, or should it be dropped?"; *not* "Should the *Daily Bugle* continue to print the Drewson Pegark column?") Again, in the light of prestige effects, "How do you feel about the federal government's farm price program?" is preferable to "How do you feel about President Kennedy's farm price program?" if attitude toward the program, not toward the President, is the variable of interest to the researcher.

A different type of prestige bias may occur when a respondent is asked a question the answer to which may (he thinks) affect the way he is perceived by the interviewer. People may be reluctant to admit ignorance of an event or problem if the interviewer gives the impression that it is generally known, and they may not want to admit behavioral sins of omission or commission (e. g., having read a risqué book or not having read a current best-seller). Sometimes a researcher may build in a face-saving device for the respondent by asking, for example, whether he plans to read the best-seller. (Validity will be low as to "plans," but those who have read the book will say so, whereas those who have not done so but who might otherwise have fibbed may save face by telling of their "plans.")

Similarly, filter questions designed to test awareness of a subject about which more detailed questions will be asked of those who *are* aware may be so phrased as to avoid giving the impression that awareness is necessarily widespread or desirable. "Have you happened to read about any press-medical codes of co-operation?" was an innocent-appearing question about a much-publicized subject. As phrased, the question made it easy for the uninformed doctor. Allen H. Barton warns (facetiously) against carrying this technique too far: "Many people have been killing their wives these days. Do you happen to have killed yours?"[41]

Because of a tendency of respondents to favor certain positions in a list of alternatives (the first in most instances, the last in opinion questions requiring a good deal of thought), the researcher often will rotate the order in which response categories are presented. Some ingenious procedures have been used to achieve such random allocation.[42]

Question Sequence

A number of factors will influence the way in which the researcher orders his questions. Broad, general questions usually will be followed, not preceded, by more specific queries. Whenever possible, questions will be grouped in such a way as to make the progression through the series seem meaningful and logical, and transitions will be provided. Sensitive questions which might abruptly end the interview usually will be reserved until other important items have been answered.

Insofar as he can, the study director will make sure that an early question does not structure responses to a later item. One journalism researcher found (through a pretest) that the word "business," used in an early question to refer to retailers, was interpreted as again referring to retailers in a later question which was intended to measure public opinion about profits in heavy industry. Sometimes a single pretest will disclose such difficulties, particularly if interviewers probe for the meaning of ambiguous or inconsistent responses. On occasion it may be desirable to pretest two or more forms of the same question.

Classification data (age, sex, education, occupation, etc.) usually are filled in at the end of an interview, but some survey people have used such items as openers because they seemed innocuous and unlikely to lead to emotional responses. Opening the interview with biographical queries may have unanticipated consequences, particularly if the respondent has to tell something about himself (e.g., substandard income, unemployment) which proves embarrassing. Although most classification information is obtained by questioning respondents, it may be desirable to have interviewers estimate certain characteristics. (In a panel study, for example, a woman may be more willing to submit to a series of interviews if she has not been asked her age.) Types of data gathered by this method (observation) have even included complex indices of social status.

Probes, Pilot Studies, and Pretests

The author has already expressed a bias in favor of structured questions and "respondent coding" for most survey purposes. Open questions, accompanied by probes, are still necessary at the pilot-study stage, when tools are being sharpened and tentative hypotheses are becoming more clearly formulated, and a few open questions may be needed in almost any survey using interviewers.

The term "pilot study" usually is used to describe an exploratory, small-scale field inquiry. A schedule or questionnaire may be pretested either in a pilot study or in a less formal tryout designed merely to show up imperfections in the measurement instrument. Pretesting helps determine what the respondent will tolerate in terms of questions and interview length, and it helps to identify bad questions. Indicators of question inadequacy may include suspiciously high "don't know" frequencies or a tendency of respondents to modify the question as they answer it.

One advantage of including probe questions in the pretest process ("Just what do you mean by that?" "In what way?") is that they may show up question deficiencies which would not otherwise be apparent. Take the following item asked of doctors:

> Some people who have studied press-medical relations have pointed out two actions a newspaper man may take which are likely to lead to a conflict of interests:
>
> a. He may ask for information which, if given, would violate the doctor-patient relationship.
>
> b. He may cause the physician embarrassment among his professional colleagues by quoting him or using his name in a story.
>
> In your opinion, is either of these problems a very serious one?
> ——Yes, (a). ——Yes, (b).
> ——No, neither is a very serious problem.

There was nothing in the distribution of responses to evoke suspicion, but a "Comment" line, retained even in the main study for "catharsis" purposes, provided a partial equivalent (for a self-administered questionnaire) of probing by an interviewer. It became apparent that the question could mean either of two things to a respondent: Did he think the events occurred? Or did he think they would be a "serious problem" if they did occur? So, in the main study, respondents were asked:

> Have you ever had either or both of these experiences?
> ——Yes, (a). ——Yes, (b). ——Yes, both (a) and (b).
> ——No, neither.

Whereas only 27 per cent claimed to have had either experience, 58 per cent of the pretest respondents rated one or both problems as "serious"! In its final form the question was at least tied down to the doctor's own experiences, as he remembered them.

Probe questions are essential where open questions are used, in order to get additional information and to insure "unidimensionality" of responses. These functions are possible, however, only when the interviewer understands fully the purpose of the question.

In a penetrating analysis of the relative merits of "poll" and "open" questions, Lazarsfeld pointed out several years ago[43] that most of the functions of open questions can be taken over by well-designed sets of closed questions. Some functions, however ("discerning influences on opinion," "clarifying statistical relationships" through deviant case analysis), cannot. The same author also has shown[44] that "why" questions have to be devised skillfully in order to tap different kinds of influence on a belief or a behavior reported by an interviewee. Thus purchasing-behavior "why's" might refer to sources of influence (an advertisement, an individual), qualities of the product (style, color), or the buyer's own impulses.

Lazarsfeld has shown how, by use of concrete, specific subsets of questions, the investigator can get at the kinds of influence in which he is interested. Furthermore, he can so arrange the questions that they fit "the experience of the respondent." Hence, if an interviewee says he went to a movie primarily just to "see a show," he may be asked about when the decision was made and who may have influenced it. If he says he attended to see a specific picture, he may be queried about how he learned about the picture and about the aspects of what he read or heard that attracted his interest. The development of elaborate subsets of "why" questions requires careful planning and rigorous pretesting, but the present author believes this procedure will be more fruitful in most media surveys than a relatively ambiguous type of "why" which permits responses in several different dimensions.

Question Validity

When the survey researcher asks a factual question he wants an accurate response, and when he tries to tap an attitude area, he hopes for a true expression of the respondent's predispositions.

The problem of providing a frame of reference for interpreting answers to opinion questions has been a matter of serious concern to survey people for a long time. One possible procedure is Gallup's "quintamensional" design,[45] which proceeds from (1) a filter question tapping a respondent's knowledge of an area to (2) an open question about how the issue might be resolved, through (3) a specific, dichotomous question ("Would you like to see your congressman vote for the ——— bill?") and other questions which deal with (4) reasons for the respondent's belief and (5) the intensity with which the belief is held.

Some researchers have tried to furnish a frame of reference for each respondent by giving him a minimum amount of information as background for an opinion question. This does not put him on an equal footing with other respondents. Instead, it forces him to a quick decision which may be at variance with what he would decide under more normal circumstances. Moreover, it is virtually impossible to get across to a previously uninformed interviewee the full meaning of a concept like "closed shop," "reciprocal trade agreements," or "farm price supports at 90 per cent of parity."

Where an evaluative response is called for, a comparative frame of reference may be provided by the researcher. In the survey reported by Paul Lazarsfeld and Harry Field[46] in *The People Look at Radio,* interviewees were asked to make an over-all appraisal of five institutions, one of which was radio. Views concerning broadcasting were more meaningful when they could be expressed and assessed in relation to opinions about churches, newspapers, schools, and local government.

Factual filter questions are ordinarily used to reduce the universe to those having knowledge of an issue. Chilton R. Bush at Stanford once suggested an alternative approach whereby a filter-type opinion question provides a basis for weighting responses to more specific questions. Thus an interviewee who thinks ill of most newspapers is "weighted in" less heavily (with respect to his opinion of a local paper) than a respondent who thinks well of most papers but attacks his hometown paper.

Error magnitude in fact questions can sometimes be assessed by comparing responses with external validation data. Where opinion questions seem likely to embarrass respondents or to elicit self-conscious replies, the researcher may resort to indirect questioning. Thus he may ask respondents how they think people behave in a given situation or react to a certain idea. (Example: "Why do some people give so little to the Red Cross?") It should be pointed out, however, that indirect questions, when they ask the respondent about other people's beliefs, values, opinions, behavior, or motives in order to get at his own characteristics, assume an intervening process of projection whereby the individual does ascribe to others something which would be painful for his ego to admit. Unfortunately, it is difficult to separate such projections from an honest effort to appraise other people. In general, the researcher will get some of both elements, both across interviewees and in the individual interview.

Projective *tests,* in contrast, consist of extremely ambiguous stimuli (e.g., an ink blot, an outline sketch of two human figures talking to each other, a picture amenable to many divergent interpretations). To the extent that the essential feature of ambiguity is lacking, the subject's opportunity to impose his own feelings, beliefs, or value structure on the stimuli is sharply reduced. Interpretation of responses, of course, is a task for the specialist. Very often the reliability of projective tests will be low—that is, the ambiguity which facilitates projection may also lead to error of measurement.

The Mail Questionnaire

Whereas the field survey is the most expensive data-gathering procedure the communications researcher is likely to use, the mail questionnaire yields data at low cost. And because almost anyone with mimeograph machine, envelopes, and stamps can send out a questionnaire, the procedure has been grossly misused, often by investigators who have overlooked the fact that analysis of mail questionnaire data can be as costly or more costly than processing data obtained by interviewing.

The following quotations illustrate the fact that research specialists have disagreed on the utility of mail questionnaires for specific purposes but have been nearly unanimous in their acknowledgment of weaknesses inherent in the method.

Quinn McNemar, in a searching review of achievements in opinion-attitude methodology, made this observation in 1946: "Mail schedules or the telephone may satisfy the less scrupulous but such methods should be taboo."[47] Six years later two sociologists proferred this somewhat more temperate statement in a research-methods textbook: "In spite of many abuses, the mailed self-administered questionnaire remains a useful technique in sociological research. So long as this method is employed in appropriate research designs, it can frequently be rewarding." [48]

Disadvantages of the Procedure

The present author would agree that mail questionnaires are overused and misused, but he also believes the method has acceptable applications in mass communication research. One way to delimit the types of study in which the procedure is most legitimate is to outline the disadvantages of this method of data-gathering. To the extent that the investigator can show that these drawbacks are inoperative or minimally operative in a study, use of a mail questionnaire may be justified. Some of the most frequently raised criticisms follow:

1. The original sample may be drawn from an inaccurate or incomplete list, catalogue, card file, or other directory-type source. Mobility of people tends to make for early obsolescence of such lists.

2. People who respond often differ from nonrespondents in certain known characteristics (e.g., socio-economic status, education, sex). To the extent that these characteristics are related to the variables being studied, estimates or population characteristics will be biased. In general, the more opinionated or interested will reply, the uninterested and apathetic will not.

3. There is no sure way to control the sequence of stimuli. Consequently, some respondents will read the entire questionnaire before answering any questions, and others will skip around. Incomplete answers and item omissions will occur, whereas in an interview or audited self-administration situation this problem can be avoided.

4. The questionnaire may be filled out by someone other than the intended respondent. (Married individuals may assign the task to their spouses, businessmen to their secretaries, poorly educated folk to their high-school-age children, and so on.)

5. There is no opportunity to probe, to obtain answers in depth.

The first objection—the lack of an adequate catalogue of the population—is most serious when the researcher wants a general-population sample in a given geographic area. Directories are apt to be woefully incomplete and inaccurate. Certain special groups, on the other hand (e.g., members of specific organizations), may be so scattered as to be inaccessible for interviewing except at great cost, yet correctly and completely listed in an up-to-date directory. The author, in a study of relationships between the press and public school superintendents in California,[49] had available a directory which yielded an extremely accurate mailing list. (No questionnaire was returned as undeliverable.)

It is in the sample from a heterogeneous universe that one is likely to encounter the largest and most predictable bias from nonresponse. Researchers have been aware for decades of the tendency of mail questionnaires to attract responses from the better educated, the more prosperous economically, the more opinionated, and so on.[50] How can this problem be dealt with? One way is to restrict the use of mail questionnaires to studies in which the survey subject is likely to be of marked interest to the sample. Careful design of the questionnaire and covering letter, along with pretests, may help maximize response. Follow-up mailings can be used in an effort to induce every person to return the form.[51]

Beyond such efforts to minimize bias by maximizing response, the researcher can make allowances or corrections for bias that may exist in incomplete returns. Separate tabulation of responses to different mailings may provide clues to the presence or absence of bias. In some studies the researcher may have data for the full sample or the full population on variables which are related to the variables measured in the survey. Those who respond can at least be checked for representativeness on these variables, and if there are serious discrepancies, weighting procedures or other allowances may be made in computing population estimates.[52]

Morris Hansen and William Hurwitz [53] suggest a double sampling procedure which permits rigorous control of response bias in mail surveys. A probability subsample of nonrespondents is interviewed to provide estimates of the characteristics of the entire nonrespondent group. Even where the subsample must be so small as to result in a fairly large sampling error, it at least provides an unbiased estimate of the group's answers and makes it possible to estimate over-all sampling error.

Where interviewing is not feasible, it is sometimes possible to obtain at least some information about nonrespondents by mailing a double postcard to them which includes one or two questions on background variables and/or a question on one of the principal dependent variables covered in the questionnaire. If responses to this procedure include a large proportion of those who failed to return the original questionnaire, the results can be used to compare the two groups on classification variables or on at least one of the dependent variables.

Unfortunately, many communications researchers who have used mail questionnaires have dutifully reported the response rate but have failed to indicate whether any data were available concerning the crucial question, how (and how much) did the no-answer folk differ from those who did answer? With this question completely unanswered, adequacy even of a high response rate remains in doubt.

The third objection to mail questionnaires—incompleteness of answers, omission of items, and skipping around—points up less serious but extremely troublesome problems. The effective sample size for some or all items often will be smaller than the number of questionnaires returned.[54] Yet, if the sample consists of highly motivated, interested people, it is reasonable to suppose they may also be responsive to appeals (in the questionnaire itself or the covering letter) to answer every question, to fill in the items in the order in which they appear, and to permit no one else to fill out the forms for them (objection 4). The obverse of this argument is that omissions and incomplete answers indicate an uninterested respondent, and lack of interest among potential respondents will result in a low response rate.

F. F. Waisanen[55] described a study in which response was almost doubled by means of telephone calls in which prospective respondents were told that a questionnaire was being mailed and were personally asked to fill it out and return it. In most studies the researcher will want to tell the questionnaire recipient who the sponsors of the study are, why he is being queried, and why he ought to co-operate. Varying results have been obtained with different types of response incentive, but there is some evidence that an altruistic type of appeal may be more effective than monetary or other special inducements.[56]

Certainly the respondent should always be given detailed instructions. Often it may be desirable to assure him of anonymity. Where second- or third-wave mailings are planned, the investigator must have some record of replies unless he is willing to subject the entire sample to the annoyance of a pleading reminder. Some researchers have obtained a record of those answering by providing a postcard to be signed and mailed separately when the unsigned questionnaire is returned.[57] In the school-superintendents study (see Note 49), the author's geographically scattered respondents were identified by postmark. In a later study in which respondents were physicians and newspaper editors, the author used a more straightforward procedure without eliciting objections: Attention of questionnaire recipients was called to the fact that return envelopes were serially numbered, and it was explained that a "clerk" would open the envelope, check off the respondent's name, and discard the envelope. Respondents were told that this was done in case it should prove necessary to send out reminders.

The fifth major objection to the mail questionnaire—the problem of obtaining "depth" and the inability to probe—suggests that the procedure should be restricted not only to certain types of population (e.g., literate people) but also to subject matter which does not require such probing. The circumstances under which mail questionnaires are filled out will limit the value of data yielded by open questions. Moreover, for many respondents (particularly those relatively low in interest or verbal ability) the open question may substantially reduce the response rate, just as questionnaire length does. (Different investigators have reached different conclusions concerning the effect of length on response rate. It seems likely, however, that for a given interest level increasing the length will reduce response.)

Highly motivated and interested respondents (e.g., newspaper editors in the author's press-medical study) may need space in which to write (if they wish) comments concerning their responses to structured questions. This enables the respondent to let off steam by making the kind of aside he would make to an interviewer.

The mail questionnaire is not generally suitable for obtaining data on media exposure. Such measurement is fraught with serious problems, some of which are mentioned in other sections of this chapter. The biases and other difficulties inherent in the mail questionnaire may merely compound the difficulty of the task.[58]

Uses of the Mail Questionnaire

In designing a mail "ballot," the investigator may avoid practices he would follow in an audited, self-administered questionnaire. He may abandon the usually desirable practice of continuous numbering of items and instead separately number each subsection in order to minimize the apparent length, or he may reduce spacing to make the questionnaire seem shorter. Compression is of course less desirable than an appeal which will interest respondents enough to make them less conscious of questionnaire length.

Frequently, in the self-administered questionnaires, the researcher may present a single question (or a group of closely-related questions) on each page. This is rarely practicable in a mail survey (unless the questionnaire is exceedingly short), but the form can be so constructed as to place on a later page (with respect to a given question) any item which logic or a pretesting indicates might contaminate responses to the earlier item. (An example would be the situation in which a general question is asked about television program preferences, after which a checklist of programs or program types is provided in an effort to elicit more specific information. The checklist should not appear on the same page as the more general question.)

Precoding for punchcard processing can result in a mail questionnaire's being cluttered with unexplained numbers which may either puzzle or annoy respondents. This result is not inevitable, but the researcher should assure himself (by pretesting) that the precoding is handled in such a way typographically that it does not prove troublesome. In assessing questionnaire length, the researcher should take account of the amount of reading which the questionnaire entails. Multiple-choice questions may be easy to answer once the respondent moves his pencil, yet they may require a great deal of time and effort for slow readers. The language used in any self-administered questionnaire must, of course, be simple enough to be understood readily.

Provision of a stamped, addressed envelope is a standard practice in mail questionnaire studies. Postage stamps may bring in a higher return rate than do business-reply (franked) envelopes, and special-issue stamps sometimes elicit significant response gains.

In several communication studies in which mail questionnaires have been used, the population under scrutiny has consisted of media personnel or news sources. Charles T. Duncan,[59] for example, used a 1-in-10 sample of weekly newspapers in the United States for an exploratory inquiry into how much coverage weeklies give to news of local government. His response rate was only 37 per cent, but his central findings are meaningful even if a response bias is assumed.

That is, if the weekly press people who bothered to answer the questionnaire were (and this is what the results indicate) giving less than adequate attention to local government news, then it is reasonable to suspect that attention was even less adequate in the case of those who did not respond.

Mitchell Charnley,[60] in a mail questionnaire study, sought answers to questions concerning the personnel and facilities of radio newsrooms. His findings (based on an effective response rate of 52 per cent) provided new and useful data.

If researchers confine the mail questionnaire to exploratory studies of accurately catalogued and otherwise inaccessible populations, they will be on relatively safe ground, particularly if they also:

1. Work assiduously at the task of maximizing response rate.
2. Provide instructions and a format which spell out the respondent's task and make it reasonably easy.
3. Attempt to obtain at least some evidence concerning the representativeness of the obtained sample as compared with the sample which was drawn.

Other Problems and Procedures

The author has tried, wherever possible, to illustrate field research problems and principles with examples drawn from the mass media field. In selecting topics for emphasis he has used as his principal criterion the probable utility of a procedure or seriousness of a problem in the work a beginner in communications research might do. A secondary standard, however, has been the availability of material in other sources. The purpose of this section is to call attention to certain key topics with which the communications researcher needs to become familiar yet can find treated more than adequately in other publications. Some of these sources are cited below.

One research tool which was not described in detail is the self-administered questionnaire which is audited by survey personnel. An example of the use of this technique is found in the consumer brand-preference studies carried out by a number of daily newspapers. In the 1962 St. Paul study questionnaires were sent to a probability sample of 4,561 households, with a return rate of 70.4 per cent. Respondents filled out the questionnaires and brought them to the survey office, where a staff member went over each form, making sure that all items were answered and clearing up any "confusion" on the part of respondents. The incentive to return the questionnaires was two shopping bags full of grocery and household items.[61] Such studies provide detailed, cumulative data concerning preferences on a large number of consumer items each year, mainly to supply market data to advertisers.

Some consumer analyses have been based on area sampling methods and in-the-home interviewing. For example, this is the procedure used in the *Minnesota Homemaker Surveys* and in *Consumer Inventories* conducted for an Oregon newspaper.[62] The method eliminates much nonresponse bias and permits relatively accurate estimation of sampling error. Respondents are interviewed in their homes so that an auxiliary check can be made on brands then on hand.

Another type of inquiry in which the self-administered questionnaire may be helpful is the study of attitudes toward mass media or attitudes hypothesized as related to audience or communicator behavior. Some attitude measurement instruments are more easily administered as written tests than by interviewing, but errors and omissions tend to be numerous unless forms are audited before the respondent gets away. Where small accessible groups constitute the population of interest (university students, members of an organization), group administration of questionnaire materials may be a satisfactory procedure.

Careful instructions and careful auditing are important, if audited self-administration is to take the place of interviewing. If a mailed appeal is used, nonresponse bias is likely to be high unless survey representatives call at the addresses to which questionnaires have been sent.

The panel method, in which a sample of respondents is reinterviewed through time, can be useful in media research, particularly in studies of the long-range effects of mass communication. Laboratory experiments have again and again demonstrated the influence of media content upon captive audiences, but such effects have been less easy to establish when audience members select content in terms of their interests and predispositions. The panel provides a means of assessing such influence through time, provided attention accorded members does not in itself modify their attitudes or media exposure or turn them into "professional critics."

Advantages of the panel method include the ability to study

change in verbal or nonverbal behavior, the reasons for change, and the changers themselves. If two successive studies with independent samples disclose a small shift in favor of a certain editorial practice, we do not know what turnover (shifts in both directions) led to the small net change. Such information is provided by a panel study. A secondary advantage of the panel method in this situation is a reduction in sampling error. (Responses in the two waves are correlated.) Then, too, repeated interviews may be used simply for the purpose of obtaining increasingly detailed information, not about changes, but about past experiences and more perdurable beliefs and opinions of the respondent.[63]

Disadvantages of the panel include bias resulting from refusals and attrition, the problem of providing adequate incentives to forestall such factors, and frozen responses or sophistication as a result of reinterviewing. Where panel members are supposed to keep track of their own behavior (purchases, TV viewing diary, etc.), their record-keeping may be sporadic and inaccurate.

Audience research was spawned of radio's need, decades ago, for data on audience size at least comparable to the circulation figures which printed media used in their dealings with advertisers. The assessment of size of audience is still a problem area in the media field, despite numerous advances and qualitative improvements in audience surveys in recent years. The novice journalism researcher should be familiar with the recognition-type newspaper readership surveys conducted under the auspices of the Advertising Research Foundation, as well as with similar studies conducted elsewhere according to the same basic principle developed a quarter of a century ago by George Gallup: Have the reader show you what he has read.[64]

Magazine researchers have done some impressive work in the audience measurement field since World War II. Probability samples have largely replaced quota sampling; elaborate "confusion control" safeguards have been built into measurement or interviewing procedures to forestall inflation of estimates through "recognition" of what has not been seen before; and intensive studies have been made of audience overlap, audience accumulation, and depth of reading. Large samples (often 7,500 and upward) and unbiased sampling methods have provided valid and useful data on the audiences reached by different magazines.

Various developments in newspaper and other audience research have been described elsewhere by the present author.[65] D. B. Lucas and S. H. Britt[66] provide an excellent general survey of audience research, describing in detail the procedures used by commercial research agencies in studies involving magazines, radio, television, and other media.

Attention has already been called to the danger, in surveys, of straining respondent's memories. In mass media research remedies have included reinstating the stimulus (as in the recognition-type readership study), partial reinstatement (e.g., with a roster listing TV programs), and concurrent measurement of audience behavior ("coincidental" phone call survey, and Nielsen and Arbitron meter devices which electronically record TV operation).

In 1955 the Advertising Research Foundation conducted an elaborate $100,000 comparative study of aided recall, recognition, and "reader interest" methods of measuring magazine ad readership. The then technical director of ARF, in a later review of the findings, suggested that "recognition ratings are a rough indicator of reader behavior, perhaps a guide to some kind of psychological contact more substantial than mere visual exposure."[67] Such findings, he opined, may be of real help to artists and copywriters, but "allowance must be made for large absolute errors which cannot readily be detected under the usual recognition procedures." Recognition scores did *not* appear to be measures of simple memory, inasmuch as there was no systematic drop-off in scores over time. Aided recall scores, based upon detailed interviews in which respondents were required to produce answers to questions about the appearance and content of ads, were relatively hard to replicate, but they did "behave like a measure of memory"—that is, the scores declined as the span between time of reading and time of interview increased.

Certainly no one has yet developed the "perfect" method of measuring radio and television audiences. In 1960 a committee of the American Statistical Association conducted a rather elaborate investigation of the methods used by the different broadcast rating services in obtaining data on audience size. Participants in the inquiry included well-known specialists in statistics and in survey methodology. Their report,[68] prepared for a Congressional subcommittee, provides a critical review of the sampling, interviewing, and other research methods used by the major rating services, as well as a detailed, annotated bibliography on the subject. There is need (as the committee points out) for continuing methodological research in broadcast audience measurement, given the fact that ratings often differ substantially according to the particular method used.

Written in an easily understood style, the committee report clarifies and interprets principles of research design and research reporting which have implications beyond the particular problem of estimating radio and TV audience size.

The perceptive reader will have noted that there is a kind of continuum from unreliable verbal reports to reliable verbal reports to direct observation of human behavior. Even direct observation is, of course, filtered through the observer. For the most part verbal reports are more reliable when they deal with recent behavior. Respondents, however, may not always be willing to report that behavior (e. g., not reading a newspaper yesterday, if they think of themselves as regular readers). One way around this difficulty is to ask people about their usual or regular or habitual behavior, with a follow-up question tapping the specific behavior in the most recent situation.

Sometimes the researcher may need both kinds of data. In the press-medical study mentioned earlier in this chapter, the researcher wanted to know the extent to which reporters went over their notes with doctors after interviewing them as news sources. Two questions were asked of doctors, the first dealing with what reporters usually did, and the second with what the reporter did in the case of the last news story for which the survey respondent was a source. The second question was the more defensible measure of reportorial behavior, but the first was a better indicator of the image the doctor had of newsmen—the kind of behavior which seemed to him to fit the reporter.

One other point. There has been considerable controversy in recent years over the merits of "motivation research." Market researchers have been trying to study motives for a long time, and the only really new element here is an emphasis on depth interviews, projective techniques, and other procedures used by clinical psychologists. The "MR" trend can be helpful in communications research and other areas if it does not lead to abandonment of sound sampling procedures and to disproportionate reliance on indirect or projective measurement procedures which are generally low in reliability. Certainly there is danger in the use of clinical tools by non-clinicians in a research setting which precludes clinical insights. Most motivation research methods require field workers with highly developed, professional skills.[69]

Some useful and important motivation studies have been done in the media field. One of these was Burleigh Gardner's *Women and Advertising*,[70] an extremely interesting study of women's attitudes toward different types of magazines and of the part magazines play in the lives of their readers. Techniques included projective questions, cartoons, and "Q-sort" procedure. Findings were related to American social structure, social change, and the relative isolation of the "middle majority woman" in present-day America. In short, the study was "theoretically oriented," even though it was conducted for a commercial client.

Field research in mass communication is improving. It is being applied to problems more important than mere size of audience, and researchers themselves are becoming increasingly adept at relating their studies to theory, at formulating hypotheses, at sampling adequately, and at minimizing the biases in their questions and in the way they ask them. Communications research specialists have learned a great deal from their colleagues in the behavioral sciences, many of whom are studying communication problems. Social scientists have sometimes found the media know-how of the communications researcher helpful. And industry, meanwhile, has become increasingly attentive to what the communications researcher can offer.

Used in combination with other research procedures described in this book, field research can continue to provide needed answers to important questions about communicators, "gatekeepers," audiences, effects, and the communication process itself.

REFERENCES

1. Roy E. Carter, Jr., "Newspaper 'Gatekeepers' and the Sources of News," *Public Opinion Quarterly*, 22 (1958), 133–44; Walter Gieber, "How the 'Gatekeepers' View Local Civil Liberties News," *Journalism Quarterly*, 37 (1960), 199–205.
2. W. F. Whyte, *Street Corner Society* (Chicago: University of Chicago Press, 1943).
3. W. F. Whyte, "Observational Field Work Methods," chap. 14 in Marie Jahoda, M. Deutsch, and S. W. Cook (eds.), *Research Methods in Social*

Relations (New York: Dryden Press, 1951), II, 493–513; S. M. Miller, "The Participant Observer and Over-Rapport," *American Sociological Review*, 17 (1952), 486–91.

4. "Problems of Inference and Proof in Participant Observation," *American Sociological Review*, 23 (1958), 652–60.
5. Donald T. Campbell, "The Informant in Quantitative Research," *American Journal of Sociology*, 60 (1955), 339–42.
6. Arthur H. Vidich and Gilbert Shapiro, "A Comparison of Participant Observation and Survey Data," *American Sociological Review*, 20 (1955), 28–33. See also Arthur Vidich, "Participant Observation and the Collection and Interpretation of Data," *American Journal of Sociology*, 60 (1955), 354–60.
7. H. F. Brandt, *The Psychology of Seeing* (New York: Philosophical Library, 1945); Tore Hollonquist and Edward A. Suchman, "Listening to the Listener," in Paul F. Lazarsfeld and Frank N. Stanton (eds.), *Radio Research: 1942–43* (New York: Essential Books, 1944), 265–334.
8. Leo Bogart, "How Do People Read Newspapers?" *Media Scope*, 6 (January, 1962), 53–56, 58, 60.
9. Walter A. Steigleman, "Do Newspaper Headlines Really Promote Street Sales?" *Journalism Quarterly*, 26 (1949), 379–88.
10. W. Lloyd Warner and Paul S. Lunt, *The Social Life of a Modern Community* (New Haven: Yale University Press, 1941), 54.
11. Mildred Parten, *Surveys, Polls, and Samples* (New York: Harper, 1950), 83; M. D. Kaplon, "The Observational Method in Radio Audience Measurement," *American Psychologist* (1947), 335.
12. H. C. Ludeke and R. A. Inglis, "A Technique for Validating Interviewing Methods in Reader Research," *Sociometry*, 5 (1942), 109–22.
13. D. B. Lucas and S. H. Britt, *Advertising Psychology and Research* (New York: McGraw-Hill, 1950), 438–39.
14. Walter Gieber and Walter Johnson, "The City Hall 'Beat': a Study of Reporter and Source Roles," *Journalism Quarterly*, 38 (1961), 289–97.
15. Robert P. Judd, "The Newspaper Reporter in a Suburban City," *Journalism Quarterly*, 38 (1961), 35–42.
16. Charles E. Swanson, James Jenkins, and Robert L. Jones, "President Truman Speaks: A Study of Ideas vs. Media," *Journalism Quarterly*, 27 (1950), 251–62, and "A Study of Who Believes What," *Journalism Quarterly*, 28 (1951), 39–48.
17. J. G. Ferraby, "Planning a Mass Observation Investigation," *American Journal of Sociology*, 51 (1945), 1–6. See also Leonard W. Doob, *Public Opinion and Propaganda* (New York: Holt, 1948), 191–97, and H. D. Willcock, "Mass Observation," *American Journal of Sociology*, 48 (1943), 445–56.
18. R. F. Bales, *Interaction Process Analysis* (Cambridge, Mass.: Addison-Wesley, 1951); L. Carter *et al.*, "The Relation of Categorizations and Ratings in the Observation of Group Behavior," *Human Relations*, 4 (1951), 239–54, and "A Note on a New Technique of Interaction

Recording," *Journal of Abnormal and Social Psychology,* 46 (1951), 258–60; E. D. Chapple, "The Interaction Chronograph: Its Evolution and Present Application," *Personnel,* 25 (1949), 295–307.

19. Herbert H. Hyman, *Survey Design and Analysis* (Glencoe, Ill.: The Free Press, 1955). See also Hans Zeisel, *Say It With Figures* (New York: Harper, 1957), and Fred T. Schreier, *Human Motivation: Probability and Meaning* (Glencoe, Ill.: Free Press, 1957).
20. For a lively "debate" on the use of significance tests in survey research, see Hanan C. Selvin, "A Critique of Tests of Significance in Survey Research," *American Sociological Review,* 22 (1957), 519–27, and Leslie Kish, "Some Statistical Problems in Research Design," *American Sociological Review,* 24 (1959), 328–37.
21. Roy E. Carter, Jr., Verling C. Troldahl, and R. Smith Schuneman, "Interviewer Bias in Selecting Households," *Journal of Marketing* (in press). Studies of the *sampling variability* associated with quota sampling are reported by Frederick F. Stephan and Philip J. McCarthy in *Sampling Opinions* (New York: Wiley, 1958), a nonmathematical treatment of problems in sample design and execution.
22. "Some Advantages of Telephone Surveys," *Journal of Marketing,* 20 (1956), 278–81. See also Ralph H. Oakes, "Differences in Responsiveness in Telephone vs. Personal Interviews," *Journal of Marketing,* 19 (1954), 169.
23. Morris H. Hansen, William N. Hurwitz, and William G. Madow, *Sample Survey Methods and Theory,* Vol. I: *Methods and Applications* (New York: Wiley, 1953). Readable introductions to the subject are Philip J. McCarthy, *Sampling: Elementary Principles* (Ithaca, N. Y.: Cornell University Press, 1951), and Leslie Kish, "A Two-Stage Sample of a City," *American Sociological Review,* 17 (1952), 761–69. A revision of the McCarthy pamphlet appears as chap. 20 in Jahoda, Deutsch, and Cook (eds.), *Research Methods in Social Relations,* II, 643–80.
24. W. Edwards Deming, *Sampling Design in Business Research* (New York: Wiley, 1960).
25. Charles E. Osgood, George J. Suci, and Percy H. Tannenbaum, *The Measurement of Meaning* (Urbana, Ill.: University of Illinois Press, 1957).
26. Robert K. Merton, Marjorie Fiske, and Patricia Kendall, *The Focused Interview* (Glencoe, Ill.: The Free Press, 1956). For a major application of the procedure see Merton's *Mass Persuasion* (New York: Harper, 1946). Nondirective interviewing is described in Carl Rogers, "The Non-Directive Method as a Technique for Social Research," *American Journal of Sociology,* 50 (1945), 279–83.
27. Margaret Chandler, "An Evaluation of the Group Interview," *Human Organization,* 13 (1954), 26–28. For a general discussion of the advantages and disadvantages of the "lively bull sessions" sometimes yielded by the group interview, see George Horsley Smith, *Motivation Research in Advertising and Marketing* (New York: McGraw-Hill, 1954), chap. 6.
28. Paul B. Sheatsley, "The Art of Interviewing . . .," chap. 13 in Jahoda

et al. (eds.), *Research Methods in Social Relations,* II. See also Eleanor E. and Nathan Maccoby, "The Interview: A Tool of Social Science Research," in Gardner Lindzey (ed.), *Handbook of Social Psychology* (Cambridge, Mass.: Addison-Wesley, 1954), I, 449–87. For a thorough treatment of the use of open questions, see Robert L. Kahn and Charles F. Cannell, *The Dynamics of Interviewing* (New York: John Wiley and Sons, 1957). A useful training item is J. Stacy Adams' *Interviewing Procedures: A Manual for Survey Interviewers* (Chapel Hill, N. C.: University of North Carolina Press, 1958).

29. Lester Guest, "A New Training Method for Opinion Interviewers," *Public Opinion Quarterly,* 18 (1954), 286–99.
30. See Leslie Kish, "A Procedure for Objective Respondent Selection Within the Household," *Journal of the American Statistical Association,* 44 (1949), 380–87.
31. Alfred Politz and Willard R. Simmons, "An Attempt to Get the Not-at-Homes into the Sample Without Callbacks," *Journal of the American Statistical Association,* 44 (1949), 9–42. See also Willard R. Simmons, "A Plan to Account for Not-at-Homes by Combining Weighting and Callbacks," *Journal of Marketing,* 19 (1954), 42–53. For a discussion of methods used to discourage refusals, see W. L. Slocum, L. T. Empey, and H. S. Swanson, "Increasing Response to Questionnaires and Structured Interviews," *American Sociological Review,* 21 (1956), 221–25.
32. The research is summarized in Herbert Hyman *et al., Interviewing in Social Research* (Chicago: University of Chicago Press, 1954). A brief overview of the problem is provided by Harper W. Boyd, Jr., and Ralph Westfall, "Interviewers as a Source of Error in Surveys," *Journal of Marketing,* 19 (1955), 311–24. See also the *American Journal of Sociology,* September, 1956, devoted entirely to the interview in social research.
33. Hyman *et al., Interviewing in Social Research,* 137.
34. *Ibid.,* 198 ff.
35. Lawrence Podell, "The Structured Interview as a Social Relationship," *Social Forces,* 34 (1955), 150–55.
36. David Riesman and Nathan Glazer, "The Meaning of Opinion," *Public Opinion Quarterly,* 12 (1948), 633–48. For a discussion of the problem of *deference* to the *middle*-class interviewer, see Gerhard E. Lenski and John C. Leggett, "Caste, Class, and Deference in the Research Interview," *American Journal of Sociology,* 65 (1960), 463–67.
37. For the researcher with sufficient time and resources, Guttman scaling (via the intensity function) furnishes a possible way out of this dilemma. See Edward A. Suchman and Louis Guttman, "A Solution to the Problem of Question 'Bias,'" *Public Opinion Quarterly,* 11 (1947), 445–55. Raymond Franzen and Robert Williams, "A Method for Measuring Error Due to Variance Among Interviewers," *Public Opinion Quarterly,* 20 (1956), 587-92, have suggested a useful statistical approach for determining the degree to which given questions are sus-

ceptible to interviewer effects. Resulting data could be used to build up a library of acceptable and unacceptable questionnaire practices.
38. Stanley L. Payne, *The Art of Asking Questions* (Princeton: Princeton University Press, 1951).
39. Charles E. Swanson, "Midcity Daily: The News Staff and Its Relation to Control," *Journalism Quarterly,* 26 (1949), 20–28; Edwin C. Braman and Robert L. Jones, "Television Owning and Newspaper Advertising Reading," *Journalism Quarterly,* 30 (1953), 489–501; Raymond B. Nixon, "Changes in Reader Attitudes Toward Daily Newspapers," *Journalism Quarterly,* 31 (1954), 421–33.
40. James E. Brinton, Chilton R. Bush, and Thomas M. Newell, *The Newspaper and Its Public* (Stanford, Calif.: Institute for Communicative Research, Stanford University, 1958).
41. Allen H. Barton, "Asking the Embarrassing Question," *Public Opinion Quarterly,* 22 (1958), 67–68.
42. A. J. Kinard, "Randomizing Error in Multiple-Choice Questions," *Journal of Marketing,* 19 (1955), 26–63. For a stimulating reappraisal of the whole subject of biased questions, see Eugene Litwak, "A Classification of Biased Response," *American Journal of Sociology,* 62 (1956), 182–86. Litwak points out that some of the rules for question design must vary according to the researcher's purpose. Thus the loaded question in one survey may be the purposive extreme item in another, and the much-decried vague question may have desirable exploratory or projective uses.
43. Paul F. Lazarsfeld, "The Controversy over Detailed Interviews—An Offer for Negotiation," *Public Opinion Quarterly,* 8 (1944), 36–60.
44. Paul F. Lazarsfeld, "The Art of Asking Why," *National Marketing Review,* 1 (1935), 32–43.
45. George Gallup, "The Quintamensional Plan of Question Design," *Public Opinion Quarterly,* 11 (1947), 385–93.
46. Paul F. Lazarsfeld and Harry Field, *The People Look at Radio* (Chapel Hill, N. C.: University of North Carolina Press, 1946), 5 ff.
47. Q. McNemar, "Opinion-Attitude Methodology," *Psychological Bulletin,* 43 (1946), 328.
48. William J. Goode and Paul K. Hatt, *Methods in Social Research* (New York: McGraw-Hill, 1952), 170.
49. Roy E. Carter, Jr., "The Press and Public School Superintendents in California," *Journalism Quarterly,* 31 (1954), 175–85. The response rate of 80 per cent apparently was par for the course. See J. R. Shannon, "Percentage of Returns of Questionnaires in Reputable Educational Research," *Journal of Educational Research,* 42 (1948), 138–41.
50. Daniel Katz and Hadley Cantril, "Public Opinion Polls," *Sociometry,* 1 (1937), 155–79; C. F. Reuss, "Differences Between Persons Responding and Not Responding to a Mailed Questionnaire," *American Sociological Review,* 8 (1943), 433–38; E. A. Suchman and B. McCandless, "Who Answers Questionnaires?" *Journal of Applied Psychology,* 24 (1940), 758–69.

51. One of the most elaborate methodological studies yet made of the mail questionnaire is described by Christopher Scott of the British Government Social Survey in "Research on Mail Surveys," *Journal of the Royal Statistical Society, Series A*, 124, Part II (1961), 143–205. Useful advice on follow-up mailings is offered by Lester R. Frankel, "How Incentives and Subsamples Affect the Precision of Mail Surveys," *Journal of Advertising Research*, 1 (September, 1960), 1–5.
52. J. A. Clausen and R. N. Ford, "Controlling Bias in Mail Questionnaires," *Journal of the American Statistical Association*, 42 (1947), 497–512.
53. Morris H. Hansen and William N. Hurwitz, "The Problem of Non-Response in Sample Surveys," *Journal of the American Statistical Association*, 41 (1946), 517–29. Useful tables are presented whereby the necessary number of interviews can be determined, given data on costs, response rate, and other factors.
54. Raymond D. Lawrence, in studying the characteristics of Kansas newspaper publishers, obtained a high response rate when he asked for biographical information, a low rate when respondents were queried about income. "Kansas Publishers, a Professional Analysis," *Journalism Quarterly*, 15 (1938), 337–48.
55. F. F. Waisanen, "A Note on the Response to a Mailed Questionnaire," *Public Opinion Quarterly*, 18 (1954), 210–12.
56. Goode and Hatt, *Methods in Social Research*, 177 ff. For a recent discussion of gains effected through (a) use of an airmail stamp on the return envelope and (b) a "token" gift (10¢), see Andrew E. Kimball, "Increasing the Rate of Return in Mail Surveys," *Journal of Marketing*, 25 (1961), 63–64.
57. See *Statistical Reporter* (Washington, D. C.: Director for Statistical Standards, Bureau of Budget, Executive Office of the President, April, 1952), 72–73; Don Cahalan, "Effectiveness of a Mail Questionnaire Technique in the Army," *Public Opinion Quarterly*, 15 (1951), 575–78.
58. George W. N. Riddle, "Validity of Readership Studies," *Journal of Marketing*, 18 (1953), 26–32; Clifford F. Weigle, "Two Techniques for Surveying Newspaper Readership Compared," *Journalism Quarterly*, 18 (1941), 153–57.
59. Charles T. Duncan, "How the Weekly Press Covers News of Local Government," *Journalism Quarterly*, 29 (1952), 283–93.
60. Mitchell V. Charnley, "The Radio Newsroom: A Descriptive Study," *Journalism Quarterly*, 28 (1951), 189–95.
61. *1962 Consumer Analysis* (St. Paul: St. Paul *Dispatch* and *Pioneer Press*). For a discussion of some limitations of a brand preference study in which respondents returned questionnaires themselves, see Arthur Highman, "The Audited Self-Administered Questionnaire," *Journal of Marketing*, 19 (1955), 155–59.
62. *Minnesota Homemaker Survey No. 14* (Minneapolis *Star* and *Tribune*, 1961); *Top Ten Brands* (Portland: Dan E. Clark II and Associates, Inc., 1955).

63. Murray Wax and Leopold J. Shapiro, "Repeated Interviewing," *American Journal of Sociology*, 62 (1956), 215–17. The authors point to an approach in dynamic psychology which suggests that people are generally complex and stable and that a "prolonged siege" may be necessary if maximum information is to be obtained. For general discussions of the panel method, see Hans Zeisel, *Say It with Figures* (New York: Harper, 1957); Paul F. Lazarsfeld and Morris Rosenberg (eds.), *The Language of Social Research* (Glencoe, Ill.: Free Press, 1955), 231–59; Patricia Kendall, *Conflict and Mood* (Glencoe, Ill.: Free Press, 1954).
64. George Gallup, "A Scientific Method for Determining Reader Interest," *Journalism Quarterly*, 7 (1930), 1–13. See also Ralph Nafziger, Malcolm MacLean, Jr., and Warren Engstrom, "Useful Tools for Interpreting Newspaper Readership Data," *Journalism Quarterly*, 28 (1951), 441–56; Robert L. Jones and Leslie A. Beldo, "Methodological Improvements in Readership Data Gathering," *Journalism Quarterly*, 30 (1953), 345–53.
65. Roy E. Carter, Jr., "Field Research in Journalism: A Tentative Review and Appraisal," *Journal of Marketing*, 21 (1956), 137–48.
66. See note 13 *supra*.
67. Raw data are reported in Advertising Research Foundation, *A Study of Printed Advertising Rating Methods* (New York: Advertising Research Foundation, 1955–57), I, II, III. Interpretations are those of Darrell B. Lucas, "The ABCs of ARF's PARM," *Journal of Marketing*, 25 (1960), 9–20. See also Ray Lapica, *SPONSOR All-Media Evaluation Study* (New York: SPONSOR Services, 1954).
68. William G. Madow *et al.*, *Evaluation of Statistical Methods Used in Obtaining Broadcast Ratings* (Washington: American Statistical Association, 1961), issued by U. S. Government Printing Office, Washington, as House Report No. 193, 87th Congress, 1st Session (report of the Committee on Interstate and Foreign Commerce).
69. For an insightful discussion of problems and limitations in motivation research, see Paul F. Lazarsfeld, "Reflections on Business," *American Journal of Sociology*, 65 (1959), 10–13. British psychologist H. J. Eysenck has published a rather hyperbolic but convincing criticism of the "pseudo-scientific 'explanations'" which MR sometimes produces concerning consumer behavior: "What's the Truth about Psychoanalysis?" *Reader's Digest* (January, 1960), 1–6. Motivational research techniques are described and criticized from many points of view in Robert Ferber and Hugh G. Wales (eds.), *Motivation and Market Behavior* (Homewood, Ill.: Richard D. Irwin, Inc., 1958).
70. Prepared for *Good Housekeeping* by Social Research, Inc., Chicago, 1954.

5

Statistical Methods in Communication Research

JOHN E. ALMAN AND
DAVID M. WHITE

THIS CHAPTER discusses statistical methods that are the common tools of research in the social sciences. We shall be concerned with the rationale behind these methods and with fostering an understanding of criteria useful for the selection of appropriate methods for a particular problem. We assume that the reader has some familiarity with the elements of statistics—the mean, standard deviation, the correlation coefficient, the normal curve. And we shall not emphasize the mechanics of the various procedures. These are well covered by various statistical works, some of which are among the references listed at the end of this chapter. It is our observation that mastery of the mechanics of statistical procedures is often reached long before genuine understanding filters through.

To aid in understanding the commonly used statistical tests and procedures, we emphasize the underlying rationale in an expository fashion that avoids mathematical abstractions insofar as possible. For the serious reader we intend that this chapter supplement a good textbook in statistics. To the extent that methods particularly appropriate to journalism research can be cited and discussed, we do so, although the methods discussed are on the whole common to the social sciences in general, and there are no statistical methods peculiar to journalism research.

We shall be concerned entirely with the notion of *statistical inference,* which may be described in a general way as the science of making objective generalizations from limited and fallible information. In journalism research we often are concerned with the characteristics of the various communication media, or how people think about or react to these media. Whether the units of measurement of our research are media or people, we have an embarrassingly large number of them to observe—so large, indeed, that no research project can do better than to observe a small sample. However we select the units we actually observe and whatever are the observations we make on them, there is always a crucial question to be answered. How can we generalize from those we have actually observed to the far greater domain of those we theoretically might have observed? And when we have made our generalizations from observed data, can we make any objective statement about the reliability of our conclusions? In a general sense the answers to these questions are found in the methods of statistical inference.

Problems of Sampling

We note first that any sample of observed data implies a population of units, all of whom it is theoretically possible to observe and measure. A population is usually thought of as being unlimited in number, even though common sense tells us there must be limits. For our purposes it will be sufficient to say that populations are normally very large relative to the resources of a research project for making observations. A population is defined if we can state at least one characteristic whereby we can decide whether or not a given observed unit belongs to the population. For example, we can define a population by the phrase "newspaper readers." This is too general to be useful since it can include any person reading a newspaper in any place at any point in time. A somewhat sharper definition might be something like "subscription readers of a certain magazine for a given issue." Now if we wish to examine the likes and dislikes, attitudes and habits, of persons included in this definition, these persons must be coralled and interviewed in some way. We recognize that (1) it is normally impossible to interview all such persons, and (2) even if this could be done, we would realize intuitively that long before we reached the end of the list of names, we would have a pretty good idea of how these readers think, or act, or believe. This is equivalent to stating that we do not need to observe the entire population; we can obtain essentially the desired information from a portion of the population, i. e., a "sample," and from the sample we can predict how the unobserved portion of the population thinks, or acts, or believes. To complete the picture we perceive what seems intuitively sound: the larger the sample, the more confidently we can state conclusions about the entire population.

A restriction must be placed on the above, however. Suppose that in polling our hypothetical subscribers, we started with those living in New York City and proceeded generally to interview subscribers according to city of residence. It seems obvious that before we could claim to speak for the population of subscribers, we should have to cover all geographical areas in which they lived. We might guess, for example, that the subscribers living in New York City are not similar in their attitudes and beliefs to all subscribers; that is, New York City subscribers form a biased sample of the population of subscribers. To obtain a reasonable estimate of the characteristics of a population it is necessary that the sample not reflect unduly the characteristics of any particular subgroup. A sample that meets this criterion cannot be secured by the process of noting biases in the sample, for this implies that we know the characteristics of the population and its possible subgroups. Such a sample can be obtained only through a random process of selection. Such a process is one in which every member of the population has an equal chance, with known probability, of being included in the sample. For example, given the entire subscription list of a magazine in an alphabetical sequence by name, we select every hundredth name, producing thereby a one per cent sample.[a] By this procedure we could be reasonably confident that the characteristics of the sample would reflect those of the population.

It is obvious that we do not always have a situation in which a random sample can be secured from a prepared list of names. For example, change our definition to read "newsstand readers" instead of "subscription readers" and the difficulties of securing a random sample increase manifoldly. Nevertheless, the science of statistics is built on the assumption that our samples are random samples from populations. The difficulties in defining appropriate populations and

[a] Strictly speaking, this procedure does not produce a truly random sample. There are certain minor biases in sampling an alphabetically arranged list, but for large samples from a long list of names the objections are trivial.

in securing random samples are legion and cannot be discussed at length in this chapter.[b] Yet, if we are to generalize from a sample to a target population, we must have some assurance that, in the statistical sense, the sample can represent the population. This situation cannot truly be assured unless the samples are obtained from a defined population by some random process. An excellent discussion of the problems of random sampling is found in W. G. Cochran *et al.*,[1] and other references.

Let us assume we can define our target population, such as our subscription readers, and can obtain random samples from that population and observe their characteristics. We make the following observations about these samples: (1) We would expect the characteristics to be different on the average from sample to sample, even though the samples are truly randomly chosen. (2) We would expect the variation in average values from sample to sample to be smaller as the samples are increased in size. These observations are two basic principles of statistical inference.

To illustrate, using our population of subscription readers, suppose we obtain by a random process a sample of one hundred such readers and find that twenty-five out of the one hundred read a certain article. We estimate, then, that 25% of the population reads the article. This is our best estimate; indeed, it is our only estimate of this percentage. But if we had obtained other similar samples, we would have obtained other percentages, each of which is an estimate of the unknown percentage in the population. It is meaningless to ask which is the best, of course; it is meaningful only to ask how much variation we can expect among these estimates. In fact, it would be decidedly advantageous if our original estimate of 25% could be reported with a proviso such as "I am reasonably sure that the true percentage in the population lies between 21% and 29%," i.e., $25\% \pm 4\%$. Such a statement allows us to make a generalization from a sample together with a statement about the expected magnitude of our error of estimate. This statement requires clarification. We have stated on the basis of a single sample that the unknown true percentage lies within a given range; the statement is either true or false. If we repeated this process for many samples, each time giving an estimated percentage and a range above

[b] See Chapter 4.

and below the estimated value within which we expect the true value to lie, we could score our statements as true or false according as to whether the true value lay within or without the given range. If, in the long run, 90% of such statements are true in that the "true" percentage actually does lie within the stated limits, we may be said to have a 90% confidence interval.

Generalizing from a Sample

To state a confidence interval for an estimate of a population value obtained from a sample requires a knowledge of how these sample proportions vary from sample to sample. Under the assumption that we produce proportions from many samples of size N randomly drawn from a single population, we can expect the standard deviation of these proportions to be given by the formula

$$\bar{\sigma}_P = \sqrt{\frac{\bar{p}\bar{q}}{N}} \tag{1}$$

where $\bar{p}$ is the true proportion in the population, $\bar{q} = 1 - \bar{p}$, and N is the sample size. Since we normally do not know the true proportion, we substitute the obtained proportion as an approximation. For the example given earlier, $p = .25$, $q = .75$, and $N = 100$. From these figures we obtain not $\bar{\sigma}$, but $\hat{\sigma}$, an estimate of $\bar{\sigma}$. This turns out to be 4.33%. To use this figure to obtain the confidence interval, we assume that the sample percentages for this example are approximately normally distributed—a fair assumption—and note that 1.96 standard deviations above and below the expected value account for 95% of the area under the normal curve. We can set our confidence limits as approximately $25\% \pm (1.96)(4.33)$, or $25 \pm 8.5\%$. Thus when we report the sample estimate of 25% and state we are "95% confident that the true percentage lies between 16.5% and 33.5%," we have really stated that we have followed a procedure for setting the interval that would result in the true value actually falling within the interval 95 times out of 100 in repeated sampling from the same population. This is a somewhat involved way to state what seems at first glance to be a simple statement. However, the literature on confidence intervals is extensive, and the concepts stem from precise mathematical thinking. For a more detailed discussion of confidence limits, the reader is referred to P. O. Johnson.[2]

The above brief discussion of confidence intervals suggests one way in which we may generalize from a sample. We now give an example in which the kind of generalization is somewhat different. Suppose we define two populations of readers of a newspaper: newsstand buyers and home delivery readers. Setting aside problems of defining and obtaining samples of these two populations, we assume that we have obtained the desired samples and the percentage of subjects in each sample who regularly read a certain feature. Suppose we have interviewed one hundred subjects in each sample with results as shown below.

TABLE 1

	Do read the feature	*Do not read the feature*	
Home delivery	25	75	100
Newsstand	35	65	100
Total	60	140	200

Our interest now centers on the contrast between the two categories of readers, which shows a difference in readership of ten out of one hundred. The problem may be restated by pointing out that, while the sample of newsstand readers shows a higher readership percentage, this higher percentage may be an accident of the sample, and it may be that in the populations no difference exists. The latter statement hypothesizes a "true difference" of zero, referred to as the *null hypothesis*. If we assume, for the moment, that the null hypothesis is true, we logically can pool the two groups together to form a single sample of readers from which we estimate that 30% reads the feature. We then ask if the percentages for the separate groups differ by no more than could reasonably be expected if we examined two random samples from the populations with the same readership percentage. What could be "reasonably expected" can be determined only if we know something of how variable such differences can be in repeated random sampling.

It can be shown for the case at hand that the standard deviation of such differences, varying around the "true" difference of zero, is 6.5%. If we assume that these differences follow a normal curve distribution, as they do quite well when the samples are this large, we may picture the situation by the figure on page 134.

We observe that a deviation from the expected value of zero is $10/6.5 = 1.54$ standard units on the normal curve scale; the area of either tail is approximately 6%. Since we can expect both plus and minus deviations if the null hypothesis is true, we conclude that in repeated random sampling we could expect to obtain differences as

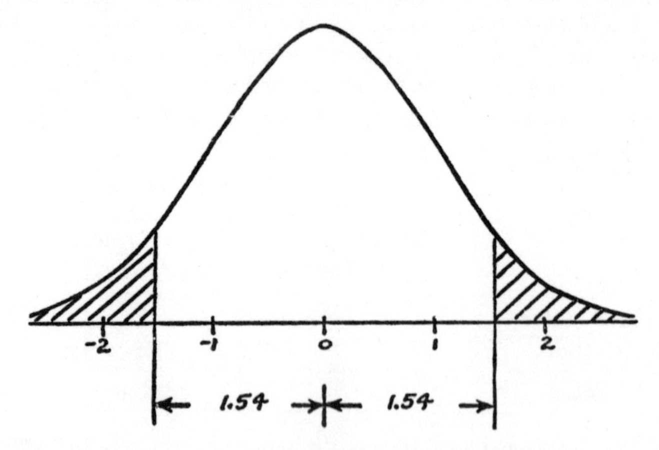

observed or greater in either direction about twelve times out of one hundred. If we adopt the convention that we shall reject the null hypothesis if differences equal to or larger than the obtained difference appear five times out of a hundred or less, we must accept the null hypothesis for this example.[c]

The above approach is described by the phrase, "testing a hypothesis." The hypothesis under test is the null hypothesis, i. e., that a zero difference characterizes the population sampled. The larger the difference obtained in the samples, the less confidence we have in accepting the hypothesis of zero differences. Our "confidence" is measured by the relative frequency of occurrence in random sampling of deviations from zero difference of a given magnitude or larger. If this relative frequency is five out of one hundred, we may reject the null hypothesis "at the 5% level of significance." That is to say, if we repeated this theoretical experiment many times, with the pooled percentage estimate the same each time, we would

[c] The numerical solution to this example is best handled by the Chi-square test for the fourfold table referred to later in the chapter. The present example is concerned with the rationale, not the computing procedure.

expect to be wrong in rejecting the null hypothesis no more than five times out of one hundred.

We can be wrong in rejecting the null hypothesis, no matter what size difference is actually obtained. It is easy to see that we would have less chance of being wrong if we insisted that the difference should be large enough to reach the 1% point on a normal curve instead of the 5% point. Indeed, we could reduce our chances of being wrong in rejecting the null hypothesis to as small a value as we pleased, simply by insisting on a sufficiently large difference. The fallacy, of course, is that by this process we continually increase our chances of being wrong in not rejecting the null hypothesis. Somehow we must steer a careful course between these two kinds of error.

The first error, that of rejecting the null hypothesis when in fact it is true, is known as a Type I error; the error of accepting the null hypothesis when it is in fact false is a Type II error. The first is the error of finding differences where none truly exist; the second is the error of not recognizing true differences. The inescapable fact of making decisions from partial information—i. e., from a sample of a population—is that the possibility exists of making one or the other type of error, whichever way the decision is made. The methods of statistics provide ways of making decisions so as to allow a direct estimate of the probability of making a Type I error; indeed, the investigator can set this risk himself merely by selecting the proper point along the normal curve baseline to make this risk of error as small or as large as he pleases. However, an estimate of the probability of making a Type II error, as F. Mosteller and R. R. Bush [3] put it (p. 291), ". . . is not constant, rather it depends on the wrongness of the null hypothesis, the sample size, the significance level chosen, and the particular method of testing significance." An excellent discussion of the power of a test of the null hypothesis, i. e., the probability of not making a Type II error, is given by Mosteller and Bush (pp. 290–300).

Since the power of a statistical test refers to its ability to recognize true differences, the researcher in journalism should be cognizant of this important aspect of statistical tests. Much of the research in journalism arises because someone has an idea that certain differences exist and can be demonstrated. For example, methods of presentation are chosen because someone thinks one method is better than another for capturing the interest of readers. In statistical language we hypothesize a zero difference, design an experiment to test this hypothesis, and rest our case on its outcome. Parenthetically, we would point out that no one really expects the null hypothesis to hold exactly; in practical research we are usually, although not always, looking for situations where the departure from the null hypothesis is substantial. It is here that the economics of research sometimes makes difficulty; for the research budget often demands that samples be kept as small as possible, consistent with the desired outcomes. But without a way of making a practical determination of the size of samples sufficient for the job, we usually make our samples as large as possible. By so doing there is often considerable waste in time and money in the mechanics of collecting and processing the data. Consideration of the power and operating characteristics of statistical tests of significance should be examined carefully in the planning stages of a research project, not after the data are collected. The reader is strongly urged to read carefully the excellent discussion by Mosteller and Bush on this important topic.[4]

Nominal and Scaled Data

We proceed now to discuss the observed characteristics of people and media that enter into communications research and the ways in which our observations of these characteristics are recorded, i. e., the raw data of research. These considerations have important bearing on the choice of the appropriate statistical techniques.

When we observe people we often place them into categories, e. g., male or female, in occupational groups, by political affiliation, and the like. We define, usually in advance, several mutually exclusive categories and insist that each person observed shall be counted in one and only one of the categories. The results of observation are tables showing the number of persons falling into each category. When observations are recorded in terms of two or more characteristics taken simultaneously, the resulting frequencies are expressed in a contingency table, e. g., registered voters counted by sex and by expressed party affiliation.

Data expressed in terms of the numbers of observations that fall into each of several mutually exclusive categories are usually called *nominal* data. The key characteristic of nominal data is that no order relationships among the several categories necessarily exist. Religious preference, for example, provides a set of categories among which no "greater than" or "less than" relationships exist. Occupational categories are generally considered to provide nominal data, though it is possible to argue that such categories can be arranged in an order approximating a scale of social status. In the latter case the occupational groups may be said to provide *ordinal* data in that a natural ordering of the categories is recognized. If we go one step further to develop a scale of social status, placing each occupational category at some point on the scale, then the data are said to be *scaled.* In many instances ordinal data are treated as though they were nominal, i.e., the natural order among the categories is ignored. Often the intrinsic difficulties in defining a defensible scale of measurement are such as to make it preferable to treat the data in a conservative fashion by ignoring order.

When the ordered categories of ordinal data are assigned to points along a scale, we are assuming the existence of an underlying continuous scale of measurement. As with our social status example, it may be impossible to make a precise measurement for each person observed; the best we can do is assign all persons in a category to the same point on the scale. If we can have reasonable assurance that the intervals between points represent equal distances on the underlying scale, then our data are expressed on an *interval* scale. Finally, if our interval scale has a true zero point, we then have a *ratio* scale. In practice, ratio scales usually are those for which the units of measurement are inherent in the characteristic observed, e.g., the number of years a household has had a TV set.

Statistical methodology, generally speaking, requires only that we distinguish between nominal and scaled data. The techniques applicable to these two kinds of data are different. For nominal data the basic statistic is Chi-square; this provides us with the means of comparing sets of frequencies and drawing inferences about their differences in probabilistic fashion. Analysis of variance and correlation methods are basic for scaled data. For statistical purposes, even though the issue is not clear, we must decide whether our data are to be treated as nominal or scaled. The statistical techniques are unconcerned with the validity of the decision; in the interpretation of the results of statistical analysis, however, the investigator must take into account the nature of the data.

The nature and definition of scales appropriate to ordinal data is more properly a measurement problem, a matter taken up at greater length in Chapter 7. However, the statistician cannot be unconcerned with the nature of the data. Treating as nominal data that which is expressed in ordered categories may result in overly conservative conclusions from the statistical tests. The reverse holds, for we can be led astray by crude and ambiguous scales of measurement and place more faith in our statistical results than the underlying data warrant.

A variant of ordinal data occurs when the observations themselves are ranked, as opposed to placing them into ordered categories. Ranked data imply that an order discrimination can be made for every pair of observations, even though nothing can be said about the distance between each pair of items in the ranking. As an example of ranked data, we might ask observers to rank five articles in order of "readability." This implies that no objective measure of readability is used, but rather that the observer subjectively compares the five stories by pairs to make his final rank order decisions. Ranking is usually limited to a small number of items and to situations in which measurement must be intuitive and subjective. The number of pairs increases rapidly as the number of items increases, and human observers have difficulty in dealing with a large number of discriminations. Nevertheless, ranking methods are used and under the right circumstances can be the most efficient method of recording the results of observation. Statistical methods appropriate to ranked data exist and are discussed in a later section under the general heading of nonparametric methods.

To round out the discussion of the various kinds of data, we need take note of the concept of a *variable*. Quite generally a variable is any characteristic of the units to be observed that varies over the population of units. The importance of the term comes when we classify the observable characteristics among independent and dependent variables.

Independent variables. These are characteristics of the observed units that are inherent and not subject to control by the investigator or are characteristics to be controlled and manipulated by the study. Independent variables are usually antecedent in nature; they set the stage for the observations that are the point and purpose of the study.

Age, sex, income, occupation, and education are observable characteristics of persons drawn in a sample; it is rather rare that at least some of these characteristics do not have a bearing on communications research.[5] The investigator may search for differences in another characteristic that can be associated with these variables. Or he may use certain of these descriptive variables to confine his study to particular strata of the population. For example, he might use sex and age for the selection of units to be studied, as would be the case if the reactions of elderly males (defined as age 65 and over) to a television program were desired.

The independent variable is also the kind the experimenter manipulates in setting the conditions under which an experiment operates. For example, in a newspaper readability study a variable is the type of item—news, feature, sports, editorial—that is presented to the observers. Or perhaps one is concerned with students' recognition of bias in newswriting; the kind and degree of bias are controlled in the readings presented to the student. Because of their obvious relationship to psychological research, these variables may be described as stimulus variables. More often than not these will be categorical in nature, representing classification of the stimuli into mutually exclusive categories.

Dependent variables. In a broad sense the dependent variable is a record of the response of a subject to a stimulus. The hypotheses which provoked a study can be stated in terms of the dependent variables. Often we are concerned with searching for differences in the dependent variables that can be related to the structure of the stimulus patterns or associated with varying characteristics of the subjects observed. Or we may be interested in predicting the kind and degree of a response from the antecedent variables.

The methodology of statistical inference is chiefly concerned with placing independent and dependent variables in juxtaposition and drawing inferences concerning the relationship between them. The choice of statistical method depends on both the kind of data and the nature of the relationship under investigation.

The Chi-Square Test

We examine first a situation in which the dependent and independent variables are expressed as nominal data. Each unit observed is placed into one of the mutually exclusive categories defined by the combination of the two variables, i. e., a two-way classification scheme. The units are classified, or selected, according to an a priori consideration; they are also observed and classified by "outcome," the dependent variable. Our task is to draw an inference about the relationship, or lack of relationship, between the two variables. As an example, suppose our units are newspapers and our independent variable is the type of paper—large city daily, small city daily, weekly. The outcome, the dependent variable, is that of political position—Republican, Democrat, Independent. The data (fictitious) are recorded in Table 2.

TABLE 2

	Republican	*Democrat*	*Ind.*	*Total*
Large city dailies	12	3	2	17
Small city dailies	27	11	10	48
Weeklies	21	16	8	45
Total	60	30	20	110

The null hypothesis states that political position is independent of type of newspaper. To make this statement more objective, we observe that, when all types of papers in the sample are pooled, the numbers of papers in the three political categories are in the ratio 6:3:2. If the null hypothesis is to be acceptable, then the numbers in each row of the table must be approximately in this same ratio. Since each type of paper is represented by a sample of such papers, we can allow some departure from these ratios owing to the vagaries of sampling. How much to allow requires a statistical test—for these data the Chi-square test. Without formally giving a computational procedure—any statistical text gives all necessary details—we first note that the ratio 6 : 3 : 2 allows us to calculate an expected value for each cell if the null hypothesis is true. For example, the expected number of Republican large city dailies is 6/11 of 17, or 9.3; for Republican small city dailies, 6/11 of 48 or 26.2, leaving 24.5 as the expected value for Republican weeklies. In similar fashion, using the ratio 3/11, expected values for the Democratic column are calculated as 4.6, 13.1 and 12.3. Finally, by subtraction, the expected values for the Independent column are 3.1, 8.7, 8.2. We see that in every cell there is a discrepancy between the observed and expected value. We now divide the square of the difference between the observed and expected value for each cell by the expected value. The sum of the quantities so obtained is the statistic Chi-square; symbolically this is written as

$$\chi^2 = \Sigma \frac{(fo - fe)^2}{fe} \qquad (2)$$

where *fo* and *fe* refer to the observed and expected frequencies, respectively, and the indicated summation is over all cells of the table. For the illustrative example given $\chi^2 = 3.9$.

To evaluate the obtained Chi-square for acceptance or rejection of the null hypothesis, we note that the expected frequencies, which are merely the numerical expression of the null hypothesis, are derived from the data at hand. The sample sizes (17, 48, 45) must be considered fixed in the sense that we are inquiring into sampling variation of samples of these sizes. In a similar sense the column totals must be considered fixed in that they represent the best available evidence as to the political line-up in the population of newspapers as evidenced by the total sample of 110. Now observe that, with these marginal frequencies fixed, we can select any four numbers to go into any four of the cells (provided, of course, that any such number did not exceed a corresponding marginal frequency), and the remaining cells are automatically determined by subtraction from the marginal frequencies. This table of data, then, has four degrees of freedom.[d] From a table of the probability distribution of Chi-square (see any statistical textbook) we find that for a table with 4 d. f. we could expect to obtain a value of Chi-square at least as large as 3.9 about 40 times out of 100, if the null hypothesis is true. Hence the probability of making a Type I error—rejecting the null hypothesis when it is actually true—is .4; if we have made an a priori agreement to reject the null hypothesis when the probability of

[d] Notice the general principle of determining degrees of freedom. In each column we fix the column total; we lose thereby one degree of freedom from the three cells, leaving two for each column. But the last column has no degrees of freedom since the row totals are also fixed. In general, we note the number of observable quantities and subtract the number of totals fixed by the conditions of the null hypothesis. This principle reappears often. Degrees of freedom hereafter are abbreviated to d. f.

making a Type I error is equal to or less than .05, we accept the null hypothesis, thereby concluding that there is no evidence from these data of a relationship between political position and type of newspaper.

As another example of the use of Chi-square, suppose subjects are asked to state one of two positions on a controversial subject; after a lapse of time during which the topic receives heavy news and editorial page coverage, they are asked to state their position again. The data for one hundred subjects might appear as in Table 3 below.

TABLE 3

		After		
		For	*Against*	
Before	For	40	19	59
	Against	11	30	41
		51	49	100

To assess properly these data we must be clear as to the hypothesis under test. We note first that the subjects who do not change their position shed no light on what took place during the interval of time. Only the thirty subjects who switched position provide information. Clearly, if the direction of change is evenly divided among the thirty, one can conclude that change is an individual matter and that there is no evidence of "trend." Hence, the degree of departure from a 50–50 split among the "changers" is the key to the appropriate statistical test. For this case Chi-square is calculated as shown below.

$$\chi^2 = \frac{(19 - 11)^2}{30} = 2.13$$

This Chi-square has just one degree of freedom since the two frequencies (19 and 11) must add to 30. For d. f. = 1 Chi-square must be at least 3.84 to be significant at the 5% level of confidence; hence we accept the conclusion that there is insufficient evidence of trend. The null hypothesis that we accept here states that we have drawn a sample of thirty "changers" from a population in which change is equally likely to take place in either direction. We conclude our data are compatible with this hypothesis. Stated differently, we can ask how likely we are to find as large a departure from a 50–50 split of the changers in many, many samples of thirty each from a population in which the 50–50 split is true. From a table of the probabilities associated with values of Chi-square we find that splits that are this extreme or more so occur with a frequency of about fifteen times out of a hundred. Thus, our probability is .15, and since it is greater than .05, we agree to accept the null hypothesis.

In general the Chi-square statistic is appropriate in any situation where an observed distribution of frequencies is compared with a hypothesized distribution; the observed distribution represents one sample from a population defined by the hypothetical distribution. The test itself specifies whether the departure from the null hypothesis—agreement between the observed and hypothetical distributions—is sufficient to reject the null hypothesis at a given risk, say 5/100, of making a Type I error. Any data that are ordinarily summarized by means of proportions or percentages can be subjected to a Chi-square test provided that a meaningful null hypothesis can be stated. We note parenthetically that, when the data are expressed in terms of percentages, the frequencies from which the percentages are derived should be used in calculation, not the percentages themselves.

For all its apparent simplicity, the literature on the Chi-square test is extensive, and it is too often misused. Some limitations on Chi-square are summarized herewith.

1. The expected values in the cells must not be too small. What is too small is not subject to easy definition, but expected values less than ten in any cell should suggest caution. If one entire category—a row or a column—has small expected values, it is often possible to make a meaningful combination of the row (or column) with another, thus raising the magnitude of the expected values in the combined row or column. If the data are in the form of a two-way dichotomy—a four-celled table commonly referred to as a "two-by-two" table—Yates's correction [e] may be used in the calculation of Chi-square. If expected cell frequencies are small, this correction leads to a more realistic evaluation of the probability of being wrong in rejecting the null hypothesis, e.g., without the correction the estimated probability of a Type I error is too small. Yates's correction is valid regardless of the size of the cell frequencies but produces negligible effect when frequencies are large. For a more complete discussion of

[e] See, for example, George W. Snedecor, reference 7, p. 217.

the effect of small expected values in the cells the reader should consult references such as Johnson [6] and Snedecor.[7]

2. Responses tabulated must be mutually exclusive in the sense that the response of each unit or subject is tallied only once. Multiple responses per unit are utilized only if the entire data table is concerned with a single unit. In this case we are not sampling individuals, but the responses of a single individual.

3. All responses must be counted. Consider the following simple example. Suppose two groups of subjects are asked to respond Yes or No to a question. We obtain for group A fifteen Yes responses, and nineteen such responses for group B. It might seem at first glance that we could test the split between 15 and 19 against the hypothesis that they should split "50–50," i.e., 17, 17. This fails to take into account the No responses in the group, which is equivalent to ignoring the number of persons in groups A and B. The appropriate test stems from a two-by-two table whose columns are the Yes and No response categories and whose rows represent groups A and B.

For a more detailed discussion of Chi-square and its rationale the reader is encouraged to examine the discussion of the Chi-square in several of the works given in the references at the end of this chapter. It should be made clear at this point that the utility of Chi-square extends considerably beyond its usage as a test of the independence of rows and columns in a two-way table of frequencies.

Analysis of Variance

We turn now to methods for the analysis of scaled data. For such data the primary statistic descriptive of a sample of units is the arithmetic mean. We are frequently concerned with contrasting two or more groups of subjects with respect to their mean levels of response—mean ratings, mean scores, mean frequency of mention, and the like. The groups of subjects whose means we wish to contrast differ in at least one characteristic, and the purpose of the research is concerned with how a change in that characteristic affects the mean level of response. This is the problem we tackle by means of analysis of variance.

The term "analysis of variance" is misleading, in a sense, because we are really interested in analyzing differences among means. However, the term takes on meaning if we recognize that differences among means is merely another way of saying that means *vary* from sample to sample. It is the variation among sample means that we analyze.

As a starting point we need to consider how means of samples vary when we draw samples from a population by a purely random device. As an example, suppose we roll three dice, count the "pips" showing, and record this as a "score." Each roll is a sampling unit; each score may vary between 3 and 18. Suppose further that we agree to call ten rolls a sample, for which we compute the mean by summing the scores and dividing by ten. We continue the process until we have many such samples. Intuitively it seems evident that (1) the means of these samples will vary, and (2) the variation in mean values will be smaller than the variation in scores. Some reflection about dice will lead us to expect that the mean score for a very large number of rolls will be about 10.5 and that the means for our samples of ten rolls each will vary around this value.

We evoke this model of a random sampling device to point up the fact that differences among means of samples occur even though the samples are indistinguishable in any logical sense. Thus, even though the samples in a research study differ in some important characteristic, e. g., sex, age, economic status, we cannot claim that the level of response is affected by this characteristic unless we can demonstrate greater mean differences than we would expect if the samples are generated by a random device. This is the essential task of the method of analysis of variance.

The measure of variability of scaled data that we use is the *variance*. In words, the variance is the average squared deviation from the mean. In symbols this is written as

$$s^2 = \frac{\sum^{N}(X - \bar{X})^2}{N}$$

where s^2 denotes the variance, X is an observed value of scaled data, $\bar{X}$ is the mean value for the sample, N is the number of units in the sample, and $\sum^{N}$ indicates the operation of summing the N values of the squared deviations. The square root of the variance is the standard deviation, s. The numerator in the above formula is the sum of squares of deviations from the mean, usually abbreviated to "sum of squares," or, more simply, to s. s.

The above definition of the variance refers to the *sample* variance, i. e., the variance computed from a sample of data. Conceptually, however, we will deal with the population variance, denoted henceforth by σ^2. This measures the variability of our scores in the population from which we draw samples; assuming that our population can never be measured *in toto*, this variance can never be known exactly, though it can be estimated from a sample of data. (When we wish to refer to an *estimate* of the population variance we will denote such by $\hat{\sigma}^2$.)

To return to the problem of the variability of means of random samples from a population, we can speak of the population variance of means, denoted by $\sigma^2{}_m$, by thinking of the means of many samples as constituting single observations, i. e., "scores." A general relationship between the variance of means and the variance of scores in the population can be stated thusly: the variation among means of random samples decreases in proportion to the increase in sample size. In symbols,

$$\sigma^2{}_m = \frac{\sigma^2}{N}$$

where N is the size of sample. We can algebraically rearrange the above and write

$$\frac{N\sigma^2{}_m}{\sigma^2} = 1$$

In truth, the above expresses our expectancy, i. e., that if we calculate the variance of means of many random samples we *expect* the ratio to be one. Even if the number of samples is very large and the population variance is known with certainty, we expect the ratio to be very close to one but not necessarily exactly one. Such uncertainty expresses the fact that in actuality we can deal with only a finite amount of data; we cannot continue indefinitely the process of drawing random samples. So, in practice we can only estimate the variance of sample means from data, just as we can only estimate a population variance. Substituting the notation for estimates, we can write for the above ratio

$$F = \frac{N\hat{\sigma}^2{}_m}{\hat{\sigma}^2}$$

This, the F-ratio, is the fundamental relationship of analysis of variance. To make use of it we argue as follows: Think of each sample as being randomly drawn from a population. Let every population from which a sample is drawn have a common variance, σ^2. If every population has a common mean value, we expect the F-ratio to be unity. However, if the populations have different mean values we expect the F-ratio to be larger than unity, for the measure of the variance of the means must reflect the differences in the population means. Thus, the magnitude of the F-ratio reflects the differences among the population means.

In practice we have several samples of subjects; each sample differs from another on some characteristic which the experimenter feels will affect the mean value of the response variable. If he is wrong, the means of his samples will differ only by amounts reflecting random sampling variability, and the F-ratio will be predictably near unity. Thus, F can be used to *test* the experimenter's hypothesis that the means of the populations from which his samples are drawn are different. One needs to know, then, how large F can be before one is willing to reject the hypothesis of equal population means. More precisely, one needs to know the probability of obtaining an F of a given magnitude or larger under conditions of true random sampling of populations with equal means. Such values of F have been computed from mathematical theory and are available in tables.

To obtain F we need estimates of the population variance and of the variance of means. So we digress for a moment to see how, in general, we obtain estimates of population variances. The formula given at the beginning of this section defines the sample variance, in which we use the deviations of the scores from the sample mean. To estimate correctly the population variance, however, we should express each score as a deviation from the population mean, which we denote by μ. In symbols, then,

$$\hat{\sigma}^2 = \frac{\sum^{N}(X-\mu)^2}{N}$$

This formula can be rewritten as

$$\hat{\sigma}^2 = \frac{\sum^{N}[(X-\bar{X})-(\bar{X}-\mu)]^2}{N}$$

After some algebra the above becomes

$$\hat{\sigma}^2 = \frac{\sum^{N}(X - \bar{X})^2}{N} + (\bar{X} - \mu)^2$$

The first term on the right is the simple variance, s^2; solving for this term,

$$s^2 = \hat{\sigma}^2 - (\bar{X} - \mu)^2$$

This formula asserts that the sample variance is smaller than the correct estimate of the population variance by an amount equal to the square of the deviation of the sample mean from the population mean. Thus, the sample variance is said to be a *biased* estimate of the population variance.

Now if we compute s^2 for many samples and averages, the first term on the right can be taken as a true estimate of the population variance, and the second term as a true estimate of the population variance of means. Symbolically we write this as

$$\bar{s}^2 = \sigma^2 - \sigma^2{}_m$$

But we have already stated that $\sigma^2{}_m = \sigma^2/N$ under conditions of random sampling, hence

$$\bar{s}^2 = \sigma^2 - \sigma^2/N = \frac{N - 1}{N}\sigma^2$$

from which

$$\sigma^2 = \frac{N}{N - 1}\bar{s}^2$$

For a single sample, we obtain from the above an estimate of the population variance, thus

$$\hat{\sigma}^2 = \frac{Ns^2}{N - 1}$$

Since Ns^2 is the sum of squares of deviations from the sample mean, we can write, finally,

$$\hat{\sigma}^2 = \frac{\sum^{N}(X - \bar{X})^2}{N - 1}$$

Thus, to obtain an unbiased estimate of a population variance the sum of squares of deviations from the mean must be divided by *one less than* the number of observations. We say that the number of *degrees of freedom* for the variance is $N-1$. The principle is general; whether the observations represent measurements on single units or mean values, we always take the degrees of freedom to be one less than the number of observations.

This detour into the notion of degrees of freedom and unbiased estimates of population variance has a purpose. The F-ratio requires unbiased estimates of population variances, the key to which is the use of degrees of freedom as the divisor of the sum of squares of deviations.

To illustrate the use of the F-ratio, we use the following set of fictitious data. We suppose we have observations on forty subjects, subdivided into four groups of ten each. Each group of subjects may be thought of as a sample from a population. We assume that the four populations sampled have the same value of variance and wish to examine the hypothesis that they have equivalent mean values. If this hypothesis is credible, the value of F should be near unity.

In Table 4 below we give the value of each observation, its deviation from the mean of the subgroup, and the square of each deviation. Each column is summed.

TABLE 4

	Group 1			*Group 2*			*Group 3*			*Group 4*		
	Obs.	*Dev.*	*(Dev.)*^{2}									
	X	$X-\bar{X}$	$(X-\bar{X})^2$	X	$X-\bar{X}$	$(X-\bar{X})^2$	X	$X-\bar{X}$	$(X-\bar{X})^2$	X	$X-\bar{X}$	$(X-\bar{X})^2$
	10	1	1	9	3	9	13	2	4	11	3	9
	13	4	16	12	0	0	10	—1	1	6	—2	4
	8	—1	1	14	2	4	14	3	9	8	0	0
	7	—2	4	11	—1	1	10	—1	1	7	—1	1
	11	2	4	10	—2	4	12	1	1	7	—1	1
	9	0	0	13	1	1	10	—1	1	5	—3	9
	9	0	0	15	3	9	8	—3	9	9	1	1
	10	1	1	10	—2	4	10	—1	1	9	1	1
	6	—3	9	12	0	0	9	—2	4	12	4	16
	7	—2	4	14	2	4	14	3	9	6	—2	4
	90	0	40	120	0	36	110	0	40	80	0	46
Mean	9			12			11			8		
Estimate of Variance		40/9			36/9			40/9			46/9	

The grand mean is found by summing all observations and averaging,

$$\text{Grand mean} = 400/40 = 10$$

The estimate of the variance of means is found as follows:

$$\frac{(9-10)^2 + (12-10)^2 + (11-10)^2 + (8-10)^2}{4-1} = 10/3$$

Hence,

$$N\hat{\sigma}^2_m = 10(10/3) = 33.33$$

To obtain $\hat{\sigma}^2$ we average the estimates of variance for each group, thus

$$\hat{\sigma}^2 = \frac{40/9 + 36/9 + 40/9 + 46/9}{4} = \frac{36}{162} = 4.50$$

Then F becomes

$$F = 33.33/4.50 = 7.41$$

We note immediately that the value of F is much larger than one, which suggests that the means are more variable than could be accounted for by random sampling theory. But before we have a definitive answer we must ask what is the probability that we could obtain a value of F at least this large if we had randomly sampled populations with equal means. This question can be answered by consulting a table of F-values, which can be found in most statistical texts. For these data the numerator of F was calculated from 3 d. f., the denominator from 36 d. f. For this combination of degrees of freedom the critical values of F are found to be as follows:

$$F(5\%) = 2.86; \qquad F(1\%) = 4.38$$

Thus, when randomly sampling populations with equal means, four samples of ten each, we can expect to obtain a value of F at least as large as 2.86 about five times out of one hundred; a value of F at least as large as 4.38 is expected to occur about once in one hundred samples. The probability of obtaining a value of F as large or larger than 7.41 then must be considerably less than 1%, and we conclude that the most credible explantion of our data is that we are sampling populations that have different means. This suggests, of course, that we must look to the manner in which the four groups were formed or treated to explain the differences among mean values we have observed.

Calculations for the analysis of variance by the above method are awkward; a simpler procedure, for which a desk calculator is desirable, is given below.

(1) Calculate the sum of the squares of all of the observations. Denote this quantity by S_2.

(2) Square each sum of X and sum these squares, dividing by the number of observations in each group. Denote this by S_g.

(3) Square the grand total and divide by the total number of observations. Denote this quantity by S_1.

$$S_2 = (10)^2 + (13)^2 + \cdots + (12)^2 + (6)^2 = 4262$$

$$S_g = \frac{(90)^2 + (120)^2 + (110)^2 + (80)^2}{10} = 4100$$

$$S_1 = (400)^2/40 = 4000.$$

The numerator of F is given by

$$N\hat{\sigma}^2{}_m = \frac{S_g - S_1}{4-1} = 100/3 = 33.33$$

as before, and the denominator is given by

$$\hat{\sigma}^2 = \frac{S_2 - S_g}{40-4} = 162/36 = 4.50$$

The quantity $S_g - S_1$ is the sum of squares of deviations "among group means," and $S_2 - S_g$ is the sum of squares "within groups." The total sum of squares is given by $S_2 - S_1$. Division of each sum of squares by the appropriate degrees of freedom gives mean squares. The conventional form for recording the results of an analysis of variance is given below, using previously obtained results.

Source of Variation	*d.f.*	*Sum of Squares*	*Mean Square*	*F*
Among groups	3	100	33.33	7.41**
Within groups	36	162	4.50	
Total	39	262		

Note that the total degrees of freedom is one less than the total number of observations and must equal the sum of the degrees of freedom for each component. Similarly, the total sum of squares $(S_2 - S_1)$ must exactly total the sums of squares for each component. The ** after F signifies that F is larger than the tabled 1% value of F. If F is greater than the tabled 5% value, but not as large as the 1% value, a single * is placed beside the value of F. If F is smaller than the tabled 5% value the asterisk is omitted, and the result is said to be nonsignificant.

It is worthwhile to stress an assumption made in the above development of analysis of variance. We assume that the groups are samples from populations having a common variance, σ^2. We estimate this common variance by pooling, i. e., averaging, estimates obtained from each group separately. If the estimates of variance from the separate groups vary widely, the assumption of a common variance is dubious. In case the assumption is far from the mark, we know from theory that the tabled values of F are incorrect for the stated levels of probability, erring on the low side. Indeed, the tabled values of F are derived from the assumption that we are sampling *normally distributed* populations with a common variance. One must be cautious, therefore, when the estimates of variance from each group give evidence of heterogeneity of variance. Fortunately, the F test is not particularly sensitive to moderate departures from the assumptions, and the given levels of probability can be taken as reasonably close approximations to the true probabilities. We note, parenthetically, that the issue is of importance only when the result of the F test is marginal, i. e., the probability is close to the 5% level. When obtained F values are either well above or well below the 5% critical value, the issue is more academic than practical.

One way of correcting for heterogeneity of variance is to use a data transformation. A common situation is to have a response variable for which the observations tend to become more variable as the mean level increases. If the group standard deviations increase approximately proportional to increases in mean value, the appropriate transformation is the logarithm of the observation; if the variances are proportional to the means, the square root of the observed value is the transformation required. After the original data are transformed (rounding off to three digits), the analysis of variance is carried out in the usual manner as though the transformed values were the original observations. A number of authors treat data transformations at length; see, for example, Johnson.[8]

The t-test. A special case that arises often is an experiment in which the mean responses of just two groups are contrasted. The usual statistical test for this case is the t-test. This test antedates analysis of variance in the literature, but it is easy to show that t can be computed from the analysis of variance procedures given above. For this special case, F is the square of t. The usual formula for t is merely an algebraic rearrangement of the analysis of variance formulas.

As an example of the t-test we use data from a study by Robert Jones.[9] He defines samples of "Combined Writers-Metropolitan Newspapermen" and "Senior Students" (in journalism). For each sample, means and standard deviations of scores on the Three-Key Michigan Vocabulary Test are given in Table 5.

TABLE 5

	n	*Mean*	*Std. Dev.*
Combined Writers-Metropolitan Newspapermen	82	65.85	6.95
Senior Students	83	62.94	5.45

The mean difference, 2.91, is the quantity under test. The usual formula for t is given below.

$$t = (\bar{X}_1 - \bar{X}_2)\sqrt{\frac{(n_1 + n_2 - 2)n_1 n_2}{(n_1 s_1^2 + n_2 s_2^2)(n_1 + n_2)}}$$

Substituting observed values in the formula,

$$t = (65.85 - 62.94)\sqrt{\frac{(82 + 83 - 2)(82)(83)}{[(82)(6.95)^2 + (83)(5.45)^2(165)]}}$$

from which $t = 3.00$. Referring to tabled values of t (found in most statistical texts), using $n_1 + n_2 - 2 = 163$ degrees of freedom, we find that this value exceeds the 1% value, hence we conclude that there is a significant difference between the two samples with respect to mean level of performance on this test.

It is interesting to note that the formula for t combines $n\hat{\sigma}^2_m$ and $\hat{\sigma}^2$ in the following manner. Algebraic manipulation of the analysis of variance formulas shows that

$$N\hat{\sigma}^2_m = \frac{n_1 n_2(\bar{X}_1 - \bar{X}_2)^2}{n_1 + n_2}$$

and

$$\hat{\sigma}^2 = \frac{n_1 s_1^2 + n_2 s_2^2}{n_1 + n_2 - 2}$$

The square root of the ratio of the above yields directly the formula for t.

The Design of Experiments

In a sense, a discussion of analysis of variance is equivalent to a discussion of the design of experiments. We experiment to test the validity of hypotheses about the effect of a stimulus variable upon the mean level of response, assuming that variation in levels of the stimulus variable does not affect the variability of the responses. The previous discussion used only one stimulus variable, "group," varied over four levels in our fictitious example or over two levels in Jones's study. But a design can involve more than one independent variable in a variety of ways. We sketch out a few of the more common designs below and suggest that further reading in a book such as that by E. F. Lindquist[10] will give much more insight into the wealth of possibilities in more complex designs.

The key to the concept of experimental design lies in the notion of *replication.* Multiple observations with all independent variables held constant are replications. We can replicate by observing a number of subjects under presumably identical conditions, using a separate group of subjects for each level of the independent variables. Or we can replicate by observing the same subject under several conditions. In the first approach the subjects are categorized according to the condition under which they are measured; in the second, the observations are categorized according to each condition under which a subject is observed. The first can be described as "replication by subjects," the second as "replication by trials." Designs involving combinations of both of the above are frequently used to allow examination of several independent variables at once. A good example of a complex design is the study by M. E. Wrolstad.[11] It is concerned with relationships among several principles of typographic design and the preference patterns of adult observers. It uses both replication by subjects (independent variables are three levels of age, three levels of education, and sex), and replication by trials for two stimulus variables (symmetric versus asymmetric approaches to typography, and five principles of typographic design—balance, contrast, proportion, rhythm, and unity). The resulting analysis of variance enabled the author to investigate not only the effect of each independent variable by itself but to examine possible interrelationships among the independent variables as well.

Another example of a study using both replication by subjects and replication by trials is that by J. B. Haskins.[12] He was concerned with the investigation of appropriateness of typeface for magazine articles of different type and mood. He used ten typefaces for the main title of each of ten articles, one hundred combinations in all. In order to avoid asking subjects to respond to all one hundred combinations, each respondent saw only ten of the one hundred combinations in a Latin square design in which each typeface and each article were seen only once by a particular respondent. The response variable was a six-point scale for rating "appropriateness."

To illustrate analysis of variance where two stimulus variables are used in conjunction we use data given by Haskins.[13] Here the observation is the mean appropriateness rating given each combination of typeface and article by thirty persons. The analysis of variance model can be described as a two-way classification with a single entry per cell; each row determines a typeface, each column an article. It is the variation among the row and column means we wish to analyze; the cell entries provide the means of estimating a population variance for the denominator of the F test.[f] For this example each typeface is a "subject" and each article is a "trial," hence the design is one of replication by trials. We reproduce (p. 156) only the row and column means from Haskins' table.[14]

The lower the mean value, the more appropriate the typeface is judged to go with the article. For this design we calculate

$$S_T = \frac{(38.47)^2 + (26.87)^2 + \cdots + (26.63)^2}{10} = 817.4376$$

$$S_A = \frac{(27.13)^2 + (28.67)^2 + \cdots + (30.74)^2}{10} = 802.3994$$

[f] The analysis we give is not that given by Haskins; we use his data to illustrate a simple case of replication by trials. Haskins gives a fuller analysis based on all variables in his design. Our analysis gives a somewhat conservative test for significant variation in row and column means.

	Typeface	*Mean*	*Article*	*Mean*
(G)	Mistral, 72 pt.	3.847	a	2.713
(K)	Bernhard Modern Roman, 48 pt.	2.687	b	2.867
(Q)	Bodoni Open, 72 pt.	2.616	c	2.614
(F)	Bodoni, 60 pt.	2.350	d	2.684
(L)	Cheltenham Bold, 48 pt.	2.487	e	2.740
(M)	Futura Light, 48 pt.	3.009	f	2.747
(T)	Futura Bold, 48 pt.	2.420	g	2.681
(H)	Kaufmann Bold, 72 pt.	2.880	h	2.844
(R)	Liberty, 72 pt.	3.298	i	3.293
(J)	Caslon Oldstyle Italic, 48 pt.	2.663	j	3.074

(Note that *sums,* i. e., ten times each mean, are used in the above arithmetic.) The subscripts T and A refer to typefaces and articles respectively; the divisors are ten each, since each sum that is squared is made up of ten observations. In addition we calculate the sum of squares of all one hundred entries in the table, yielding $S_2 = 828.4825$. To obtain S_1 we square the grand total and divide by 100; i. e.,

$$S_1 = (282.57)^2/100 = 798.4581$$

The sum of squares among typeface means is given by $S_T - S_1$; for article means it is given by $S_A - S_1$. The population variance, the estimate of which is used as the denominator of the F test, is here defined as the variance not accounted for by the variation among row and column means. Subtracting the sum of squares for articles and typefaces symbolically

$$\begin{matrix} \text{(total)} & \text{(typefaces)} & \text{(articles)} \\ (S_2 - S_1) - & (S_T - S_1) - & (S_A - S_1) \end{matrix}$$

which yields algebraically

$$S_2 - S_T - S_A + S_1$$

This is the "error" sum of squares which, upon division by the appropriate degrees of freedom, gives the denominator of the F test. Degrees of freedom for error are found by subtracting the d. f. for typefaces (9) and the d. f. for articles (9) from the total d. f. (99), or 81 d. f. for error. The analysis of variance table is given on page 157. We note the over-all differences in appropriateness among type-face means are highly significant, as are those among articles. The F values are not as high as those reported by Haskins, since the error variance here used includes variation due to the effect of combinations of typeface and article.

Source of Variation	*d.f.*	*Sum of Squares*	*Mean Square*	*F*
Typefaces	9	18.9795	2.1088	24.05**
Articles	9	3.9413	.4379	4.99**
Error	81	7.1036	.0877	
Total	99	30.0244		

Multiple Comparisons. The analysis of variance for Haskins' data tells us that the subjects perceive significant differences in appropriateness among the ten typefaces. However, it does *not* tell us if the subjects can effectively discriminate among all pairs of typefaces with respect to the criterion. More specifically, can we arrange the typefaces in rank order by their mean appropriateness scores and report this as a definitive rank order without ties? To answer this question requires a procedure for making *multiple comparisons.* D. B. Duncan [15] gives a procedure, and Henry Scheffé [16] discusses several alternate procedures. We use Duncan's to complete the analysis of Haskins' data.

Duncan's procedure requires that means be arranged in rank order. He then considers the least significant difference between two adjacent means, between means separated by one, separated by two, and so on. The greater the number of intervening means, the larger the difference required before a significant difference between a particular pair is claimed. Applying Duncan's procedure we divide the error mean square, .0877, by the number of replications, 10, and take the square root to obtain .09365, an estimate of the standard error of the mean in the population.

Duncan provides tables showing the least significant difference, in standard error units, between mean values, taking into account the number of means (when arranged in rank order) over which the difference is taken. He provides these values for the 5% and 1% levels of significance; we use (p. 158) his 5% values for 81 d.f.

The test proceeds as follows: Starting with F we test the difference, F — G, F — R, etc., until a nonsignificant difference is found. Underscore the nonsignificant means as shown. We see that F is significantly different from J and all to the right of J; F, T, L, and Q are underscored. We then test the difference T — G, T — R, etc., finding that T is significantly different from H and all to the right; T, L, Q, J, and K are underscored. This process is continued to produce the pattern of underscoring shown below. Any two means *not* underscored by the *same* line are significantly different; conversely, any two means underscored by the same line are *not* significantly different.

Number of Means	2	3	4	5	6	7	8	9	10
Duncan's Least Significant Difference	2.81	2.96	3.06	3.13	3.19	3.23	3.27	3.31	3.33
x .09365	.263	.277	.287	.293	.299	.302	.306	.309	.312

The mean values for typefaces are arranged in rank order below, using Haskins' alphabetic codes.

F	T	L	Q	J	K	H	M	R	G
2.35	2.42	2.49	2.62	2.66	2.69	2.88	3.01	3.30	3.85

Some conclusions can be drawn immediately. It seems clear that G (Mistral) and R (Liberty) are deemed less appropriate than the others; M (Futura Light) is distinguishable from all but H, and the discrimination between typefaces is poorer toward the more appropriate end of the scale. Some cautions about generalizations must be made. First, insofar as the over-all appropriateness of the typefaces is concerned, much depends on whether the articles used can be thought of as a random sample of articles from the particular magazine used; restrictions or biases in the selection of articles restrict the generality. Secondly, the range of typefaces selected for comparison obviously affects the comparisons made; the F value for typeface means would be much lower, for example, if G, R, and M were eliminated. (This would not constitute a valid test, however; obviously if these typefaces had not been used in the original experiment, some adjustment of the perception of the appropriateness scale by the respondents would have taken place, e.g., H would probably have received a higher mean score than it did in the actual experiment.)

A third point is that certain typefaces were perceived as much more appropriate for *certain articles* than their over-all average would suggest, e.g., R was judged the most appropriate typeface for article i. Clearly, if more articles similar to i had been included in the sample of articles, R would probably indicate a higher level of appropriateness. For more detail on the relationship of typeface to certain articles the reader is referred to Haskins' paper.

Duncan's procedure will not necessarily make the rank order of means definitive, just as it fails to do so in Haskins' study. It does tell the investigator about how far he can go in accepting the rank order of means and to what extent he must see ties in the ranks. In general, whenever over-all mean differences are found to be significant by analysis of variance, a multiple comparison procedure should be used to throw further light on the differences among pairs of means that are of real consequence. We note, incidentally, that a multiple comparison procedure is *not* appropriate unless the overall F is significant.

Intersubject variability. Whenever human subjects are used in experiments the variability from subject to subject is an important source of sampling error. The ideal way to control this source of error is to use a design that measures each subject under every condition of measurement, i.e., allows each subject to act as his own control. This often proves to be impractical for two reasons.

1. The number of combinations of measurement conditions may be too large to be practical. Human subjects, particularly volunteer, will become fatigued, lose interest, and even rebel if too many tasks are presented to them. (In Haskins' study each subject should have rated each of the one hundred combinations of typeface and article. Such was obviously impractical, hence the design required each subject to make only ten ratings.)

2. The effect of each "stimulus" must be temporary and entirely dissipated before the next stimulus is applied. It is obvious that, when learning and practice effects accompany the successive presentation of stimuli, the results obtained are related to the order of presentation and to the magnitude of practice effects.

The extreme example of (2) above occurs when each subject has no further value as a subject after exposure to one condition of an independent variable. (A simple example is that of comparing two methods of teaching; a subject cannot be exposed to more than one method. In this case only replication by subjects can be used.) In many cases order effects are not sufficiently strong to preclude use of replication by trials and can be minimized. The stimuli can be presented to each subject in a random sequence, thus randomizing order effects over combinations of the independent variables. Another means is to counterbalance order effects by means of a "cross-over" design in which the several possible orders of presentation are systematically distributed over individuals selected at random. However, a cross-over design is impractical when the number of stimuli is large, for the number of possible orders increases much more rapidly than the number of stimuli. (With only three stimuli there are 6 possible orders, 24 with four stimuli, 120 with five, etc.)

With two or more independent variables it is possible to mix replication by trials with replication by subjects, using different groups of subjects for levels of independent variables that cannot be handled by multiple measurements on the same subjects. Suppose, for example, each subject is asked to react to several stimuli (using a rating scale) under a specific criterion for making his judgments. Though the experiment involves multiple criteria, each subject is unaware of this; he must make his judgments under the criterion provided to him. The total group of subjects is split into random subgroups for the assignment of criteria, but each subject in a subgroup responds to the same stimuli under the same instructions. Thus to examine differences among criteria we are replicating by subjects; to look at stimulus effects we are replicating by trials.

The appropriate analysis of variance for the above example is discussed by L. S. Kogan[17] and as a Type I design in Chapter 13 of Lindquist.[18] This is the simplest example of a "mixed" design; more complex ones arise when we increase to two or more the number of independent variables that are treated by replication of subjects, replication by trials, or both. Wrolstad's study, for example, uses three independent variables replicated by subjects, two replicated by trials. Lindquist discusses and gives examples of several of the more complicated designs that mix replication by subjects and trials.

When two or more independent variables are used and it is impractical to use replication by trials at all, we use a different group of subjects for *each* combination of the independent variables; such designs are described as *factorial*. For example, we have two levels of one independent variable, three of another, and four of a third; this is described as a $2 \times 3 \times 4$ factorial design. The assignment of a particular subject to one of the twenty-four possible combinations is best done by a random mechanism, although this is not always possible. In some cases a characteristic of the subject himself determines which treatment condition he receives, e.g., age, sex. In other situations subjects are required to be used in intact and predetermined groups, e.g., as when using elementary school children as subjects with access to them necessarily in the classroom. In the latter case the experimenter must have some assurance that the intact groups do not differ appreciably on some characteristic that affects the dependent variable. For example, suppose an experiment involving reading of passages from newspaper stories uses the several sections of a large course in newswriting as the basis for assignment of treatment condition, all students in a section tested under the same conditions. Variation from section to section in average reading ability could affect markedly the results of the experiment, thus *confounding* readability with the independent variables. If it is not possible to control average reading ability through randomizing the assignment of subjects, it is still possible to provide *statistical* control through the *analysis of covariance.* For this method it is necessary to have for each subject an independent measure of reading ability. Variations in the means of the dependent variable are adjusted for concomitant variation in reading ability means. The method is fully described in many texts (cf. Lindquist,[19] McNemar[20]) and is not detailed here.

In a factorial design, or a mixed design, where two or more independent variables are treated by replication by subjects, it is necessary that the number of subjects assigned to each combination of the independent variables be equal, or at least in proportion. With disproportionate subclass frequencies comparisons are made among means based on varying numbers of cases; the F-ratios resulting from the analysis of variance may be over- or under-estimated; adjustments are required. C. R. Rao gives the procedure for making the proper adjustment for a factorial design involving two independent variables. If there are more than two levels of both variables the arithmetic calculations are formidable, and approximate methods of adjustment are given by Rao and others authors (cf. Walker,[21] Wert[22]).

For three or more independent variables the correction for disproportionate cell frequencies is so formidable that it is preferable to equalize the cell frequencies prior to the analysis of the data. Cases must be discarded, making use of a table of random numbers, until all cell frequencies are equalized. Obviously this is wasteful of data and is not practical for use in studies involving few subjects. (Wrolstad,[23] who used replication by subjects on three independent variables, applied this technique to reduce to twenty-four the subjects per cell.) As a last resort, one analyzes the data in parts, arbitrarily reducing the number of variables examined to the point where disproportionate cell frequencies are no longer a problem. Lest the point be missed, we note that unequal cell frequencies constitute no problem if there is only *one* variable treated by replication by subjects.

It is no exaggeration to say that the selection of an experimental design contains in it the specification of the subsequent analysis of the data and that a poorly designed experiment cannot be rescued by the power of statistical techniques. Even though the effects of poor design can sometimes be ameliorated by careful analysis, sophisticated statistical techniques are poor substitutes for good design. This requires not only a knowledge of the analysis appropriate to the design but must also look carefully at the assumptions that underlie the analysis and the weaknesses and strengths of a particular design. Nor is good design sufficient. Of parallel importance are the measuring devices used and the extent to which they generate data meeting the requirements of the statistical procedures to be employed —as well as, of course, the extent to which they measure appropriately and reliably the responses or traits which they presume to assess.

Nonparametric Statistics

Included in this category are statistical tests and techniques having in common freedom from the assumption that the distribution of the dependent variable is normal, or approximately so. Many of these tests depend not at all on the magnitudes of the observations but derive all information from the order relationships existing among them. They are useful when samples are small, when the observations are all too obviously skewed in distribution shape, when little is known about distribution shape, or when the data contain a seemingly disproportionate number of extreme values. If some or all of these conditions hold, the results of an analysis of variance may leave the issue in doubt simply because of doubt of the validity of the assumptions necessary to analysis of variance.

Nonparametric tests have in common the basic advantage of guarding against the Type I error (the error of finding differences where none truly exist) with known probability. As a trade for this advantage they have the disadvantage of lower power, i.e., are less sensitive to true differences. As they are conservative in rejecting the null hypothesis, one can use them for any data and feel confident that significant results truly do reflect real differences. When samples are small, they require less effort than analysis of variance and are sometimes referred to as "quick and dirty statistics."

Many nonparametric treatments of data use the Chi-square test. Two examples will suffice. The first is an example of a case in which a scaled variable is reduced to nominal data for the test; here the scaled variable is age of the recipient of a mail questionnaire where the names and ages are taken from an organizational directory. Because the distribution of ages in the population encompassed in the directory is irregular, and because the experimenter feels that the effects of age are only reflected in broad age groups, he chooses to express age in the broad categories shown below. He tests the hypothesis that the distributions of ages among persons responding to the questionnaire and those not responding are similar. The data are given below.

	Under 30	*30–49*	*50 and over*	*Total*
Respondents	20	38	32	90
Nonrespondents	16	20	34	70
All	36	58	66	160

We obtain for this contingency table Chi-square = 1.80. For 2 d.f. Chi-square must reach 5.99 to be significant at the 5% level; hence we conclude that there is no evidence from these data that respondents and nonrespondents differed appreciably in their age distributions. (We make the additional note that a *t*-test of the difference in mean age might be an unnecessarily sensitive test, since a small difference in mean age even though significant may be trivial in the context of the experiment.)

A second example concerns data that show strong skewness and extreme values. The dependent variable is the number of names of newspaper columnists that an interviewee can recall as authors of columns he has read within the past six months. The independent variable reflects the classification of respondents as "business" or "professional." The data (fictitious) are below.

Number of mentions of Columnists	*Professional*	*Business*	*Combined*
0	3	6	9
1	9	16	25
2	18	19	37
3	37	32	69
4	31	28	59
5–6	24	19	43
7–9	15	12	27
10 and up	21	10	31
Total	158	142	300

We first note that for the "combined" column the first four categories account for roughly half of the cases (140). If, in the populations sampled, there are no differences between the two classes with respect to the mean number of mentions we would expect to find about the same proportion of cases above the dashed line in each of the two categories. This leads to the following two-by-two table.

	Professional	*Business*	*Total*
3 or less	67	73	140
4 or more	91	69	160
Total	158	142	300

For this table, Chi-square = 2.09, a nonsignificant value. (At the 5% level Chi-square is 3.84 for a table with one d.f.) This use of Chi-square is often called the Median Test because we split the distribution at or near to the median. It is easy to apply and is particularly useful when either or both ends of the distribution are "open."

A quick test for the difference between two sets of paired data is the Sign Test, a substitute for the t-test for paired data. Here one merely records whether the difference between two paired measures is + or —. If the null hypothesis holds, both signs should appear equally often. Significant values for the frequency of + or —, whichever is smaller, are tabled for a range of sample sizes in a number of texts (cf. Siegel[24]), or Chi-square can be computed. Suppose, for example, we scan twenty pairs of observations, finding four negative differences, fifteen positive differences, and one tie. Discarding the tie, thus using an effective sample size of 19, we can calculate Chi-square from the following formula. N is the effective sample size, n is the number of + or — signs, whichever is smaller.

$$\chi^2 = \frac{(N - 2n - 1)^2}{N} = \frac{(19 - 8 - 1)^2}{19} = 5.26$$

The figure 5.26 exceeds the 5% critical value for one d.f. (3.84); hence the two sets differ in level of response.

A number of nonparametric procedures have been developed for data that are given in the form of ranks. Ranked data represent an ordinal scaling for which nothing is assumed about the relative magnitude of the difference between any pair of ranks. Rankings arise in situations where respondents can recognize a "greater than" relationship between two stimuli, even though they have no scale for expressing "how much greater." By implication, at least, if a set of stimuli are ranked by an observer he has made a "greater than" comparison for every pair of stimuli. However, ties are allowed in ranking procedures; in some techniques using ranked data special provision is made for dealing with ties. Ranking methods are available as a substitute for the *t*-test and for one-way and two-way analysis of variance. For these procedures the reader is referred to Sidney Siegel.[25]

As a final footnote to this brief discussion of nonparametric methods we point out that they do not serve as equally powerful substitutes for analysis of variance procedures when the data conform in reasonable fashion to the assumptions of analysis of variance. The computational ease of these techniques, particularly when samples are small, is not per se a reason for using them in preference to analysis of variance. But when the distributional character of the data is skew or quite unknown, or when the scales of measurement cannot be justified as interval scales, there are good arguments for using these methods.

Correlation

So far the discussion of statistical methods has concerned situations in which only one dependent variable has been measured. Suppose we measure more than one dependent variable on the same subjects, then desire to study the relationship among the variables. The appropriate measure of the relationship between two variables is the ordinary product-moment coefficient of correlation, r. Since an elementary discussion of this statistic can be found in every textbook on statistical methods, we shall be concerned here with a number of uses to which this statistic can be put in research.

As an index of the strength of a relationship between two variables, common usage seems to be to designate a correlation of .1 to .3 as "low," .4 to .6 as "moderate," and .7 to .9 as "high." This scale must be used with caution, however, for often a relationship must be judged high or low according to the magnitudes of correlations usually found in like situations. A correlation of .7 may be considered low when one is describing the estimated reliability of a psychometric instrument; on the other hand, a correlation between two "items" of a psychometric instrument may be judged "high" if it reaches .3.

Statistical Prediction

The coefficient of correlation may be thought of as an index that describes how well one variable may be predicted from another. For example, the score on a test of English usage given at the beginning of the semester may be used to section students in newswriting, i. e., predict the level of performance as measured by a subsequent grade. The effectiveness of the prediction of a course grade must be assessed in retrospect. For a group of students completing newswriting, all of whom have taken an English usage test, we calculate the correlation between the two variables. From the value of r, and the means and standard deviations, we can write an equation by means of which, knowing a student's test score, we may predict his grade. For example, suppose the test has a mean of 60, a standard deviation of 8, the course grades a mean of 2.4 (on a scale from 0 to 4.0) with a standard deviation of .8. The correlation between test and grade is found to be .6. The regression equation for prediction is

$$Y = .06X - 1.2$$

where Y is the *predicted* value of grade, and X is the actual value of a test score. For example, for a student scoring 70 on the test, his predicted grade is $(.06)(70) - 1.2 = 4.2 - 1.2 = 3.0$.

The prediction process may be extended by using several predictor variables, X_1, X_2, X_3, etc. Symbolically, the form of the prediction equation becomes

$$Y = b_1X_1 + b_2X_2 + b_3X_3 + \cdots$$

where the b's may be thought of as "weights" attaching to each predictor variable, and the process of prediction is one of "weighting and adding." The b's are the best weights in the sense that they produce a smaller average squared error of prediction than any other possible sets of weights. The above describes the method of *multiple regression,* a powerful approach to any research situation in which prediction of future performance is central to the study. Just as the simple coefficient of correlation describes the power of one variable to predict another, the correlation between the predicted and actual values of Y—the *multiple correlation*—describes the predictive power of a team of predictors. This predictive power increases with the square of the multiple correlation, not with the first power. For example, referring to the example described earlier, we may have a correlation of .5 between the English usage test and course grade. We now use two other tests as predictors as well, correlating respectively .4 and .3 with course grade. Using the team of three predictors we might obtain a multiple correlation of .6. The gain from .5 to .6 must be evaluated by comparing the ratios of the squares of the r's, $.36/.25 = 1.44$, i.e., a gain of 44% in predictive power.

The literature on multiple regression is voluminous and should be studied with care before undertaking to utilize the method in research. The various studies to which reference is made below discuss this topic in detail. A comprehensive discussion with detailed examples is found in C. H. Goulden.[26] A recent bibliography is given by C. J. Hoyt and M. D. Johnson.[27] When several predictors are used, the amount of calculation involved can be formidable. However, the use of calculating machines and punched card and electronic computers make such studies feasible.

Reliability of Measurement

Another use of the correlation coefficient is as an index of the reliability of a measuring instrument. When we make physical measurements such as length, weight, temperature, and the like, we use instruments whose reliability of measurement is rarely open to serious question. Several persons measuring the same quantity with the same instrument may be expected to obtain the same result or very close thereto. Instruments measuring variables important in the social sciences rarely have such intrinsic reliability. It is incumbent on a researcher who uses an unproven psychometric instrument to assess its reliability.

The reliability of a measuring device expresses the confidence that our measurements are replicable, i. e., if remeasured under the same conditions the same results will be obtained. If reliability is something less than perfect, however, the second set of measures will not be exactly equivalent to the first. The index to describe such an imperfect relationship is the coefficient of correlation between the pairs of measures. Reliability may be estimated by administering the same instrument to the same subjects at two different times (test-retest method), by administering two equivalent forms of the instrument at two different times (alternate form method), or by splitting a test into two random halves and correlating one half-score against the other. (In the latter case allowance must be made for the fact that the scores so correlated are derived from a test only half as long as the test whose reliability is being assessed. The Spearman-Brown formula makes the proper allowance for the length of test. See, for example, J. P. Guilford.[28]

Another approach to the reliability of a measuring instrument composed of a number of items is that of considering each item of the instrument as providing a single evaluation of an individual. The sum of all such item "scores" is the final score for the individual. Items may be questions, problems, ratings, or any stimulus of any kind such that the response can be quantified. Items may be scored as right or wrong, agreeing with or not agreeing with a standard response, or may be scaled, such as is often done to indicate strength of agreement or disagreement. All such, by implication, have the property that the summation of item scores provides a meaningful index of the individual.

We can form an index of the reliability of the subjects' total scores by an appeal to analysis of variance logic. Let each item score be the entry in a cell of a two-way table, where the rows represent persons, the columns items. The row sums (or means) represent the scores of the persons measured. Let each cell entry be represented as the sum of the "true" item score plus the error of measurement.[g]

$$x = t + e$$

where x is the item score, t is the true item score, and e is the error of measurement; e may be positive, negative, or zero. We assume that errors of measurement are uncorrelated with the true score and, for convenience, agree to express x and t as deviations from the grand mean. Summing and averaging over the items give us row means which we designate by the subscript p to indicate they reflect the "score" for each person. Thus

$$x_p = t_p + e_p$$

The population variance of x_p is given by the well-known expression for the variance of the sum of two measures,

$$\sigma^2_x = \sigma^2_t + \sigma^2_e + 2\sigma_t\sigma_e r_{t,e}$$

where $r_{t,e}$ is the correlation between true score and error of measurement. But we assume this to be zero; hence the third term on the right vanishes. In solving for the variance of true scores,

$$\sigma^2_t = \sigma^2_x - \sigma^2_e$$

Hence, the variance of true scores is smaller than the variance of actual scores by an amount equal to the variance of errors of measurement. We now define our index of reliability as the ratio of the variance of true scores to the variance of actual scores, or

$$r = \frac{\sigma^2_x - \sigma^2_e}{\sigma^2_x}$$

We note that, if $\sigma_e^2 = 0$, $r = 1$, i.e., perfect reliability. If $\sigma_x^2 = \sigma_e^2$, $r = 0$, and the scores have no reliability. This is equivalent to saying that the variation among subject scores is no more than we would

[g] The error of measurement must not be confused with our ordinary notion of an error in the response. An item for which a subject gives the "wrong" response may be truthfully revealing that the subject does not know the "right" response, i.e., the measurement error is zero.

expect if the item scores were random variables. This index is obtainable directly from the analysis of variance of the two-way table; since the estimates of population variance are mean squares we can write

$$r = \frac{\text{m. s. (rows)} - \text{m. s. (error)}}{\text{m. s. (rows)}}$$

Returning to Haskins' data, we can calculate the reliability of the mean typeface scores as

$$r = \frac{2.1088 - .0877}{2.1088} = .958$$

a high degree of internal consistency among the items (articles) that make up his measuring device.

The above approach to reliability is due to Hoyt,[29] though proposed in a different form earlier by G. F. Kuder and M. W. Richardson [30] in their Formula 20. Hoyt's formula and K-R 20 are algebraically equivalent. As an index of the reliability of a measuring device over time it is biased on the high side, for any component of measurement error introduced by random variation in the response patterns of individuals over time is not taken into account by this method.

If we define the reliability of a set of items in terms of the average correlation among pairs of items, we have a different situation. This form of reliability is applicable to a design where the items are judges making the same ratings on a set of individuals; we choose to ask the question, "How reliable, on the average, is any single judge?" This is answered by the average correlation among pairs of judges and is given by intraclass r, due to R. A. Fisher.[31] Using again the notation of analysis of variance for the two-way table, we have

$$\text{Intraclass } r = \frac{\text{m. s. (rows)} - \text{m. s. (error)}}{\text{m. s. (rows)} + (k-1)\ \text{m. s. (error)}}$$

Again by using the analysis of Haskins' data,

$$\text{Intraclass } r = \frac{2.1088 - .0877}{2.1088 + (9)(.0877)} = .697$$

This is considerably lower than Hoyt's measure of reliability given earlier, as it should be, for no one article on the average should give as reliable an index of typeface appropriateness as given by the composite of all articles.

Both Hoyt's and intraclass r can be expressed in terms of the F ratio used to test for significance among the row means in the analysis of variance.

$$\text{Hoyt } r = \frac{F - 1}{F}$$

$$\text{Intraclass } r = \frac{F - 1}{F + k - 1}$$

Another form of reliability, applicable to the case of judges rating individuals, is one in which the average correlation is obtained between any one judge and the average rating by all other judges except himself. This might be called "consensus" reliability. Again in terms of the F ratio for row means,

$$\text{Consensus reliability} = (F - 1)\sqrt{\frac{k - 1}{(F - 1 + k)(Fk - F + 1)}}$$

Again by use of Haskins' data,

$$\text{Consensus } r = 23.05\sqrt{\frac{9}{(33.05)(217.45)}} = .816$$

This index of reliability is higher than that given by intraclass r, since each judge is correlated with a more reliable criterion. However, it still reflects the reliability of a single judge's ratings in the sense of measuring the extent to which a judge is consistent with the consensus of his peers, averaged over all judges.

Which of the methods of assessing reliability is used must depend on the purpose of the measuring device and its ultimate usage. It seems clear that there is no such thing as *the* reliability of an instrument, and one can only select that method that seems most appropriate and report the method used. The literature on test reliability and other aspects of evaluating psychometric instruments is amazingly extensive. Many authors give thorough discussions of various aspects of test reliability, including J. P. Guilford,[32] P. O. Johnson,[33] E. Haggard,[34] R. L. Thorndike,[35] and H. Gulliksen.[36]

Multivariate Analysis

Multiple regression analysis is part of a more general area, multivariate analysis. In general, whenever we measure several different variables for a group of subjects or groups of subjects, we need the methods of multivariate analysis to evaluate the interrelationships of the variables. Here we enter a field in which some understanding of the mathematics involved is essential, and the computational labor can become formidable. Availability of automatic computing machines has gone far to free the researcher from days, even weeks, of labor at the desk calculator. The subject of multivariate analysis can be discussed only briefly here, and some of its possibilities indicated.

We note first that, given several measurements on each unit in a sample, the simple correlations among all pairs of variables show a complex pattern of interrelationships. These will suggest that each variable to a greater or lesser extent is measuring something in common with every other variable. We might suppose, indeed, that the number of underlying traits we are actually measuring is fewer than our nominal measurements would indicate. Or we might hypothesize that these underlying traits "cut across" our measuring instruments and should be labeled in some way more generally than we have labeled our instruments. The questions raised by the above statements lead to methods of *factor analysis.* While there are several methods of factor analysis in the literature of psychometrics, the two main schools of thought are those of L. L. Thurstone's *centroid* method and H. Hotelling's method of *Principal Components.* The original contributions of these authors have been elaborated on in many subsequent articles and books, some of which are given in the references at the end of this chapter.

One of the few studies in the field of journalism research employing a factor analysis approach is by M. S. MacLean, Jr., and W. R. Hazard.[37] In this study the response variables are interest ratings (a 5-point scale on each of 31 pictures); ratings were made by 152 women. The table of intercorrelations (465 in all) among all pairs of pictures were analyzed by factor analysis with the results that the thirty-one pictures could be classified into six groups with respect to interest. In general we can say that the groupings are such that the intercorrelations between pictures in the same group are on the average relatively high, between pictures of different groups relatively low. While such groupings could conceivably be made by inspection, it is doubtful that any two investigators could arrive at the same set of groupings by such an approach. Factor analysis provides a systematic and objective means of arriving at such groupings. Another study using the method is by D. W. Twedt.[38]

All methods of factor analysis lead fundamentally to the same result, that of analyzing a complex pattern of relationships among many variables into a pattern of fewer and more general variables derived from the original measurements. Each new variable is a weighted combination of the original measurements. The centroid method and a number of variants of it have been used widely, since the computational procedures can be handled on an ordinary desk calculator, although for a large study the computational burden is substantial. The Hotelling method involves a much heavier computational burden and is not feasible for even a moderate-size study without the use of automatic computing machines. With these machines the methods of factor analysis become much more attractive as research tools and should see increasing use in the future.

While the complete solution of the Hotelling method requires a sophisticated mathematical argument, the basic logic of the process can be stated simply. The following equation, identical in appearance to that used earlier to describe the multiple regression problem, states that by applying a series of weights to a series of test scores we arrive at a single score for each individual Y. This score is described as a *linear combination* of the original scores, "linear" in that only the first powers of the original scores are used.

$$Y = w_1x_1 + w_2x_2 + \cdots + w_nx_n$$

where n is the number of measures used in the study. The w's are the weights attaching to each x score. In Hotelling's solution the weights have the property of making the variance of the Y's as large as possible. This is equivalent to maximizing individual differences among the subjects. The mathematical solution produces more than one set of weights; each set of weights yields a value of Y for each subject. The values of Y so obtained have the interesting property of being uncorrelated over the sample of subjects. This leads to the interpretation that the several Y's measure different and unrelated traits. However, one must be exceedingly cautious in seizing on this mathematical property and glibly endowing it with meaning. The task of evaluating and interpreting a factor analysis study requires a sound knowledge of the method and the measuring instruments used. Two basic references for the interested reader are Godfrey

Thompson[39] and Thurstone.[40] Guilford[41] gives a good introduction to the centroid method. A recent bibliography is given by H. Solomon and B. Rosner.[42]

A variant of multiple regression analysis that has some of the properties of factor analysis is the method of *discriminant analysis.* This case arises when we wish to predict group membership for a set of individuals. In retrospect we examine several distinct groups of individuals through a series of measurements. We can obtain a single discriminant score on each subject by using a linear combination of the measurements, i. e.,

$$Y = c_1x_1 + c_2x_2 + \cdots$$

which is exactly the same equation we have written before. However, we now desire the weights, here denoted by c's to be determined so that the mean values of Y for each subgroup are as well separated as possible. When translated into mathematical terms, this property leads to a solution that obtains several sets of weights, similar to the Hotelling solution of the factor analysis problem. From these sets of weights values of Y can be calculated, and these Y's are uncorrelated over the entire sample of subjects. By calculating the several values of Y for a given subject and comparing his Y-scores with corresponding ones for the group means, we can find the group, or groups, to which he seems most closely related. This finding has obvious connotation for the guidance and classification of persons. The complete solution of the discriminant problem for multiple groups is fairly recent, but a sizable bibliography has accumulated in the past few years. For this bibliography the reader is referred to Note 42. The computational burden is very heavy, but the method is manageable if automatic computing equipment is used.

The methods of multivariate analysis place a heavy burden on the researcher, both in the study necessary for understanding and in the volume of data processing and computing as well. Because of these factors little use of the methods can be found in the literature of journalism research. However, for the courageous who are willing to study and use the methods, the rewards should be high. The raw material of journalism research, people and media, involve the interplay of many variables. To examine these variables one at a time is to ignore their interrelationships in which it is likely that revealing information lies.

Conclusions and Indications

Much of our discussion of statistical methods has led to tests of significance wherein we claim to be making decisions based on uncertain evidence. We accept or reject the null hypothesis at a given level of confidence. Yet it is rare that the end point of a piece of research is a decision as to a course of action; our so-called decisions are really *conclusions* about our data that we offer and bolster with the objectivity of a test of significance. In addition, it is unusual to find these conclusions stated with the crispness that we like to associate with decisions. They are likely to be hedged with the recognition of possible bias in the sampling of experimental units, lack of real knowledge of the distribution of the variables in the population, weaknesses in the measurement device, and the like. It is proper that reservations about conclusions be clearly stated and not left for the reader to infer; yet there is more to the point.

Ideally, an experimental study is planned for specific analyses to be made from the data. These analyses directly test the hypotheses upon which the study was built. In practice, research is not this simple. It often happens that the analyses to be made—at least some of them—are suggested to the researcher during and after the process of collecting the data and *by the data themselves.* The latter situation, in its extreme form, is the case where an unforeseen effect is noted in the data, and a test of significance is then applied to validate the conclusion. Unhappily the usual significance levels for the test no longer apply, for we may be seeing only a fortuitous quirk of the data; it was this quirk that called our attention to the hypothesis that is tested. Such a situation calls for clear thinking on the part of the investigator to recognize it and for candor in reporting it. He must clearly distinguish those hypotheses that were truly preplanned for test from those that developed during the course of examining the data. Indeed, the latter should be treated as *indications,* not conclusions.

Indications come about as a result of the process of "digging into the data" and are not to be derided. Statistical tests of significance are essentially conservative; they are designed to permit conclusions to be stated with a known level of confidence. Yet there is often more information in a set of data than can be formally extracted in the form of statistically validated conclusions. Part and parcel of research is the planning of the next study from the present; indications and suggestive effects are central to this process. Indeed, nonsignificant results may be—and often are—taken as indications of effects that should be re-examined in a new study with an improved design.

John Tukey gives a "caveat about indications." Because he says it so well he is quoted here at length.[43]

"It may be that the central problem of complex experimentation may come to be recognized as a psychological one, as the problem of becoming used to a separation between indication and conclusion. The physical sciences are used to 'praying over' their data, examining the same data from a variety of points of view. This process has been very rewarding and has led to many extremely valuable insights. Without this sort of flexibility, progress in physical science would have been much slower. Flexibility in analysis is often only to be had honestly at the price of a willingness not to demand that, what has *already* been observed shall establish, or prove, what analysis *suggests*. In physical science generally, the results of praying over the data are thought of as something to be put to further test in another experiment, as indications rather than conclusions.

"If complex experiment is to serve us well, we shall need to import this freedom to reexamine, rearrange, and reanalyze a body of data into all fields of application. But we shall need to bring it in *alongside*, and not in place of, preplanned analyses where we can assign known significance or confidence to conclusions about preselected questions. We must be prepared to have indications go far beyond conclusions, or even to have them suggest that what was concluded about was better not considered. The development of adequate psychological flexibility may not be easy, but without it we shall slow down our progress."

We remake the point that both have their place in research. The distinction may not always be clear, especially when a suggested effect is bolstered by a test of significance. It is all too easy to rationalize that the unplanned analysis really represented an a priori hypothesis. Particularly when the initial planning of a study is fuzzy, it is easy to make the tacit assumption that the tests of significance resulted from preplanned analyses and to leave the reader of the research report with this impression. One must depend on the perspicacity and integrity of the investigator to stay clear of this temptation.

Some Final Thoughts

We close this chapter with some remarks about statistical methods in general. In spite of the fact that statistics is a mathematical subject and requires a high degree of mathematical sophistication for complete understanding, it by no means follows that one must be a mathematician to make intelligent use of the methods outlined in this chapter. It is necessary, however, that the student be willing to devote time and effort to understanding both the rationale and the procedures of these methods. It is essential that not one but several of the references given below be studied. Often understanding comes only after examining the treatment given a particular method by several authors. Also, it is almost self-evident to point out that statistical methods are "learned at the calculating machine." In other words, only after a method has been applied to real data, not once but several times, does understanding come.

Few researchers in a specialized field such as journalism can be expected to be experts in statistical methods as well. Hence we suggest that the aid and counsel of a qualified statistician be sought whenever available. We cannot emphasize too strongly that this assistance should be utilized in the planning stages of a piece of research. File cabinets are full of unpublished studies that came to nought because poor and uninformed planning produced data that did not yield the hoped-for evaluation of the hypotheses with which the investigator started.

Current trends in research emphasize teamwork in research. Just as a competent statistician should be on the research team, so should a person competent in the field of data-processing machines and methods. Research in the social sciences is leaning more and more upon punched card machines and electronic computers as research tools. In this field, too, "a little knowledge is a dangerous thing," and the specialist in machine methods belongs on the research team in the planning stages.

The matter of proper planning of a research study has many ramifications. Indeed, it might be said that practically all of the hard thought and effort comes at this stage. For a well-planned study the execution, collection, and processing of the data are mechanics; the statistical analysis and interpretation of results straightforward. The hard work is done early in the game.

REFERENCES

1. W. G. Cochran, F. Mosteller, and J. W. Tukey, " Principles of Sampling," *Journal of American Statistical Association*, 49 (1954), 13–25.
2. P. O. Johnson, *Statistical Methods in Research* (New York: Prentice-Hall, 1949), chap. 6.
3. F. Mosteller and R. R. Bush, " Selected Quantitative Techniques," chap. 8 in G. Lindsey (ed.), *Handbook of Social Psychology* (Cambridge, Mass.: Addison-Wesley, 1954), I.
4. *Ibid.*
5. W. Schramm and D. M. White, "Age, Education, Economic Status: Factors in Newspaper Reading," *Journalism Quarterly*, 26 (1949), 149–59.
6. Note 2 *supra.*
7. George W. Snedecor, *Statistical Methods* (5th ed.; Ames, Iowa: Iowa State College Press, 1956).
8. Note 2 *supra.*
9. Robert L. Jones, "A Predictive and Comparative Study of Journalism Personnel," *Journalism Quarterly*, 31 (1954), 201–14.
10. E. F. Lindquist, *Design and Analysis of Experiments in Psychology and Education* (Boston: Houghton Mifflin, 1953).
11. M. E. Wrolstad, "Adult Preferences in Typography; Exploring the Function of Design," *Journalism Quarterly*, 37 (1960), 211–23.
12. J. B. Haskins, " Testing Suitability of Type Faces for Editorial Subject Matter," *Journalism Quarterly*, 35 (1958), 186–94.
13. *Ibid.*, 189.
14. *Ibid.*
15. D. B. Duncan, " Multiple Range and Multiple F Tests," *Biometrics*, 11 (1955), 1–42.
16. Henry Scheffé, *Analysis of Variance* (New York: Wiley, 1959).
17. L. S. Kogan, "Analysis of Variance—Repeated Measurements," *Psychological Bulletin*, 45 (1948), 131–43.
18. Note 10 *supra.*
19. *Ibid.*
20. Q. McNemar, *Psychological Statistics* (2d ed.; New York: Wiley, 1955).
21. H. Walker and J. Lev, *Statistical Inference* (New York: Holt, 1953).
22. J. E. Wert, C. O. Neidt, and J. S. Ahmann, *Statistical Methods in Educational and Psychological Research* (New York: Appleton-Century-Crofts, 1954).
23. Note 11 *supra.*
24. Sidney Siegel, *Non-Parametric Statistics for the Behavioral Sciences* (New York: McGraw-Hill, 1956).
25. *Ibid.*
26. C. H. Goulden, *Methods of Statistical Analysis* (2d ed.; New York: Wiley, 1952).

27. C. J. Hoyt and M. D. Johnson, "Regression and Correlation," *Review of Educational Research,* 24 (1954), 393–401.
28. J. P. Guilford, *Fundamental Statistics in Psychology and Education* (New York: McGraw-Hill, 1956).
29. C. J. Hoyt, "Test Reliability Estimated by Analysis of Variance," *Psychometrika,* 6 (1941), 153–60.
30. G. F. Kuder and M. W. Richardson, "The Theory of the Estimation of Test Reliability," *Psychometrika,* 2 (1937), 151–60.
31. R. Fisher, *Statistical Methods for Research Workers* (11th ed.; London: Oliver and Boyd, 1950).
32. J. P. Guilford *Psychometric Methods* (2d ed.; New York: McGraw-Hill, 1954).
33. Note 2 *supra.*
34. E. Haggard, *Intraclass Correlation and the Analysis of Variance* (New York: Dryden, 1958).
35. Robert L. Thorndike, *Personnel Selection: Test and Measurement Techniques* (New York: Wiley, 1949).
36. Harold Gulliksen, *Theory of Mental Tests* (New York: Wiley, 1950).
37. M. S. MacLean, Jr., and W. R. Hazard, "Women's Interest in Pictures: The Badger Village Study," *Journalism Quarterly,* 30 (1953), 139–52. See also R. Nafziger, M. S. MacLean, Jr., and Warren Engstrom, "Useful Tools for Interpreting Newspaper Readership Data," *Journalism Quarterly,* 28 (1951), 441–56.
38. D. W. Twedt, "A Multiple Factor Analysis of Advertising Readership," *Journal of Applied Psychology,* 36 (1952), 207–15.
39. Godfrey Thompson, *The Factoral Analysis of Human Ability* (3d ed.; New York: Houghton Mifflin, 1948).
40. L. L. Thurston, *Multiple Factor Analysis* (Chicago: University of Chicago Press, 1947).
41. Note 32 *supra.*
42. H. Solomon and B. Rosner, "Factor Analysis," *Review of Educational Research,* 24 (1954), 421–38.
43. John W. Tukey, "The Future of Data Analysis," *The Annals of Mathematical Statistics,* 33 (1962), 1–67.

6

Content Analysis in Communication Research

WAYNE A. DANIELSON

THE MESSAGE—the actual symbol sequence that is being communicated—occupies a central place in the communication process. It stands suspended in time and space between the source that created it and the destination that will ultimately receive it. It is the product of many forces, some plain and present, others obscure and remote. Observers look at the message and wonder about the person who sent it:

"Why did the source use this word rather than that one? Why did the source use this medium or channel to carry the message?"

At a deeper level the question arises: "What does the message tell us about the intelligence and aptitudes of the source, about his personality, his motives, values and goals, about his attitudes, his social situation, the groups he belongs to or desires to belong to and their influence on him?"

The message also has potential *effects* that are infinitely varied and infinitely interesting to journalists, behavioral scientists, and laymen alike. "Will the message attract attention," they ask. "Will it be correctly perceived? Will it be understood? Will it arouse motivating forces in the destination? Will it be remembered? Will it lead the final receiver to act? Will it cause his attitudes to change?"

The message, in short, contains a remarkably concentrated expression of some of the major factors involved in communication. It is perhaps because of this concentration of forces (and also because messages are sometimes more available than the people who produced or received them) that content analysis—the scientific study of messages—has become a central technique in communication research.

What is Content Analysis?

Many useful definitions of content analysis have been given.[1] An enduringly popular one by Bernard Berelson is as follows: "Content analysis is a research technique for the objective, systematic, and quantitative description of the manifest content of communication."[2] The key words are objective, systematic, quantitative, and manifest. These are the words which distinguish scientific content analysis from the ordinary, informal analysis all of us do every day in reading newspapers or magazines or listening to the conversations of our friends.

Objective means that the categories used to analyze content must be defined so precisely that different persons can analyze the same content using these definitions and get the same results. It also means that heavily *evaluative* categories and terms (good-bad, fair-unfair, beautiful-ugly) are avoided both because these terms are highly subjective and because their meaning tends to change as fashions come and go.

Systematic means that the selection of content to analyze must be based on a formal, predetermined, unbiased plan; in other words, the analyst cannot choose to examine only those elements in the content which happen to fit his hypothesis and ignore all the others. The word removes content analysis, supposedly, from the argumentative, biased collection of data to prove a point.

Quantitative means that the results of the analysis are usually expressed numerically in some way: in frequency distributions, in contingency tables, in correlation coefficients, in ratios and percentages of various sorts. The preference for quantification is understandable; there is simply much more agreement as to what is correct and incorrect procedure within the precise language of mathematics. It is always advisable, of course, to be sure that the assumptions underlying the use of numbers have been met; a fine frosting of statistics is sometimes used to conceal a crumbling analytical cake.

Manifest means that the semantic analysis involved in content analysis is ordinarily of a fairly direct and simple kind: it deals, as Harold Lasswell, Daniel Lerner and Ithiel Pool have put it, with "reading on the lines" and not "between the lines."[3] As mentioned earlier, the researcher may be interested in the forces which shaped the message or the effects the message is likely to have, but he does not code the content *in terms of* these latent forces or effects. He codes the content in fairly obvious terms of *what it says.* This should not be taken to mean that coders always agree about the manifest content of messages. The author has had many battles (particularly, it seems, with women coders) as to the proper interpretation of messages. The sentence, recorded at the faculty women's tea, "What a sweet hat you have on!" manifestly may mean to a male coder that the hat is okay, favorable, swell, good. To a female, however, it manifestly may mean that the hat is cheap, dowdy, last year's, and fifteen years too young for the wearer. The point is that manifest is a relative term. It indicates an *area* of meaning in which content analysts have traditionally tried to operate, rather than a definite point.

The Literature of Content Analysis

The student who decides to use content analysis as a major method of inquiry frequently does so on the basis of an article he has seen in a current journal, say *Journalism Quarterly* or *Public Opinion Quarterly.* Too often, however, he thinks the method is new, and he plunges bravely ahead without dipping further into the history of his technique than articles running back four or five years. In doing this, he may be making a serious error. For content analysis, much as it is known today, has a history running back to the 1920's and before that, to the establishment of the first schools of journalism early in this century.[4] Hundreds, perhaps thousands, of content analyses have been made since. And although methods and theoretical emphases have changed, the serious student can nevertheless gain a much-needed perspective and a proper feeling for the place of his study in the history of content analysis by carefully examining earlier work. In addition, he may find that some of the troublesome problems he is encountering have been encountered before and have been *solved* before; thus, he may avoid having to solve them again. In this area, as in many others, he who ignores history is condemned to repeat it.

The first major content analyses consisted mainly of subject matter classifications of newspaper content. An example of a study along these lines published in 1930 is Julian Woodward's analysis of foreign news in morning newspapers.[5] The next major use was in the analysis of political communication. The works of Lasswell and his students and associates are of importance here.[6] A book-length survey of content analysis by Bernard Berelson appeared in 1952. It contains an excellent bibliography of studies up to 1950.[7] Ithiel de Sola Pool is the editor of a book published in 1959, *Trends in Content Analysis,* a collection of papers on new approaches to the method. A greater emphasis on the use of content analysis in psychology and psycholinguistics is clearly evident. A limited bibliography updates the Berelson book to some extent.[8] The student would probably be well advised to look for recent studies in those journals which traditionally have carried content analysis studies, namely *Public Opinion Quarterly, Journalism Quarterly, Journal of Abnormal and Social Psychology* (all major sources), and the *American Journal of Sociology, American Sociological Review, Journal of Applied Psychology, Social Forces, The Annals of the American Academy of Political and Social Science, Psychological Bulletin, Psychiatry, Library Quarterly,* and others.

Major Problems of Content Analysis

Much has been said elsewhere in this book about the necessity for having a clear statement of a problem before starting out to investigate it. In content analysis the same rule applies. The method involves far too much work of a rigorous, fatiguing nature to be indulged in frivolously for purposes of fishing for a problem and a solution. Immense amounts of time and effort can be wasted in content analysis by an improperly prepared investigator. As Berelson says, "Unless there is a sensible, or clever, or sound, or revealing, or unusual, or important notion underlying the analysis, it is not worth going through the rigor of the procedure, especially when it is so arduous and so costly of effort. Content analysis, as a method, has no magical qualities—you rarely get out of it more than you put in, and sometimes you get less. In the last analysis, there is no substitute for a good idea."[9]

Assuming then, that you have a good idea, expressed in an abstract, generalized fashion, what are the major problems involved in investigating it through content analysis?

Sampling

Nowhere in social research does one escape the necessity for having a sound sampling scheme. Such a plan is especially important in content analysis. People are wordy. And one of the first problems that the content analyst faces, in almost any study he undertakes, is an immense *potential* collection of words—either distributed in space on the pages of newspapers, books, or magazines, or in time on radio or television. The material cannot be coded in its entirety; sampling in some form is a necessity if the problem is to be considered at all.

The word *potential* was italicized above because one of the chief difficulties in sampling, of course, is the *availability* of relevant materials. The messages of the mass media are ephemeral products of the modern world; they flash out upon the scene and then are gone. At the time this is being written, for example, there is no place in America where one can find a complete current collection of American daily newspapers, to say nothing of a collection with deep runs into the past. Librarians tend to save only the prestige papers of the country. Thus, as a rule, analysts who want to generalize to the American press, must plan their study in advance and *subscribe* to a sample of newspapers. If one were interested in generalizing to American newspapers, a sample could be drawn by going to the current *Editor & Publisher* yearbook and giving each newspaper listed there a number and then drawing numbers randomly from the universe so established. Since there are many more small dailies than large dailies in the nation, however, such a plan would not accurately represent the content typically seen by readers of American newspapers, most of whom live in large urban areas and read the large city newspapers. A sample designed to represent what is available to readers, therefore, would have to be weighted in such a way that papers of larger circulation had a greater chance of being selected. Such a sample is described in the International Press Institute *Flow of the News* study.[10] Other newspaper sampling methods are given in the references.[11]

After titles of publications have been selected, issues must still be sampled in *time*. This presents additional problems to the content analyst. It is well known, for example, that American daily newspapers vary in thickness during the various days of the week, due primarily to the flow of advertising which reflects the weekend buying habits of Americans. Hence, papers of Thursday are typically fat with grocery ads while Saturday papers are slim. Similarly, magazines typically have their biggest issues of the year just before and during the Christmas shopping season. Radio and television stations fill the same number of hours every day with programs, but content varies widely as audiences ebb and flow with the hours and with the seasons.

What all this implies, of course, is that the messages to be studied must be sampled in time according to a plan which takes into account the various systematic factors which may influence the occurrence and nature of the messages. A sample of newspapers which included only content from Saturday afternoon issues would be a poor sample for most analyses, for example.

A method of time sampling sometimes used in newspaper content analysis is the "composite week" technique of Robert Jones and Roy Carter.[12] In this method a "calendar" is constructed showing all the Monday issues, the Tuesday issues, etc., in the total sample of papers. Then a *subsample* is taken by randomly choosing *N* Monday papers from the Monday column on the calendar, *N* Tuesday papers from the Tuesday column, and so on. In this manner "constructed weeks" can be fashioned which will respresent the flow of news and advertising through the days of the week, and also randomly sample the total time period involved in the study. For some analyses this is a most useful method.

Establishing the Units of Analysis

Before content analysis can begin, the basic coding unit must be established. This is the smallest division or segment of the content which is to receive a score. Typical coding units are the word, the theme or assertion, the item, space and time units, and the character.[13]

Words are often easier coding units to work with than the more encompassing subdivisions of content. It is fairly easy to define a word so that others can identify it in all its variations. If the coding operation is simply to note the presence or absence of certain words (as in some of the readability formulas, for example), a high degree of coder reliability can usually be obtained. Some studies which have used words as basic coding units appear in the references.[14] Often the analyst is interested in larger units of meaning than individual words, however, and he feels that he must move to a larger unit of analysis. If the hypothesis has been expressed in a general enough manner, however, it is sometimes possible to test it using a *variety* of coding units. If the hypothesis can be tested through some count of individual words or the relationship of individual words to one another, such a method certainly deserves at least a pretest of its feasibility. If the hypothesis can be as fairly tested with a simple coding unit as with a complex one, the investigator is certainly justified in taking the easier course.

The *theme* or *assertion* is one of the most often used units of content analysis. A theme is defined as "a simple sentence . . . an assertion about a subject-matter."[15] For example, one might be interested in the attitude of an advice columnist toward various family members. Thus fathers, mothers, sisters, brothers might be significant "subject-matters." The statement, "Your father, though handsome, is a selfish, intolerant man," contains at least three assertions; namely, "Your father is handsome," "Your father is selfish," and "Your father is intolerant." It is evident that, unless the permissible referents are restricted, assertion analysis can rapidly explode a relatively small body of content into a large amount of data. The content analyst should be aware of this danger before he starts to use the method, so that he can be certain that he is coding only the content (and only the statements within the content) that are relevant to his hypothesis.

The student may wonder why content analysts make relatively little use of normal grammatical units such as the sentence or the paragraph. There is no innate reason why these units should not be used in some types of studies, and indeed they are occasionally used. However, it is ordinarily more difficult to put these units into single *categories*, if the categories are at all complex. What if a *direction* (favorable, neutral, or unfavorable) is to be assigned to a sentence, as a unit? Obviously the sentence may contain conflicting directional statements, joined by such connectors as "but," "however," or "nevertheless." Coders, faced by such conflicting statements, may not operate reliably in coding the sentence. One time they may decide that the over-all weight of the sentence is favorable; the next time they may decide that the weight is neutral or even unfavorable. The same criticism applies even more strongly to paragraphs as units.

Why then, is the most popular unit in content analysis the entire *item*, story, article, or editorial? Does not the same argument apply?

It applies, certainly, when coders attempt to place an entire article in a single complex category. Attempts to write directions for performing such feats nearly always produce frightful headaches. When careful directions are not written, coders tend to approach the task subjectively, and their classifications are not reliable. The wise student will always look for and examine with care the coder reliability figures in studies which report that complex categories were applied to coding units as large as whole stories. Often he will find that reliabilities simply are not reported. Using the entire article as a unit is defensible, however, in a variety of other situations when the classification categories are broad. For example, if one is interested in measuring *attention* paid to various categories of news, frequently the story has unity enough to enable coders to place it reliably into a single descriptive news category, or at most into two categories.[16] Using the large unit is defensible also if great amounts of material are to be coded. Somewhat lower reliabilities can then be tolerated because enough cases will be collected so that true relationships will show up in spite of a considerable amount of *random* coding error. A coding *bias,* of course, will continue to appear in spite of the large number of units coded.

Space and time units of analysis, such as the column inch (newspapers), the page or partial page (magazines), or the minute (radio and television), were widely used in early descriptive content analyses and are still used today.[17] When subtle categories are to be employed, time and space measurement suffers in the same way that item units and grammatical units suffer. Moreover, several researchers have found that space and time units (which are difficult to measure precisely) correlate highly with item units; thus, the simpler natural item coding is being more frequently employed today.[18]

A *character,* or person, or a class of persons is sometimes used as a coding unit in content analysis. All relevant information about the character is sifted out of the article or story and classified. For example, Berelson and Patricia Salter classified characters in American magazine fiction according to whether they were "Americans," "Anglo-Saxons and Nordics," or "Others." Then they examined each character as to his goals, his occupation, whether he was "approved" or not, etc. They found that, in the stories analyzed, the Americans, Anglo-Saxons, and Nordics were more often major "approved" characters and were more often interested in heart goals than were the "Others."[19] Recently, Jack Schwartz studied the portrayal of teachers in motion pictures in such terms as age, marital status, romantic involvement, relationships with students, etc. One of his conclusions was that in the movies, ". . . a successful romance for the educator exists only outside the academic pale; he leaves the teaching profession or marries someone with less education."[20] The character unit has often been used, as the foregoing examples show, to examine the extent to which the mass media perpetuate the stereotypes of our society.

The Context Unit

The basic coding unit is the smallest division of content to receive a score. Sometimes, however, a score cannot be given solely from an examination of the basic unit; the unit can be coded reliably only in terms of its *context*. Hence, a context unit—the largest division of content which may be consulted by a coder in order to assign a score to a basic coding unit—is often used in content analysis. Suppose, for example, that you were to categorize all assertions made by a source about Communists as being favorable, unfavorable, or neutral. Suppose, further, that you encountered the following assertion: "The Communists are taking over the world bit by bit." In isolation, it is impossible to code the assertion accurately. It sounds neutral or ambiguous. Only when it is placed in a context unit is the direction apparent. For example, if the sentence appears in a speech entitled, "The Red Menace," delivered at a National Association of Manufacturers Convention by a conservative Republican senator, then the correct code probably would be *unfavorable*. If the assertion appeared in a speech by a Russian astronaut to a world gathering of Communist youth, however, the correct code would undoubtedly be *favorable*. Some limits are usually placed on the *size* of the context unit which the coder is permitted to scan. Ultimately the unit could become so large that the coding of the basic unit would again become unreliable. A historian trying to analyze Jefferson's quotations concerning the press in the context of the president's entire life might encounter this problem. Then, too, as the context unit becomes larger, more time is spent scoring each coding unit. Usually, therefore, a compromise must be sought between the desirable and the possible.

A final word on the selection of units of analysis is in order.

It is certainly desirable that the student be familiar with the definitions, units, codes, and categories other researchers have used before him. He can save valuable time by following the disciplined measures others have devised. Yet he should not slavishly follow the past. From time to time, as he is developing his idea, he should attempt deliberately to break with the conventional and try to see his problem with fresh and clear vision. It is easier to say this, of course, than to do it. But it is often in such contemplative moments that insights are born which advance science not by inches but by miles.

Testing Coder Reliability

At an early stage in the research, and at intervals thereafter, the method being used in the analysis should face tests of its reliability. This means, in general terms, that the investigator puts different coders to work on the same content and checks to see whether they apply the method in the same way and obtain the same results. It may also mean that the same coders, after a time lapse, are required to recode some material coded earlier to see whether they will do it the same way the second time. Coder reliability tests are extremely important and should never be neglected unless the codes being used are so obvious that even a severe critic will concede that "on the face of it" they can be reliably used. In many cases the chief investigator or his main analysts *gradually* learn to make many subtle *qualifications* and restrictions in coding content. To the extent that these qualifications and restrictions are not plainly spelled out and incorporated in the coding directions they cannot be communicated to others, and the method is likely to become increasingly unreliable. A coder reliability check taken at intervals in the research, using newly trained coders, will forcibly remind the researcher that his intuitions and subtle feelings for content must ultimately find concrete verbal expression if others are to use his method. Reputable journals are gradually becoming reluctant to print analyses in which coder reliabilities have not been tested.

Various methods of making coder reliability tests are mentioned in the references; hence illustrations of only two methods will be given here.[21] Suppose one purpose of the analysis is to estimate the average number of page one national-international stories per issue of a number of newspapers. We might decide to test coder reliability in this instance by taking fifty newspapers from the sample and having each coder go through the papers, counting the number of national-international stories on the front page of each. We then could make a correlation matrix giving the scores assigned to each newspaper by each pair of coders. In Figure 1, for example, each mark in the scattergram represents the scores given to a particular front page of a paper by Coder A (on the vertical axis) and Coder B (on the horizontal axis). Inspection shows a high degree of agreement between these two coders. The Pearsonian product-moment correlation between the two sets of scores is .961. We might go on, from this point, and figure the product-moment correlations between the scores given by Coder A and Coder C, then Coder B and Coder C, and so on. Finally, we might present the *average* correlation as our estimate of the coder reliability in this study.

FIGURE 1

Scattergram showing the number of national-international stories found on the front pages of fifty newspapers by two coders

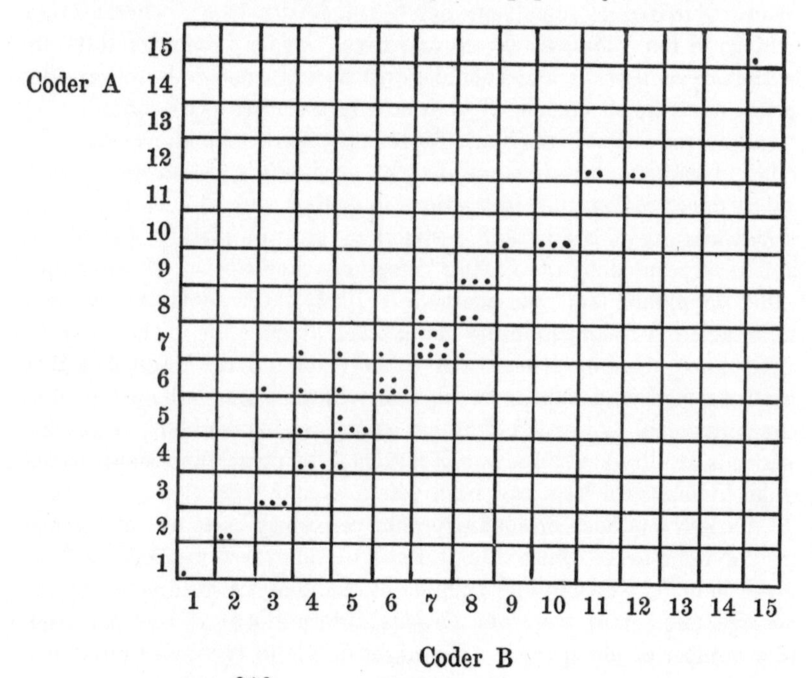

r = .916

What if the correlation coefficient is low and the scores of the two coders are disappointingly different? Obviously, at least two opportunities for errors are present: (1) A coder may be missing stories in the process of scanning the paper; or (2) A coder may be finding stories but coding them erroneously for one reason or another. Thus, it is often helpful not only to check the total score given a paper but to look into the matter further and find out whether the coders involved are coding the *same* stories in the *same* way. Such a procedure often results in a statistical measure referred to as the average percentage of agreement, which is, in one definition, the number of stories on which two coders *agree* divided by the total number of stories found by both the coders, averaged over all pairs of coders tested. Thus, suppose that in the example given, Coder B found 323 national-international stories in the fifty papers and Coder A found 341. Of the 323 stories found by Coder B, 321 were also found by Coder A. What is the percentage of agreement between these two coders? The answer is 94 per cent, because the 321 stories should be divided by the total number of stories found by both coders which is 343. An analysis of this type helps the researcher find which coders are making mistakes and what those mistakes are. (In the example, Coder A was counting stories which were less than 2 inches long and Coder B was not.)

In some tests coders are *given* a certain number of units to code (for example, a certain number of stories about crime, to be coded as juvenile, adult, or mixed crime). In this case, there is no error involved in finding the stories, and the percentage of agreement will be merely the number of items coded the same way by two coders divided by the total number of items in the test and averaged over all possible pairs of coders. This test obviously is easier than the first since the opportunity for error is less. In reading content analysis reports, it is important to note specifically how the reported percentage of agreement was obtained. Generally speaking, those coder reliability tests are most respected which are done under natural coding conditions, using natural materials, and without alerting coders to the fact that they are participating in a special test of their ability.

Testing the Validity of Results

Validity supposedly answers the question, "Does the measurement technique *measure what it is supposed to measure?*"[22] In the foregoing example the question might have been asked, "Well, I can see that you are measuring the stories you *defined* as crime stories reliably, but are those stories *really* crime stories?" The analyst, in answering this question, would probably have to defend the *face validity* of his definition of crime. He should be able to show that it encompassed only those acts generally considered by judicial authorities (which he can cite) or by the general public (as evidenced by survey data which he can cite) or by newspapermen (whom he can quote) to be truly criminal in nature, and not, for example, mere juvenile pranks or perhaps the result of panic. He may also attempt to defend the validity of his measurement device by the *known group* method. He may say, for example, "It is widely known and accepted that *The Christian Science Monitor* carries less crime news than *The New York Mirror*. In my content analysis I found an average of one story per issue in the *Monitor* and eight stories per issue in the *Mirror*. Thus, the results certainly are in accord with what we already know about these newspapers." Another way of establishing validity is by comparing results obtained by the method with results obtained by using a *different measure of the same thing*. Thus, Jones and Carter, in presenting their news hole content analysis by the "constructed week" approach, demonstrated that their results corresponded closely with results obtained by measuring the complete news hole in the traditional fashion.[23] Of course, this method of showing validity is good only if the criterion measure has previously been validated. Thus, James Farr, James Jenkins, and Donald Patterson compared their simplified readability measurement with the results Flesch had obtained using a more complex measure.[24] The validity of their technique, therefore, depends on the validity of the Flesch measure. It is always useful to inquire into the validity of the criterion measure used, since it sometimes happens that its validity has never been carefully established. Occasionally in social research *agreement* among different scientists is so vital that validity is granted to a certain measurement by *fiat*. That is, scientists agree among themselves that henceforth Concept A is Concept A and it is measured by Technique C. The author knows of no case in content analysis which really fits this definition. An example from the field of audience measurement is the commonly accepted definition of a newspaper's circulation: "It is what the Audit Bureau of Circulation says it is." Actually, the definition is a practical one and the measurement is carefully done, but it is not *the* circulation of the paper, which might be defined in many other ways. The validity of the A. B. C. definition is accepted because of the obvious commercial importance of having one accepted measurement of a publication's circulation. One of the tests of validity which is being used more and more as time goes on is the pragmatic establishment of validity by concomitant variation. This means that the author predicts that, as content varies in a certain fashion, a related variation will be found in another, independently measured phenomenon. If a check is made and the relationship is found to be as predicted, then there is some reason to believe that the measurement of the content has some validity. The logic of this deduction must be satisfying, of course, and the measure should pass other validity tests, but the pragmatic test of concomitant variation is often a hard one and is respected. The analyst whose measure passes this test can sometimes say with the inventor's justifiable pride: "You see?—It works just as I said it would!" A final test of validity, which has not often been used in large scale content analysis involves the establishment of validity by *experimental prediction.* This means that the analyst measures content prior to its publication and predicts what the nature of the reception will be when the content is transmitted. The method is logically similar to the test of concomitant variation, except that the direction of causality is clearer; that is, it is established rather definitely that differences observed in the receivers are due to prior differences in the content and not the other way around. It is an experimental rather than a correlational test and is generally thought of as being more elegant.

Uses of Content Analysis—Theory and Practice

It is probably true that some content analysts working on some problems are interested solely in what happens in the content itself and have no interest in the source that produced it or the audience that received it. Such men and such problems are rare, however. Content analysis is ordinarily employed because the analyst is interested in drawing an inference about some state in the source which originated the content, or some state in the audience or person who received it, or some more global inference about several parts or all of the communication system involved. In this section, therefore, we will look at a few studies which draw such inferences.

Drawing Inferences About Sources of Communication

Psychologists have observed that language is closely allied to thought and that many inferences as to a person's mental processes can be obtained by making a careful study of his verbal output. What is a person interested in? His speech or his writing often gives clues to his *interests.* What is a person paying *attention* to? Again, his verbal output may be a good indicator. How intelligent is the source? The words he knows and uses and the way he puts them together often provide clues to his general mental ability and to his special aptitudes as well. What are his *attitudes* toward various persons or objects in his environment? Attitudes have drive characteristics which impel the source to express them in his behavior; it is difficult for a person to keep to himself the fact that he has a strong attitude on any subject. What about enduring *personality factors*—long-term methods of relating to other people and to social situations? Again, these are often revealed in a source's speech or writing. Is the source under an *emotional strain?* Is he afraid? Anxious? In a blue mood? Sometimes we can tell by changes in the messages he produces. What *social or group influences* are operating on the source? Often these, too, are reflected in the messages he puts out, but we may have to be observant and insightful to see them. The message is a cloudy carnival mirror in which we may catch images—sometimes clear and sometimes distorted—of forces within the source of the message, and behind him, within the society and culture in which he lives.

The Institute for Journalistic Studies at Stanford University (then under the direction of Chilton R. Bush) was interested in describing certain aspects of the press coverage in California of the hotly contested Nixon-Douglas senatorial campaign of 1950.[25] In addition to describing the main issues of the campaign as seen by the twelve newspapers sampled, the analysts wished to gather some evidence on the general question: Does the editorial attitude of a newspaper toward a candidate affect communication concerning that candidate in the news columns? There is an ethical tradition in the American press that the two kinds of communication—editorial and news—are to be kept separate. Political opinions may be expressed in the editorials, but the news is to be kept objective and apolitical.[26] However, the psychological maxim that attitudes *will* influence communication in general in the attitudinal area is thought by some social scientists to outweigh occasionally the ethical restrictions, particularly when commitments are extreme. Was this the case in the Nixon-Douglas campaign? How might the hypothesis be fairly tested?

The Institute analysts examined all of the news about the campaign that appeared in the papers studied for the period of September 1 through November 7. The coding unit was the "statement," defined as an "expression which denotes a complete idea." [27] To qualify as a statement, the expression had to have one of the following referents: Douglas, the Democratic party, the administration and Democratic leaders, Nixon, the Republican party, and Republican leaders. Each statement was also classified as to its *source* (candidate, labor leader, political organization, reporter, etc.) and *direction* (favorable, unfavorable, or neutral with regard to the referent). Most statements (86% of all found) were made by the candidates themselves or by their avowed supporters. Therefore, little subjective judgment was required of the coders in classifying the statements as favorable, unfavorable or neutral because it was assumed that "every expression by such a person was only for the purpose of advancing the cause of a given candidate." [28] In every case in which a subjective determination was used, three coders agreed unanimously as to the proper direction of the statement.

TABLE 1

RELATIONSHIP BETWEEN EDITORIAL SUPPORT OF CANDIDATES AND NEWS COLUMN REFERENCES TO THEM *

	Editorial Stand of Papers Sampled					
News Column	*Supported Nixon*		*Neutral*		*Supported Douglas*	
Statements	*Douglas*	*Nixon*	*Douglas*	*Nixon*	*Douglas*	*Nixon*
Favorable	27.5%	53.8%	42.0%	34.4%	57.7%	23.2%
Neutral	30.2	35.8	38.8	46.1	38.8	38.4
Unfavorable	42.3	10.4	19.2	19.5	3.5	38.4
	100.0%	100.0%	100.0%	100.0%	100.0%	100.0%
N statements	2992	2930	528	486	707	458
N papers	9		1		2	

* Based on data from the Stanford Institute for Journalistic Studies analysis described in reference 25.

Table 1 presents the findings with regard to the question raised above. The two Douglas papers had a balance of statements in the news columns favoring the editorially supported candidate. The "no-stand" paper also favored Douglas slightly. Only two of the Nixon papers had a balance of statements favoring Douglas; all the remaining papers had a balance of statements favoring Nixon in the news columns.

These findings do not *prove* the hypothesis that the editorial position of a newspaper will influence communication in the news columns; too few newspapers were studied and too many additional factors were involved. For example, the authors say, "While 'bias' may have contributed to the favored index in some instances, some of the following considerations may also explain the scores: the relative efficiency of the candidates' news bureaus, the relative size of the newspapers' news holes, and various editorial, mechanical, and business considerations involved in the replating of pages." Clearly, however, the findings are *in accord with* the hypothesis, in general, and thus keep it in the running. The technique employed is one of the more sensitive ones devised in this difficult area, although many other studies could be cited which use different methods.[29]

Other studies which implicitly or explicitly draw inferences about sources of communication include Paul Deutschmann's study of the attention paid to ten categories of news by seven New York papers and four Ohio papers,[30] Ralph White's study of the personality of the author of *Black Boy,* using the technique of "value analysis."[31] Charles Osgood and Evelyn Walker's study of the emotional condition of individuals about to commit suicide as revealed in their suicide notes,[32] Berelson and Salter's study of cultural influences on use by fiction writers of stereotyped heroes and villains in magazine fiction,[33] and Sanford Dornbusch and L. C. Hickman's study of the historical tendencies toward other-directedness as reflected in the appeals of magazine advertising.[34] Examples need not be drawn exclusively from print media; Eugene Webb,[35] for instance, recently presented an insightful study showing that television audience ratings for various types of shows at the end of the season influence the medium's offerings of shows the next fall; that is, the law of reinforcement tends to hold here: sources (in this case networks and advertisers) tend to repeat or increase those actions which have been rewarded and cease or decrease those which have been "punished."[36]

Drawing Inferences About Receivers

Can we tell from analyzing content alone what the effects of a message will be? This question, phrased in many ways, has fascinated researchers in content analysis through the years. Can we predict what characteristics of content will command the *attention* and *interest* of audiences? Can we predict *comprehension* or "readability" or "listenability" of messages? Can we predict whether content will affect *attitudes* or arouse *emotions*? Will communication have effects on the cohesiveness or harmony of *social groups* such as the family? Will it lead to a desired *action* or to *social change*?

Efforts to answer these questions are of great theoretical importance, and in many cases, of some practical importance also. For example, a lucrative career in advertising probably awaits the man who can dependably predict audience size on the basis of a content analysis of advertising. Similarly, the United States Information Agency is probably eagerly awaiting the man who can reliably predict world attitudinal reaction by content analyzing our international communication efforts. To the young person who can predict stock market action on the basis of an objective content analysis of the news of the day will go a respectable fortune. Many other examples could be given.

There always has been a substantial risk in mass communication because of the poor feedback channels from the ultimate audience to the source. In most mass communication situations the messages are sent out, and individuals are free to respond or not respond to them. What will people do? Sources in the mass communications industry strive constantly to offer content which will meet the needs of their audiences. Yet, as a matter of fact, they often operate in semi-darkness, if not in black night, because reactions from the audience are slow in arriving and are difficult to evaluate when they do arrive. If a content analysis can be of assistance in predicting audience reactions, many people will be interested in knowing about it.

What are the factors in an advertisement which will result in high or low levels of attention being paid to that ad, as indexed by a readership study? This question was asked by Dik Twedt in a study of a business magazine.[37] Twedt correlated fifteen mechanical variables in the advertisements (such as number of colors, number of type styles used, etc.) and nineteen content variables (such as the Flesch readability and abstraction level scores, the number of "benefits" offered in headlines, etc.) with the readership scores of 137 ads. After eliminating nonsignificant correlations and after a factor-analysis study, Twedt came up with a multiple regression equation based on three factors: (1) size of advertisement; (2) number of colors; and (3) square inches of illustration. (The multiple correlation of these measures with the criterion readership scores was .76.) The equation was as follows:

$$\begin{aligned}\text{Predicted readership} \\ = 10.456 &+ 8.293 \cdot (\text{Size of ad in pages}) \\ &+ 3.869 \cdot (\text{Number of colors}) \\ &+ 0.181 \cdot (\text{Square inches of illustration})\end{aligned}$$

Twedt tested the validity of the formula by comparing the predicted and actual readership scores in six other magazines. The average (mean) correlation was .71.

What are the factors in a prose message which make it easy or hard to comprehend? Rudolf Flesch [38] decided to study this question using an interesting set of messages, *The McCall-Crabbs Standard Test Lessons in Reading.*[39] These test lessons were short reading selections followed by ten or so questions measuring the student's comprehension of what he had read. The grade score of students getting a certain number of questions correct was given beneath each selection; thus a student who answered five of ten questions correctly after reading a selection might find by consulting the table that he was reading as well as average pupils throughout the country read when they are nine-tenths of the way through the third grade.

When Flesch made his content analysis of each reading lesson, therefore, he had a convenient indication of whether the message factor he was measuring had anything to do with message comprehensibility or "readability" as he called it—he simply correlated the score obtained from message with the *grade level* of students who answered a certain proportion of the test questions correctly.

Flesch found two factors which correlated highly with this criterion: the number of syllables per one hundred words in the selection, and the mean (average) sentence length in words. The multiple correlation of these two measures with the criterion grade level scores was .70. Flesch's familiar reading-ease formula, therefore, is an adaptation of the multiple regression equation for predicting grade level from a knowledge of syllables per one hundred words and average sentence length.

The Flesch content analysis demonstrates the good sense of making use of available materials and having an outside measure of the response in the audience you wish to predict. A short list of recent studies on readability is given in the references.[40]

Other studies which draw inferences about the effects of content include John Harvey's study of the characteristics of best-selling novels,[41] Jack Haskins' study of the relationship between abstraction level, readership, and reader satisfaction in *Saturday Evening Post* articles,[42] and Percy Tannenbaum's and Mervin Lynch's attempt to predict through content analysis whether certain newspaper stories would later be classified as sensational by respondents using their Sendex scales.[43]

Generally speaking, researchers in this area have attempted to predict only the "simpler" effects of content; for example, those bearing on attention level and comprehension. Little has been done in the use of content analysis to predict emotional reactions, attitude change, action differences, etc. Sometimes researchers have not been careful to get an independent measure of the effect of the message, and consequently we find a number of studies which rely primarily on the "face validity" argument in defending the merits of the analysis.

Current Trends in Content Analysis

Students in almost any field of knowledge observe periodic shifts in direction and emphasis as major studies are made and publicized or as major figures enter and leave the field. The same is true in content analysis, and although the author lays no claim to omniscience, he would like to mention the following trends which he thinks he observes in the field as being of possible interest to students:

1. There is a divergent trend in content analysis toward simplicity and complexity of measurement. The recent book by Pool contains some of the most complex content analysis methodologies offered to behavioral science in recent years.[44] Osgood's "evaluation assertion analysis" is perhaps the outstanding example. This technique requires an involved masking out of parts of the message and the use of different coders to examine different parts of the message.

It seems to this observer to advance further toward an objective quantification of semantic analysis than any previous technique. But, though its theoretical importance is great, its potential usefulness may be limited until a sufficient supply of scientists brave enough to undertake its administration can be developed.

On the other hand, numerous advances are being made each year which actually make older content analysis techniques easier and simpler to use. New readability formulas, for example, have been developed which are easier to apply.[45] New sampling techniques have been devised.[46] Space measurement has given way in many instances to item counts, which often correlate highly with the more tedious measures.[47] The field, in short, is beginning to look more like an older science, with certain very difficult methodologies being developed on the periphery and certain established methodologies being simplified to the point that their application has almost become routine.

2. The studies cited in this chapter indicate rather clearly a long-established trend toward hypothesis-testing as opposed to purely descriptive research. This is important to the field for two reasons: (1) Hypothesis-testing is associated with validity of the measuring technique, as suggested in the section on validity. (2) Hypothesis-testing is also helpful in ridding the field of argumentative and subjective analyses of mass media "effects" which are never tested except by circular reasoning. Content analysis, in short, seems to be becoming less of a tool to use when you *cannot* examine sources and receivers and is becoming more of a tool to use when you *also* examine or interview sources and receivers. It is playing an increasingly important part in integrated studies which deal with whole communication systems or communication processes and not with isolated parts or fragments of such systems.

3. Along with the shifts outlined above, a change is occurring in the nature of the central concepts examined by the analytical method. Many earlier analyses appear to have been conducted by men who were "morally outraged" by something the mass media had done. They used content analysis at times as evidence or ammunition to denounce the source of the communication or the medium which carried it. For example, the Gabels concluded their analysis of Texas newspaper opinion in the 1940's with the following statement.

"Thus, by its own words the press of Texas stands convicted of consistent bias in favor of property rights, as against human rights. Its basic motivation is defense of the status quo. In a world of rapidly changing values, it clings stubbornly to the ideas of the past and offers no constructive program for the future. . . . These ten papers alone blanket a great state. Most of them preach an anti-democratic program. Is it any wonder that the O'Daniels and Stevensons hold great sway in Texas?"[48]

In the opinion of this author such a statement would not appear in a content analysis article in the same journal today. The point is not to argue that "moral outrage" is inconsistent with the scientific outlook but to observe that the nature of the concepts which *interest* content analysis is changing. The desire to examine *bias* in the press is changing to a desire to examine the *processes of social control* on newsroom copy. The desire to study *false claims* in advertising is changing to a desire to study *other-directedness* in advertising. The change is toward central concepts which have more to do with abstract, theoretically oriented social and psychological concepts and less to do with relatively concrete moral issues. The new studies may be less interesting to read, but they seem, to this observer at least, to be approaching science more rapidly.

4. A trend which, as this is being written, is just beginning to be observed in the field is the use of electronic computers for content analysis. Much has been said in this chapter about the tedious nature of certain aspects of content analysis—the dreary checking through page after page for isolated stories or the drudgery of counting words for readability tests. Computers, with their amazing capacity for storing information and checking facts rapidly, would seem to be ideally suited for such tasks. Certainly those types of analysis which involve searching content for the occurrence of certain words or word combinations would seem to lend themselves well to the peculiar abilities of computers. Analysts who, over the years, have tried to write objective descriptions of content classifications believe that it will be possible to adjust some of these definitions so that computers can use them, too, to make low-grade semantic decisions.[49] If computers can be programmed for certain types of analysis, it should be possible for researchers to take much larger samples of content because of the enormous speed with which the machines work. This, in time, should certainly result in sturdier generalizations than have been possible up till now. Coder reliability should cease to be a major problem, also, when machines instead of fallible humans are programmed to do the job.

5. A final trend, which has been alluded to several times, is the use of content analysis in experimentation. Experimental analysis in the form of advertising copy-testing has been around for many years. Such analysis, however, has not always been particularly profound. Perhaps a headline was changed, or an illustration was switched, or parts of the copy were rewritten for a split-run test, but few systematic content analyses were performed. Now, we are beginning to see studies in which changes in the content are systematically made and documented via content analysis, and the effects of the changes are then observed in audiences.[50] We are also beginning to see studies in which conditions affecting sources are systematically manipulated and the resulting communications of these sources are then content analyzed.[51] Both trends are healthy and should result in time in substantial increases in our knowledge of the communication process.

REFERENCES

1. For a list of definitions of content analysis, see Bernard Berelson, *Content Analysis in Communication Research* (Glencoe, Ill.: The Free Press, 1952), 14–15.
2. Ibid., 18.
3. Harold D. Lasswell, Daniel Lerner, and Ithiel de Sola Pool, *The Comparative Study of Symbols* (Stanford: Stanford University Press, 1952), 32.
4. For a description of a study made *much* earlier, see K. Dovring, "Quantitative Semantics in 18th Century Sweden," *Public Opinion Quarterly*, 18 (1954–55), 389–94.
5. Julian L. Woodward, *Foreign News in American Morning Newspapers: A Study in Public Opinion* (New York: Columbia University Press, 1930).
6. Harold D. Lasswell, Nathan Leites *et al.*, *Language of Politics: Studies in Quantitative Semantics* (New York: Stewart, 1949); Harold D. Lasswell, "World Attention Survey," *Public Opinion Quarterly*, 5 (1941), 456–62; Lasswell, "Communications Research and Politics," in Douglas Waples (ed.), *Print, Radio and Film in a Democracy* (Chicago: University of Chicago Press, 1942), 101–17; Harold D. Lasswell and Associates, "The Politically Significant Content of the Press: Coding Procedures," *Journalism Quarterly*, 19 (1942), 12–23; Harold D. Lass-

well and Joseph M. Goldsen, "Public Attention, Opinion, and Action," *International Journal of Opinion and Attitude Research,* 1 (1947), 3–11.

7. Note 1 *supra.*
8. Ithiel de Sola Pool (ed.), *Trends in Content Analysis* (Urbana: University of Illinois Press, 1959).
9. Note 1 *supra,* 198.
10. *The Flow of the News* (Zurich, Switzerland: International Press Institute, 1953), 197–99.
11. Wendell J. Coats and Steve W. Mulkey, "A Study in Newspaper Sampling," *Public Opinion Quarterly,* 14 (1950), 533–46; F. James Davis and Lester W. Turner, "Sample Efficiency in Quantitative Newspaper Content Analysis," *Public Opinion Quarterly,* 15 (1951–52), 762–63; Nathan Maccoby *et al.,* "Method for the Analysis of the News Coverage of Industry," *Public Opinion Quarterly,* 14 (1950), 753–58; and Alexander Mintz, "The Feasibility of the Use of Samples in Content Analysis," in *Language of Politics,* note 6 *supra.*
12. Robert L. Jones and Roy E. Carter, Jr., "Some Procedures for Estimating 'News Hole' in Content Analysis," *Public Opinion Quarterly,* 23 (1959), 399–403.
13. Note 1 *supra,* 135–46.
14. Note 3 *supra*; Ithiel de Sola Pool, *The Prestige Papers* (Stanford: Stanford University Press, 1952); also see the readership studies mentioned in note 40 *infra.*
15. Note 1 *supra,* 138.
16. For an example of reliable double coding of item units, see Paul J. Deutschmann, *News-Page Content of Twelve Metropolitan Dailies* (Cincinnati, Ohio: Scripps-Howard Research, 1124 Union Central Building, 1959).
17. Recent examples include James W. Markham, "Foreign News in the United States and South American Press," *Public Opinion Quarterly,* 25 (1961), 242–62; Guido H. Stempel, III, "The Prestige Press Covers the 1960 Presidential Campaign," *Journalism Quarterly,* 38 (1961), 157–63; and note 16 *supra.*
18. See James W. Markham and Guido H. Stempel, III, "Analysis of Techniques in Measuring Press Performance," *Journalism Quarterly,* 34 (1957), 187–90; and note 16 *supra.*
19. Bernard Berelson and Patricia Salter, "Majority and Minority Americans: An Analysis of Magazine Fiction," *Public Opinion Quarterly,* 10 (1946), 168–90; see also Patrick Johns-Heine and Hans H. Gerth, "Values in Mass Periodical Fiction, 1921–1940," *Public Opinion Quarterly,* 13 (1949), 105–13; Leo Lowenthal, "Biographies in Popular Magazines," in Bernard Berelson and Morris Janowitz (eds.), *Reader in Public Opinion and Communication* (Glencoe, Ill.: The Free Press, 1950), 289–98; Gerhart Saenger, "Male and Female Relationships in the American Comic Strip," *Public Opinion Quarterly,* 19 (1955–56), 195–205.
20. Jack Schwartz, "The Portrayal of Educators in Motion Pictures, 1950–

1958," paper read at the Association for Education in Journalism Convention, August 26, 1959, Eugene, Oregon. (Current source: College of Journalism and Communications, University of Illinois, Urbana, Ill.)

21. Coder Reliability studies include: Abraham Kaplan and Joseph M. Goldsen, "The Reliability of Content Analysis Categories," in Lasswell *et al.*, *Language of Politics*, 83–112; Hornell Hart, "The Reliability of Two Indexes of Newspaper Behavior," *Social Forces*, 10 (1932), 358–63; Irving L. Janis *et al.*, "The Reliability of a Content Analysis Technique," *Public Opinion Quarterly*, 7 (1943), 293–96; W. A. Scott, "Reliability of Content Analysis: The Case of Nominal Scale Coding," *Public Opinion Quarterly*, 19 (1955), 321–25; Julian L. Woodward and Raymond Franzen, "A Study of Coding Reliability," *Public Opinion Quarterly*, 12 (1948), 253–57.
22. See Paul J. Deutschmann's general discussion of reliability and validity in Chapter 7 of this book, "Measurement in Communication Research."
23. Note 12 *supra*.
24. James N. Farr, James J. Jenkins, and Donald G. Patterson, "Simplification of the Flesch Reading Ease Formula," *Journal of Applied Psychology*, 35 (1951), 333–37.
25. Chilton R. Bush, "The Analysis of Political Campaign News," *Journalism Quarterly*, 28 (1951), 250–52, for the method; see also Galen Rarick, *California Daily Newspaper Reporting of the 1950 U. S. Senatorial Campaign: A Content Analysis* (M. A. thesis, Stanford University, 1951); and "The Nixon-Douglas Campaign," (Stanford Institute for Journalistic Studies, Stanford University), a press release dated Jan. 26, 1951.
26. Canon V of the "Canons of Journalism," adopted in 1923 by the American Society of Newspaper Editors, reads as follows: "Impartiality—Sound practice makes clear distinction between news reports and expressions of opinion. News reports should be free from opinion or bias of any kind," Wilbur Schramm (ed.), *Mass Communications* (Urbana: University of Illinois Press, 1960), 623–25.
27. Note 25 *supra*.
28. *Ibid.*
29. Content analyses of press performance include: Robert Batlin, "San Francisco Newspapers' Campaign Coverage: 1896, 1952," *Journalism Quarterly*, 31 (1954), 297–303; Nathan B. Blumberg, *One Party Press?* (Lincoln: University of Nebraska Press, 1954); Charles E. Higbie, "Wisconsin Dailies in the 1952 Campaign: Space vs. Display," *Journalism Quarterly*, 31 (1954), 285–96; Malcolm W. Klein and Nathan Maccoby, "Newspaper Objectivity in the 1952 Campaign," *Journalism Quarterly*, 31 (1954), 285–96; Markham and Stempel, "The Prestige Press Covers the 1960 Presidential Campaign," *loc. cit.*; Granville Price, "A Method for Analyzing Newspaper Campaign Coverage," *Journalism Quarterly*, 31 (1954), 447–58.
30. Note 16 *supra*.

31. Ralph K. White, "Black Boy: A Value Analysis," *Journal of Abnormal and Social Psychology,* 42 (1947), 440–61. For a more general treatment of the method see White, *Value-Analysis, The Nature and Use of the Method* (Glen Gardner, N. J.: Society for the Psychological Study of Social Issues, 1951), and "Value Analysis," *Journal of Social Psychology,* 19 (1944), 351–58.
32. Charles E. Osgood and Evelyn G. Walker, "Motivation and Language Behavior: A Content Analysis of Suicide Notes," *Journal of Abnormal and Social Psychology,* 59 (1959), 58–67.
33. Note 19 *supra.*
34. Sanford M. Dornbusch and L. C. Hickman, "Other-directedness in Consumer-Goods Advertising: A Test of Riesman's Historical Theory," *Social Forces,* 38 (1959), 99–102.
35. Eugene J. Webb, "Ratings and the Content of Television," paper read at the Association for Education in Journalism Convention, August 28, 1961, Ann Arbor, Michigan. (Current Source: Medill School of Journalism, Northwestern University, Evanston, Ill.).
36. William S. Verplanck, "The Control of the Content of Conversation: Reinforcement of Statements of Opinion," *Journal of Abnormal and Social Psycholoy,* 51 (1955), 668–76.
37. Dik W. Twedt, "A Multiple Factor Analysis of Advertising Readership," *Journal of Applied Psychology,* 36 (1952), 207–15.
38. Rudolf Flesch, "A New Readability Yardstick," *Journal of Applied Psychology,* 32 (1948), 221–33.
39. William A. McCall and Lelah Mae Crabbs, *Standard Test Lessons in Reading* (New York: Bureau of Publications, Teachers College, Columbia University, 1926, 1950).
40. Edgar Dale and J. S. Chall, "A Formula for Predicting Readability," *Education Research Bulletin,* 27 (1948), 11–20, 37–54; Farr, Jenkins, and Patterson, "Simplification of the Flesch Reading Ease Formula," *loc. cit.*; Rudolf Flesch, "Measuring the Level of Abstraction," *Journal of Applied Psychology,* 34 (1950), 384–90; Paul J. Gillie, "A Simplified Method for Measuring Abstraction in Writing," *Journal of Applied Psychology,* 41 (1957), 214–17; George R. Klare *et al.,* "The Relationship of Style, Difficulty, Practice and Ability to Efficiency of Reading and to Retention," *Journal of Applied Psychology,* 41 (1957), 222–26; Richard D. Powers, W. A. Sumner, and B. E. Kearl, "A Recalculation of Four Adult Readability Formulas," *Journal of Educational Psychology,* 49 (1958), 99–105; Margaret Jean Peterson, "Comparison of Flesch Readability Scores with a Test of Reading Comprehension," *Journal of Applied Psychology,* 40 (1956), 35–36; Herbert Rubenstein and Murray Aborn, "Learning, Prediction, and Readability," *Journal of Applied Psychology,* 42 (1958), 28–32; Charles E. Swanson, "Readability and Readership: A controlled Experiment," *Journalism Quarterly,* 25 (1948), 339–43; Charles E. Swanson and H. G. Fox, "Validity of Readability Formulas," *Journal of Applied Psychology,* 37 (1953), 114–18.

41. John Harvey, "The Content Characteristics of Best-Selling Novels," *Public Opinion Quarterly*, 17 (1953), 91–114.
42. Jack B. Haskins, "Validation of the Abstraction Index as a Tool for Content-Effects Analysis and Content Analysis," *Journal of Applied Psychology*, 44 (1960), 102–106.
43. Percy H. Tannenbaum and Mervin D. Lynch, "Sensationalism: The Concept and Its Measurement," *Journalism Quarterly*, 37 (1960), 381–92. For a similar approach to sensationalism in newspaper front pages, see William Glenn Robertson, *The Spillane Ratio: Development of a Space Measurement Method for Ranking the Front Page Relative Sensationalism of United States Daily Newspapers* (M. A. thesis, University of North Carolina, 1962).
44. Note 8 *supra.*
45. Notes 24 and 40 (Gillie) *supra.*
46. Note 12 *supra.*
47. Notes 10, 16, and 18 *supra.* Also see Wayne A. Danielson, "Applying Guttman Scaling to Content Analysis," paper read at the Association for Education in Journalism Convention, August 31, 1961, Ann Arbor, Michigan. (Current source: School of Journalism, University of North Carolina, Chapel Hill, N. C.).
48. Milton and Hortense Gabel, "Texas Newspaper Opinion II," *Public Opinion Quarterly*, 10 (1946–47), 201–15.
49. Charles E. Higbie, "Computer Utilization in Planning and Executing Mass Media Performance Studies," paper read at the Association for Education in Journalism Convention, August 31, 1961, Ann Arbor, Michigan. (Current source: School of Journalism, University of Wisconsin, Madison, Wisconsin).
50. Note 43 *supra.*
51. Bradley S. Greenberg, *Performance and Message Consequences of Encoding Behavior Under Congnitive Stress* (Ph. D. dissertation, University of Wisconsin, 1961); Lionel C. Barrow, *The Effects of Cognitive Incongruity Upon Encoding Behavior* (Ph. D. dissertation, University of Wisconsin, 1960).

7

Measurement in Communication Research

PAUL J. DEUTSCHMANN

RESEARCH AT ITS BEST must be related to theory. More specifically, to be of maximum utility the research with which this volume deals must lead to the formulation and testing of hypotheses. Generally speaking, the hypothesis cannot be formulated precisely unless a means of measuring the variables has been developed. And finally, the hypothesis cannot be tested, unless means have been found to measure the variables.

Thus a first step toward measurement is the identification of the variables involved in the phenomenon one wishes to study. A variety of researchers have characterized the variables of the communication process.[1] Most agree on a list quite similar to this one:

1. The communicator (source, sometimes medium).
2. The message (content, sometimes stimulus).
3. The channel (also medium, interpersonal network).
4. The receiver (audience).

The basic problem of communication research is to discover the relationships between these variables. For example, we might seek to discover what are the effects upon the communicator as the result of his playing this social role. Taking another approach, we might concentrate upon the message, seeking to make inferences about the source of the message, his purposes, attitudes, and communication "strategy," or to make inferences about message effects upon the receiver. If we focus upon effects, defining them as changes in receivers as the result of communication, we might study changes in all four key variables. To put the latter approach mathematically, in this instance the researcher hopes to express effects as some mathematical function of various communicator, channel, message, and receiver variables—$E = f(C, M, Ch, R)$. More often, our goal is less complex, i.e., we may endeavor to hold constant all of the variables but one. Then our mathematical formula can be expressed as $E = f(C)$ or $E = f(M)$.

Rules for Measurement

Such a formulation immediately implies that there will be measurement of the variables. How do we approach measurement? W. J. Dixon and F. J. Massey point out:

> It is necessary in the investigation of any phenomenon, whether it be the study of forces of attraction by the physicist, the study of the effects of anxiety by the psychologist, the study of radiation effects on animals by the biologist, or any other research, to observe and record some characteristic of the objects under consideration.[2]

The observation and recording of some characteristic of the objects under study suggest immediately the need for a systematic approach. Indeed, unless the researcher has a system, a collection of rules which will guide him in recording observations, his observations will have little or no utility. But if he has a system, there is the possibility that his observations will result in new information about the relationships between the objects of his study. Sometimes his system or set of rules does not lend itself to recording observations in numerical form. We sometimes call data gathered under such rules "qualitative." But if his set of rules makes possible the recording of observations in numerical form, we may call it "quantitative." And if he has so systematized his observations, we may say that he is engaged in measurement.

This system may be exceedingly crude; it may simply involve splitting the observations into two categories which differ in some observable respect. Thus we classify receivers into those who have read a particular message and those who have not, ignoring differences in the amount of readership. In such a circumstance the observations are stated implicitly in numerical terms; specifically a value of 1 is assigned to each reader and of 0 to each nonreader. The proportion or percentage of readership which is reported is exactly equal to the mean we would obtain by summing all of our 1's and 0's and dividing by the number of observations.

Underlying this simple case of measurement must be a system of recording observations. It may be very crude, such as asking the respondent whether he read the particular message, accepting a statement in the affirmative as an indication of readership, and considering all other statements as an indication of nonreadership. Or it may be more complex. We might require that the individual first answer in the affirmative to a question concerning his exposure to the newspaper or magazine which carries the particular message. Only if he passed this hurdle and then answered the specific question concerning the article would he be classified as a reader. We might require that he recall some portion of the message. But such complexity would not necessarily mean that our number system be changed.

In any of the cases we have an example of measurement, accepting the word in its broadest sense. This states that measurement is the assignment of numerals to objects, events, or persons according to rules.[3] Broadly speaking, the problem of measurement involves working out rules for the assigning of numerals and understanding what limitations are imposed by the nature of these rules and by the nature of the set of numbers which will result.

It is important to note that the choice of measuring instrument—even though it might not be theoretically oriented—does often result in implicit statements about theory. Suppose, for example, you seek to measure attitude toward some social object—say, the newspaper. Perhaps you have hypothesized that attitude toward newspapers relates to readership of newspapers. Thus you will need two measures—one of attitude and one of readership.

Let us discuss the attitude measurement. A fairly common approach is to build a questionnaire composed of a number of items. You might ask whether the respondent thinks newspapers are "fair," whether he enjoys reading newspapers, whether there are many or few interesting items in newspapers, etc. In taking this approach to measurement, you have already begun to make assumptions. **First,** you have assumed that attitude toward newspapers is unitary and can be thought of as stretching from an area of extreme favorability to one of extreme unfavorability. (We often call this an attitude continuum.) You would assume that if you could find individuals who represented these polar extremes, they would answer all questions either favorably or negatively.

Since measurement is the assigning of numbers to objects in accordance with rules, the next problem is to determine how you will "score" various responses. If the questions were dichotomous, i.e., simple agree-disagree, or yes-no, or favorable-unfavorable, you probably would assign the number 1 for agree and 0 for disagree. You would then hope to sum the answers over all items, producing a score which would represent a person's attitude relative to others in the group being measured.

If there were 10 items and a person answered 6 favorably and 4 negatively, he would have a score of 6, while a person answering 4 favorably would have a score of 4. The assumptions made in such a system are that the answer to each question is a function of underlying attitude and that the total configuration of answers is also a function.

In effect, you have constructed a model. A way to appreciate this more specifically is to state the model in probability terms. For example, for the most favorable "polar" individual the probability that he will answer *any* question favorably is 1, that he will answer negatively is 0. The most unfavorable individual is characterized by opposite probabilities. We could conceive of individuals in between these extremes as having probabilities of giving favorable replies which are less than 1. This would mean that they will answer some proportion of the items favorably and some negatively. An individual with a probability of .5 would on the average answer half of the questions favorably and half negatively.

In spelling out the model, we see that each item is considered to be operating in exactly the same way. Indeed, if we could present a single item a large number of times and somehow cause the individual to forget how he had answered earlier, with sufficient trials we would expect that the proportion of favorable replies would equal his probability figure. We are attempting to approximate this by asking him a number of different questions. And we are assuming that it makes no difference which item he answers favorably.

Analyzing in Advance

If we wanted to move from measurement of individuals to measurement of the group, we would expect that every question would serve as an estimate of the favorability of attitude of the group. The proportion of favorable replies for any question would be the sum of the 1's divided by the total number of replies. In the ideal situation each item would provide exactly the same estimate of favorability for the group measured. The characteristics of the model underlying this scoring system are found in the table on page 175 (the student who recalls his algebra will probably notice the relationship between this model and the binomial theorem $[p + q]^n$). This demonstrates that there are 32 different patterns of response possible in the scoring system. (Generally, there would be 2^n patterns with n equaling number of dichotomous items.) Further, these patterns are related to six different probability levels. With this model we consider a response of 01111 as good an indicator of a (p) level of .8 as a response of 11011. Both produce scores of 4. It might be noticed also that we cannot characterize the individual exactly. We would have to assume that individuals whose true probability of a favorable response was somewhat below or above .2, for example, would tend to respond in the pattern appropriate for this probability level and would get scores of 1.

In the example we can also observe that the proportion of favorable responses for any item is exactly .5. The particular value (.5), of course, is a function of the distribution of scores in the example. If we were sampling from a population which was quite favorable toward newspapers, we might find high frequencies of score 5 and 4, leading to a higher proportion favorable for each item. However, given this model, the proportions would still all be equal. What would be necessary is that *all patterns* of response which produce a particular score be found in the same, or very nearly the same, frequency. Departures from this condition would mean that items would yield different estimates of the group proportion of favorableness.

Now it is possible to utilize a very similar system of scoring or measurement, starting with different assumptions and leading to a quite different result. Supposing that we have constructed a set of items, but instead of designing them to produce similar proportions

TABLE 1

QUESTIONS

Individuals	*Probability of fav. response*	A .5	B .5	C .5	D .5	E .5	*Score*
a	1.0	1	1	1	1	1	5
b	.8	0	1	1	1	1	4
c	.8	1	0	1	1	1	4
d	.8	1	1	0	1	1	4
e	.8	1	1	1	0	1	4
f	.8	1	1	1	1	0	4
g	.6	1	1	1	0	0	3
h	.6	1	1	0	1	0	3
i	.6	1	1	0	0	1	3
j	.6	1	0	1	1	0	3
k	.6	1	0	1	0	1	3
l	.6	1	0	0	1	1	3
m	.6	0	1	1	1	0	3
n	.6	0	1	1	0	1	3
o	.6	0	1	0	1	1	3
p	.6	0	0	1	1	1	3
q	.4	1	1	0	0	0	2
r	.4	1	0	1	0	0	2
s	.4	1	0	0	1	0	2
t	.4	1	0	0	0	1	2
u	.4	0	1	1	0	0	2
v	.4	0	1	0	1	0	2
w	.4	0	1	0	0	1	2
x	.4	0	0	1	1	0	2
y	.4	0	0	1	0	1	2
z	.4	0	0	0	1	1	2
aa	.2	1	0	0	0	0	1
bb	.2	0	1	0	0	0	1
cc	.2	0	0	1	0	0	1
dd	.2	0	0	0	1	0	1
ee	.2	0	0	0	0	1	1
ff	.0	0	0	0	0	0	0
Total Favorable Responses		16	16	16	16	16	
Total Responses		32	32	32	32	32	

of favorability, we design them to produce different proportions. We assume they will provide a variety of estimates, ranging from one which indicates a rather small proportion of favorability to another which indicates a rather high proportion. We can relate probability concepts to this approach, but in a somewhat different fashion than in our first example. We now describe each individual in terms of as many probability figures as there are items. Further, we conceptualize the answering in each case as an all-or-none affair, i. e., we say the probability of a favorable answer by a given individual on a given question is either 1 or 0. However, we relate these probability figures in a systematic fashion. We say that a person endorsing the item accepted by the smallest number of respondents has a probability of 1 for this item and has, further, a probability of 1 for a favorable response to all other items. Generally, we say that if an individual endorses a particular item, his probability of endorsing any item endorsed by a larger proportion of the sample is 1.

We can also say the obverse. If an individual fails to endorse a particular item, his probability of endorsing any item endorsed by a smaller proportion of the sample is 0. Thus we can say that if we know a given individual's score, we also know automatically his pattern of response, since one and only one pattern is associated with a particular score. The characteristics of the model underlying this scoring system can be indicated below:[4]

TABLE 2

QUESTIONS

		A	B	C	D	E	
Probability of favorable response to the item		.2	.4	.5	.6	.8	*Score*
Individual	a	1	1	1	1	1	5
	b	1	1	1	1	1	5
	c	0	1	1	1	1	4
	d	0	1	1	1	1	4
	e	0	0	1	1	1	3
	f	0	0	0	1	1	2
	g	0	0	0	0	1	1
	h	0	0	0	0	1	1
	i	0	0	0	0	0	0
	j	0	0	0	0	0	0
Total favorable responses		2	4	5	6	8	
Total responses		10	10	10	10	10	

From this we can see that there are six different scores, even as in our earlier system. However, instead of being related to a number of different patterns, each is related to a single response pattern. Further, there is a cumulative characteristic in the response pattern. (While only six patterns are given, the student will observe that the other twenty-six can occur. However, they do not fit the model.) Again we cannot characterize the individual exactly. We have to assume that individuals whose true score is somewhat below or above 1 will tend to respond 00001. If we wanted a finer measure, we would have to insert items with slightly larger or smaller probabilities of response than .8.

At this point it should be clear that, despite a number of points of similarities in these two approaches, there is a basic difference involving the types of questions used. In the first case the questions should be statements which would produce almost the same proportion of favorable responses. We might take, for example, several items which had been judged to be near the neutrality point as far as the total population was concerned. We can also see that this requirement of equality in number of favorable responses might be a very difficult one to satisfy in a practical sense. Further, we can see that the testing of the correspondence of our results to our model will be quite different. In the first system our data will fail to fit the model to the extent that possible response patterns for given scores do not appear. For example, if all of our scores of 4 are produced by a pattern 01111 in this system, the equality of proportions by items will be disturbed. In the second system just the reverse result is produced. If our scores of 4 are produced by all of the possible patterns, our assumptions concerning probabilities of response are not satisfied. On the other hand, if they are all produced by the pattern 01111, our data fit the model very well.

Determination of which model fits the data better is a matter for empirical investigation. Much work suggests that there is a tendency for respondents to be consistent from one item to another, resulting in patterns of response more nearly in line with the second model than with the first. The respondent performs, in effect, as though he had separate probability figures for each item, rather than an over-all probability figure for the attitudinal area. Thus, if he were presented with a set of items of the type called for by the first model, he should either answer all of them favorably or answer all of them negatively. This would preserve the equality of proportions the first model requires but would produce only two patterns of response as the second would require.

These two extended examples should serve to demonstrate that, when we develop a measuring instrument, certain statements about our variables are inherent. It is best to make these statements explicit, by means of an advance analysis of the sort described here. Further, this analysis has touched on some general characteristics of measuring instruments, to which we will now turn.

The Measuring Instruments

One of the first involves the number of different numerical values we may obtain, given the particular set of rules for recording observations. If the rules are such that a limited set of values can occur, we are dealing with a measuring instrument which produces a discrete set of numbers. The readership examples are of this nature—only the values of 1 or 0 may occur. We might so design a readership measure to make possible an infinite number of values. If we measured how far the reader read into the particular item and expressed the result as a proportion, we could have, at least theoretically, all possible proportions between 0.00 and 1.00. Almost all variables in the communication process are capable of such continuous measurement; however, many measuring devices yield discrete sets of numbers.

Another problem in measurement involves the number of variables which are contributing to the changes in the numbers we record in keeping with our rules. Actually, unless we have some notion of what variables are contributing to changes, our recording is fruitless. Ideally, a measuring instrument should reflect differences in just one variable (or one aspect of a variable). If it did so, we could call it unidimensional. The measurement of height with a ruler is an example of unidimensionality. The resulting set of figures varies only as height of individuals observed varies. But suppose we measured height with a flexible tape which adhered to the surface of the body. Then our resulting figure would be affected not only by height, but also by girth. We could have two individuals of the same height with different measurements, or two individuals with the same measurements and with different heights. The confounding comes from the sensitivity of our system of measurement to both factors—height and girth.

Most of the measuring devices used in communication research are multidimensional to a greater or smaller degree. It is important that we recognize their limitations. Sometimes we can change our hypotheses and systems of recording observations so that our instruments can approach unidimensionality. However, it is not necessary that we limit ourselves strictly to variables which have a surface or conspicuous "unidimensionality." Actually, it is usually more fruitful to look for hidden functional unities which will facilitate the development of devices for measuring aspects of the variables which have hitherto gone unobserved.[5]

This attention to unidimensionality suggests that one of the goals of measurement is ordinarily to locate our observations along some continuum. This may be from readership to nonreadership, from favorable to unfavorable, from informed to uninformed, from readable to unreadable. The nature of the continuum is specified by the theoretical formulation; the nature of the measuring instrument is specified by the continuum. The effectiveness of the measuring instrument is in its ability to locate observations accurately and unambiguously on the continuum.

At the same time, this does not mean that in communication research, or in any other research for that matter, we are interested only in problems which can be put into unidimensional terms. Frequently, it may be necessary for us to study problems which involve many dimensions.

What is important is to understand whether we are dealing with a unidimensional situation. Suppose, for example, we had measured four individuals and had obtained scores of 3, 4, 5, and 6. If we were assuming unidimensionality, they would be arranged in this fashion:

3	4	5	6
a	b	c	d

The linear arrangement suggests that we know at least that case "d" is greater than case "c" and so forth. However, suppose that the obtained scores actually represented a confounding of two independent factors. Then the situation would actually be of this form:

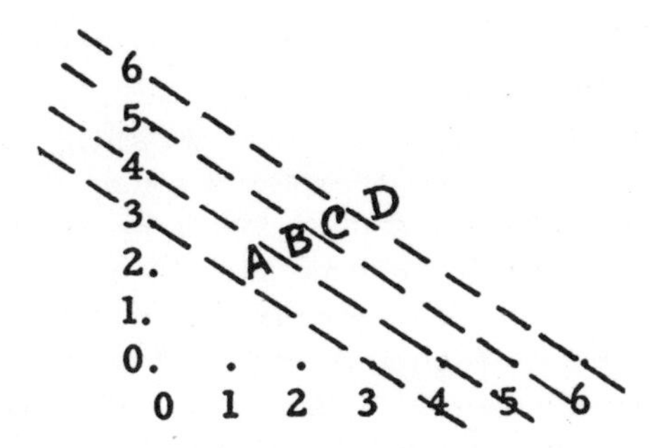

All we could know from these measurements is that the individual case could be found at some point along its appropriate line. The lines are ordered in the same manner as our points on the single continuum, but we cannot say where upon its line any individual case is located.

On the other hand, if we could identify the contribution of each of the factors to the obtained score, we could locate each case precisely. Then, it might happen that a different ordering of objects would result, as is shown here:

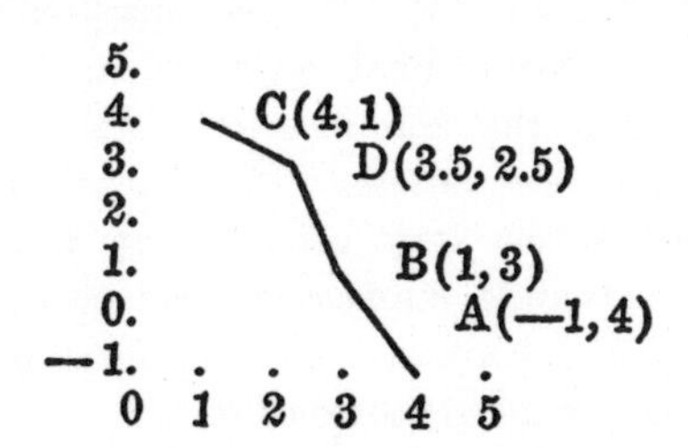

It is quite possible that a new kind of relationship would be brought out by such an analysis. For this approach to be operable, of course, requires the use of two measuring instruments, one to locate the observations upon one continuum, and the second to locate the observation upon the other. Another point which this example illustrates is that we should not add numbers which come from different continua; thus if we have a number of individual measuring instruments we wish to combine into an over-all index, we must be sure that they are combinable in the fashion that the model underlying addition specifies.

Another way to talk about measurement, which we have already partially introduced, is in terms of scales. Almost always, when we assign numbers to observations, we do so upon the assumption that some form of scale results. A scale is actually the set of numbers produced by our recording observations according to rules.[6] The measurement of height clearly produces a scale. Further, the scale is unidimensional. Beyond that, the units in the scale are equal, and we can specify the nature of 0 on the scale—or total lack of height. This is the ideal form of scale, since the measurements can be manipulated in the full sense. A given measurement which is twice another, in a numerical sense, can be spoken of as being double in respect to the variable being measured. If these criteria are met we have a ratio scale. In communication research, more often than not, we do not have such scales.

If the scale which results from the measurement lacks an objective zero point but maintains all of the other features, it is referred to as an interval scale. An example of this type is the measurement of temperature. Its prime limitation is that we lose the ability to describe the ratios between observations. For example, we cannot say that 80 degrees is twice as hot as 40 degrees any more than we can say that 10 degrees is ten times as hot as 1 degree.

The next kind of scale has even less manipulability. We step down to this variety—the ordinal scale—when we lose equality of intervals. The result is that our measurements give us information only about the ranks of observations. Thus we are reduced to working with a set of figures which state merely that this figure is greater than that one. For example, suppose we had measured the attitudes of respondents toward newspapers and had five cases for which our system of numbering produced scores of 5, 4, 3, 2, and 1. From this, we know that the case with a score of 5 is more favorable toward newspapers than the case with 4. We do not know, however, that the 1-point difference between scores of 5 and 4 is equal to the 1-point difference between scores of 2 and 1. In order to have this result—and an interval scale—we would have to be certain that a unit, no matter where it came from, was equal to every other unit.

Technically, when we have simple ordinal scales, we should use only the manipulations appropriate to a series of numbers which represent ranks. Thus we should describe the group in terms of the median rather than the mean; we should use the rank-order correlation coefficient (rho) rather than the Pearson product-moment correlation. If we do compute means and other values from rank-order observations, we must recognize the "as if" quality we have introduced; the results are based upon our assumptions that the units are equal and can be manipulated in this fashion.

Reliability of Measurement Tools

A central problem of measurement involves the reliability of the instrument. Stated simply, the problem of reliability involves the degree to which our measuring instrument would give the same values (the numbers our rules of observation produce) if we repeated the observations. If we measure height of the same object several times with a piece of string, rather than a rigid ruler, we will get a wider range of measurements from the string than from the rigid ruler. The string is stretchable and thus is not as reliable as the rigid ruler. The differences in height measurement are so small that they seem of little importance. But in communication measurement, many of our "rulers" perform as though they were made of rubber; the variation from measurement to measurement may become exceedingly gross. If the variation becomes too gross, our measurement is as fruitless as if we had no system of recording observations. There must be a relatively high positive correlation between two sets of measurements of the same thing if they are to be useful.

This is simply stated, but the problem of determining whether two sets of measurements of the same thing are very nearly similar (or reliable) is a serious one in communication research. What makes it serious is that it is often difficult to take more than one measurement. Here are some of the factors interfering with taking repeated measurements of the same objects:

1. The objects may have had a real change in position on our continuum. (The problem of learning, attitude change, mood, etc.)

2. The objects may have remained stable artificially because of "memory" of the first test. (The problem of learning introduced in the measurement situation.)

3. The objects may appear to have changed because of random errors in measurement.

In the first situation, remeasurement is possible only to the extent that the characteristic being measured is stable. If we work with a variable which fluctuates continuously, we must devise means of remeasuring over very short time-spans.

In the second, the effect of measurement might be to produce a pseudo stability because of memory of the previous testing situation. Here we have not really remeasured. This can happen when we reduce the time-span between measurements to get rid of the problem of lack of stability of the variable.

The third circumstance is usually considered to be the only one which is acceptable; indeed, it is inevitable. But even though these random errors fit the model underlying reliability, they must be limited in their magnitude. If they are too great, we will not produce useful results.

In this discussion of reliability we have been implicitly using a model. It is based on certain initial assumptions, the first of which is that any score which may result from measurement is composed of a contribution from the individual's true score and another from random error of measurement. In effect, this model deals only with the last of the reliability problems discussed above. If we look briefly at this model, we can gain a clearer understanding of the reliability problem and of the general problem of measurement.[7]

The assumption can be stated in a formula, in which the X will indicate the score of a particular individual, the T will indicate the true score, and the E the random error of measurement. Then

$$X = T + E \tag{1}$$

Since it has been assumed that the E's are random, it is reasonable to assume further that over a large number of cases the errors will cancel out. Then

$$\Sigma E = 0 \tag{2}$$

Thus the sum of the obtained scores will equal the sum of the true scores, and the mean of the obtained scores will equal the true mean

$$\frac{\Sigma X}{N} = \frac{\Sigma T}{N} \tag{3}$$

These primary formulas underlying measurement of reliability are valid to the extent that the assumptions underlying them are met. If errors of measurement are truly random, the above relations will hold.

Now let us suppose that we could obtain a genuine remeasurement of our variable. This would assume that there were no memory factors and that there were no changes in true scores. The second measures would not be exactly the same as the first, score by score, because of the random error. An individual who was somewhat above his true score on the first measure might now be somewhat below on the second. It is not necessary that individual errors be exactly compensatory in this fashion, but the sums of the two sets of errors would be compensatory. We can designate our first measurement as X_1 and our second as X_2. Then there will be respective errors, E_1 and E_2. True scores will remain the same, of course. Then

$$\frac{\Sigma X_1}{N} = \frac{\Sigma X_2}{N} = \frac{\Sigma T}{N} \tag{4}$$

It is necessary for us to make one further assumption, namely, that the error variance of the first measurement will equal the error variance of the second measurement. This seems reasonable, since there are no factors operating between the first and second measurements to produce any change in the spread of error. It should vary randomly about the mean of 0 which will result in both instances.

Now it can be shown that the variance of a sum equals the sum of the variances of the parts, plus a factor relating to the correlation between the parts. In our model, the parts of the obtained score are the true score and the error score, and since the latter are random, it can be expected that the correlation between them is 0. Thus the following relationship will hold for our first measurement:

$$s^2_{x_1} = s^2_t + s^2_e \tag{5}$$

and this will hold for the second measurement:

$$s^2_{x_2} = s^2_t + s^2_{e_2} \tag{6}$$

Since we have specified that error variances of the two measurements are equal, and since the variance of true scores will remain unchanged, then

$$s^2_{x_1} = s^2_{x_2} \tag{7}$$

which is to say that the variances of the two measurements will be equal.

By convention, the correlation between two sets of measurements of the same thing is referred to as the reliability coefficient. We can express this in the regular formula for correlation

(8)
$$r_{x_1x_2} = \frac{\Sigma X_1 X_2}{N s_1 s_2}$$

However, we may substitute equation (1) in this formula, designating the errors in the first measurement as E_1 and in the second as E_2. Then we have

(9)
$$r_{x_1x_2} = \frac{\Sigma (T + E_1)(T + E_2)}{N s_1 s_2}$$

Multiplying, we get

$$r_{x_1x_2} = \frac{\Sigma T^2 + \Sigma T E_1 + \Sigma T E_2 + \Sigma E_1 E_2}{N s_1 s_2}$$

Dividing through by N produces this result:

$$r_{x_1x_2} = \frac{s^2_T + r_{TE_1} s_T s_{E_1} + r_{TE_2} s_T s_{E_1} + r_{E_1E_2} s_{E_1E_2}}{s_1 s_2}$$

Since the correlation between true scores and error scores is 0, as is the correlation between error scores, and since the two obtained standard deviations are equal, the equation reduces to

(10)
$$r_{x_1x_2} = \frac{s^2_T}{s^2_x}$$

Substituting from equation (5) or (6) we get

(11)
$$r_{x_1x_2} = \frac{s^2_x - s^2_E}{s^2_x}$$

Equation (11) shows clearly that the correlation between the two tests, which is the "measurement" of reliability we have been explaining, is clearly a function of the magnitude of the error variance. If it were 0, our first and second measurements would be exactly the same, and the ratio between the variances of obtained scores would be 1.00, or perfect reliability. As the error variance increases relative to the magnitude of the obtained score variance, reliability will decrease.

This algebraic manipulation demonstrates the kinds of relationships which may exist when we choose a particular measuring instrument. It also shows how we can ferret out the meaning that we have built in with our assumptions by examining the results which will obtain when certain kinds of variation occur. From this, for example, we can see that if we have a sizable variance in a set of obtained scores, we can tolerate a somewhat larger error of measurement; but if we have a very small obtained score variance, we have little margin for error variance, and the chances of getting high reliability are slim.

Thus far we have concentrated upon errors in our results which are caused by the fallibility of our measuring instrument. We should remember also that errors may be produced by sampling, as we have seen in previous chapters. The sampling-error concept can be extended to the measurement of a single object. Actually, we have taken one measure, usually, out of an infinite population of possible measurements. If we were to take a larger number of measurements of each individual, our chances of error would be reduced.

Ordinarily, we think of sampling error in connection with groups, especially groups of persons. We select some part of the population, perform various operations, and arrive at a measurement of the whole sample. In this circumstance we are concerned with the degree to which our measurement might be in error because of the number of persons we have taken, rather than the number or measurements of them. This point has been introduced here because it is often discussed in terms of reliability. When we speak of the reliability of a result of a sample, we are speaking of the tendency of the given sampling procedure to produce the same result, under the same conditions. M. H. Hansen and W. N. Hurwitz use reliability in this sense, defining it as the "difference between a sample result and the result from a complete count taken under the same conditions."[8] The concept is referred to also as the precision of the result.

Our measurements, then, may be in error from both of these fallibilities, the one inherent in the measuring instrument, the other inherent in our failure to measure the entire population. If either of them is excessive, our results may be of little utility.

Validity of Measuring Devices

A final problem to consider is the validity of the measuring device. Stated in simple terms, it concerns the degree to which the device measures what we intended it to measure. It can be shown mathematically, building upon the assumptions used in the discussion of reliability, that validity cannot be higher than the square root of reliability.[9] Actually the magnitude of the validity is of relatively less concern than the demonstration that there is validity. Here, it is necessary to advance logical argument. Frequently it is necessary to utilize what is described as face validity, i. e., that the nature of the measuring instrument plainly indicates that it is measuring what was intended. Thus we can argue that a measurement of readership involving asking each respondent whether he has read a news story obviously measures readership. A critic, of course, can argue that it also measures what an individual thinks he should have read and might suggest some recall measure. The first researcher can retort that this would be more a measure of memory than of readership. Face validity, as the examples suggest, is almost always open to argument. The familiar measure of height can certainly be defended upon a face validity basis. But in communication research we face situations which are something like attempting to measure a group of clever stilt-walkers, using different length stilts concealed by their trousers. In this fanciful circumstance, we would appear to be measuring height, but actually we would be measuring true height plus the various stilts. Another approach to validity is to get common agreement among researchers to use a particular measuring instrument and to agree that it measures the variable under discussion. Such is the situation as far as intelligence is concerned. Such is not the situation concerning the measurement of radio and television audiences. A variety of measuring devices (systems of questioning respondents) are used in the field. The 1954 report of the Advertising Research Foundation was an attempt to produce agreement.[10] Thus far it has not been successful.

Another approach is to pit one measuring device against another. If we use several different instruments and obtain very similar results, it would appear that greater confidence in their validity is justified. However, it is always possible that the measurements are invalid similarly and thus give us a pseudo validity similar to the pseudo reliability produced by memory.

If we have extreme groups or individuals whose position is known, we can demonstrate the validity of our instrument upon them. The approach is to argue that these groups or individuals are obviously different and then to show that our instrument differentiates them. Thus the content analysis of papers of known biases which produces results corresponding to these biases serves as a kind of validation of the measurement.

Psychologists often have used correlations of their results with life history or clinical data. Occasionally this approach can be used in communication research. The validation of answers to marketing research questions by the inspection of pantry shelves is somewhat analogous. Such an approach is usually better if we can clearly refer to past behavior which can be described objectively.

The most rigorous test of a measuring instrument is to use it as a predictor. The commercial public opinion pollers use the results of their measurements to predict elections. By and large, they have been successful. Various measures of intelligence have been used to predict academic performance. Within the limits set by error of measurement, these have been useful as predictors. Various methods of determining the readability of messages have been devised. They are generally quite effective predictors of the degree of comprehension which the messages will produce.

In summary we need to ask these questions about our measuring instrument:

1. Does it relate satisfactorily to the theoretical formulation?
2. What rules about making observations does it imply?
3. What kinds of numbers and scales will it produce?
4. Is it measuring primarily a single factor or is it measuring several?
5. Is it reliable?
6. Is it valid?

Measurement of Effects

Our discussion of measurement can be enlarged if we consider one of the basic problems of communication research—the measurement of effects. This area has been given more study than any other aspect of the communication process. Indeed, it is next to impossible to study communication without considering measurement of effects. Broadly, effects can be described as some change in the receiver of the message. He may give attention to and perceive the message; he may learn factual material from the message; he may learn new attitudes or modify old ones as a result of the message; he may behave in a novel way; or he may modify his former behavior.

It would be ideal if effects could always be studied in terms of behavior, but this is not always possible. It has often been necessary to work in the area of information or attitude, where verbal or symbolic responses of the receiver are measured and inferences made about his information or attitude structure, which of course cannot be observed directly. It also has been necessary to work in the area of perception, where again the measurement is ordinarily of some verbal response, and the inference made to the nature of the receiver's percept. In psychological terms one might say that the communication researcher often finds himself attempting to measure intervening variables without much possibility of measuring the final effect.

Several factors make measurement of effects very difficult. Some of these have already been pointed out in the discussion of reliability. Since receivers of interest to communication researchers are ordinarily human beings, the researcher is always plagued with the possibility that the receiver will learn in the measurement situation. If he does learn, measurement will usually reflect this learning along with the learning which occurred during the communication situation under study.

Sometimes the measuring devices (as a set of factual questions) may contain information about the answers; the result will be to produce a spurious increase in the "effect" of the message. This is an even greater problem in measuring attitudes. Whenever the measuring devices contain information about what the attitudinal answers *should* be, part of the apparent effects will be measurement-induced changes. The respondent will endeavor, more often than not, to answer in a way that agrees with what he thinks the questioner wants or with what he thinks the majority would answer. Almost any direct question contains such information.

Part of this difficulty can be corrected by the use of the before/after experimental design, used by many investigators and particularly by Carl Hovland.[11] In this situation the unwanted sensitivity of the instrument is cancelled out by the use of a control group which is measured in the same fashion as the experimental group receiving the communication. Then, if there is learning from the test, or test-induced change in attitude, it should be the same for both groups. If the changes in the experimental group are beyond this in the direction hypothesized, one can say that there has been some effect from communication.

Another approach is to use a field experimental design. Here, exposure to the message takes place on a natural basis. The potential audience is studied, a measure of exposure being taken along with a measure of effect. Then the differences between the "exposed" and "unexposed" groups are determined. This approach, of course, lacks the completeness of the before/after design.

When it comes to specifying the kinds of instruments which can be used in measuring effects, an almost unlimited variety is available to the communication researcher. They range from the single question to the complex multi-item scale, from the direct approach to the most obscure projective device, from the attempt to measure mental phenomena to the measurement of physical behavior.

Measuring Effects by Behavior

One way to analyze the measurement of effects is to explore the nature of the basic question which is being asked by the researcher. When we study the size of the audience of a media message, for example, we are usually asking the receiver, "Did you perceive or give attention to the message?" All of the approaches to readership measurement are of this nature. The most frequently used device is to ask this basic question orally (or in a written form) and to have the receiver respond in words or possibly in movement, such as the marking of a newspaper or magazine article. This approach provides us with data which can be transformed into a continuous number system, but is more often transformed into the discrete "yes-no" (1–0) system. Often there is little or no theoretical orientation or implication in such studies of readership or listenership. The desire is mainly to describe the situation accurately. We have very little information on the reliability of such direct measures. The work of D. B. Lucas in magazine and streetcar-card advertising has indicated that reliability may be rather low,[12] but Daniel Starch and others have provided data which support their reliability (and validity).[13] Probably, the best we can say is that the measure of any individual receiver is not very reliable, but the measure of the group of receivers may be fairly reliable.

A measure of behavior which answers this question at least partially in the radio and TV audience measurement is provided by Nielsen's Audimeter, which electronically records whether a set is turned on or off and to which station it is tuned. The Nielsen measurement also reduces to discrete "yes-no" data and is a necessary, but not a sufficient, indication that receivers in a household are paying attention to the messsage. It is unquestionably more reliable than verbal response, since there is virtually no possibility of human error or "forgetting," which plagues the measurement of audiences with verbal questions.

Another example of measurement of behavior answering the question, "Did you give attention to the message?" is provided in the relatively old studies of such factors as motion and intensity. Studies have been made, for example, of variation in numbers of individuals stopping to look into a store window as related to variation in intensity of illumination. Here again data of the "yes-no," 1–0 variety were obtained, although it would have been possible to measure more finely, even as in readership.[14]

The eye-camera also has provided behavioral evidence of the degree of attention. The measurement is in terms of the direction and duration of fixations of the eye, recorded on a moving picture film. There is little question here of the reliability of the measurement. However, the eye-camera records are so complex that only a skilled person can interpret them. Reliability problems could arise if two or more skilled interpreters did not agree in their interpretations of a given record.[15]

If the question is shifted back to perception, we may also consider the tachistoscope as a measuring device. Here attention is forced, and the "message" is presented usually for some very brief period. Measurements of the time or intensity of exposure can be made quite precisely, depending on the nature of the equipment. However, the measurement of the receiver ordinarily cannot be behavioral but must be in the form of an oral or written report of what was seen. Again, the data are usually reduced to a 1–0 number system, under rules describing what will be considered total reproduction or nearly total reproduction of the stimulus, and what will be considered imperfect reproduction. However, the use of several different stimuli makes possible the development of scores which can have greater variation.

Another basic question which is asked in communication research of the receiver is, "Did you learn from the message?" In order to get answers to this question it is necessary to establish both the level of information before the message was received and the level after it was received. It may also be necessary to measure ability to learn, as by IQ or some other abilities test; educational level can be used as a rough measure of ability to learn when more precise data are lacking. Again some variation of the before/after technique or of the field experimental method is called for. The specific measure of information can be a single question yielding discrete, 1–0 numbers. However, with slight modifications, the single question can be transformed into a more flexible measuring device, if it is possible to investigate a communication situation in which the message content does not necessarily lead to a dichotomous question. For example, any message referring to quantities, such as numbers of years, amount of money, or perhaps the probability of an event, can be used to produce numerical responses to single questions. The results obviously will have more variation than the "yes-no" or "right-wrong" type of question.

Field Experiments on Effect

A brief report of a field type experiment will illustrate this. Thirty-three college students were asked (early in 1956) to estimate the number of years before an earth satellite or artificial moon would probably be sent aloft. After they had made this estimate several stories were published in newspapers and carried on radio and TV about the United States' plans to send a satellite aloft during the International Geophysical Year. The original mean estimate was 26.5 years. When they re-estimated after the stories had been published, the mean was 19.8 years. Data also were obtained on whether the students had seen or listened to any of the items concerning the satellite. When the estimates were broken down on the basis of this information, quite different patterns for the two groups were demonstrated. Those who were exposed had a much more nearly accurate estimate (mean of 11.2 years) than the unexposed (60.3 years) even before exposure to the items. And on the second estimate, the exposed individuals made a much greater relative change in the direction of messages (which suggested an estimate of 1 or 2 years) than did the unexposed individuals. The exposed individuals' mean estimate had been revised downward to 6.3 years, a change of 43.7 per cent, while the unexposed individuals had revised theirs to 49.0 years, a relative change of 18.3 per cent. This treatment is made possible by the expanded number system which the measuring device provides. Of course, it is possible to score the data in a way which would return to a dichotomous, 1–0 system. For example one might record the direction of change, ignoring the amounts. With these same data, the following results were obtained:

TABLE 3

	Same or higher estimate (0)	*Lower estimate* (1)	
Exposed to Message (1)	9	13	22
Not Exposed (0)	8	3	11
	17	16	

This approach yielded a Chi-square of 5.46, significant beyond the .02 level.

This small-scale study used measuring devices providing answers to the two types of questions we have discussed. Specifically, the devices obtained data on

1. Were you exposed to the messages concerning the earth satellite?
2. Did you learn anything about the expected launching date from the message?

As a by-product, this study emphasizes a fact often brought out in communication research: self-selected receivers of a message in a natural situation are often individuals who are already relatively informed about the message content. In this instance the individuals who indicated paying attention to the earth satellite stories were already better informed about it, in the sense that their original estimates showed much less error. Many studies have shown such results.

In a study of this type it is difficult to provide an estimate of reliability, since a real change in the level of knowledge being measured is hypothesized. We might look to the unexposed group for an index of reliability. But here another factor which frequently operates when measuring instruments of this nature are used comes into play. This is the matter of unreliability or change which appears to be concomitant with low interest in the subject matter of a question. Kendall has shown that the degree of change from an initial measure to a remeasure in the areas of knowledge and attitude is greater among those who have low interest than among those who have high interest.[16] In the earth satellite study the variance of the changes for the unexposed individuals was considerably greater than the variance for the exposed.

Measuring Knowledge by Scales

Another approach to measurement of knowledge, which is particularly useful in communication research, is the use of a relatively simple scale. If we construct a set of items relating to the knowledge area, we can now obtain a spread of scores based on the total of "rights." This will make possible a finer classification of our individuals. The assumption underlying the use of a device is that the collection of items form a scale and that the several right-wrong measurements provided by the items are additive. The individual who gets a larger number of items right is assumed to be at a higher knowledge level than the one who gets a smaller number right.

Several of the approaches to scaling might be used here, but the Guttman method can be used very effectively if appropriate items are developed.[17] The items must all be closely related to the subject matter being examined; in addition, they must have a cumulative quality. In knowledge testing one can think of the cumulative quality as relating to level of difficulty. The set of items should ideally contain one item which every respondent save the least informed individuals will get correct. Then successive items, each more difficult than the last, should be provided. The most informed individual should get all of the items correct. Looking at the scales in reverse, as level of knowledge drops, successively more items should be missed. It is not sufficient that just any items be missed but that they be missed in a definite pattern, following the second model introduced earlier in this chapter. If the area is scalable, it will be possible to reproduce the patterns of response of almost every individual, simply by using his total score. The degree to which the data fit the model is ordinarily expressed in what is known as the coefficient of reproducibility. This requires classification of response patterns as to the nearness of fit to the model. Failures to fit are called "errors." For example, a response pattern of 10011 would have a score of 3 but would most nearly fit the perfect type 00011. Thus it would produce one error. The pattern 11100 would most nearly fit the perfect type 11111, but would produce two errors. Such error cases are classified on the criterion of "minimum error," i. e., are assigned to the perfect type class which reduces the error to the smallest amount. Such errors are counted, and the coefficient of reproducibility is computed by the following formula:

$$1 - \frac{\text{Number of Errors}}{\text{Total Number of Responses}}$$

Guttman has set an arbitrary lower limit of .90 for C of R, in order to accept the hypothesis of scalability. In addition, other criteria must be met. There must not be more error than nonerror for any item. Items should represent a spread of marginals with very few extreme items (usually interpreted as beyond .20 or .80). Further, a sample of at least 100 is recommended.

Effects by Attitude Changes

Another question which is asked of the receiver in determining the effects of communication is, "Did your attitude change?" Measurement of attitude change produces problems parallel to those just discussed concerning level of knowledge. It is necessary to determine what the receiver's attitude was before the communication and what it was afterward. Again, an experimental approach will provide controls, or a field experimental approach will provide exposed and unexposed groups.

The problem of attitude measurement has been explored by many researchers in fields other than communication. A comparatively recently developed measuring device of considerable utility in the study of attitude is provided by Charles Osgood's semantic differential. Produced as the result of an investigation of the problem of meaning, the semantic differential is supported by a carefully developed theoretical base.[18] It utilizes the fact that words, as well as being denotative, are also connotative to a considerable extent. Investigating this, Osgood produced evidence by factor analysis that there are three principal connotative factors in almost all words. These are the evaluative (good/bad) factor, the potency (strong/weak) factor, and the activity (active/passive) factor. In a practical sense, these factors mean that words touch off connotative mediating responses within the individual, as well as denotative. Thus, whenever a source transmits a verbal message, the receiver responds to its denotation, but he also responds in a customary way to the connotative aspects of meaning. Osgood's results indicate that meaning is a multidimensional conception. As he has pointed out, however, they suggest strongly that the evaluative aspect of meaning is unidimensional and that it corresponds to what we think of as attitude. Furthermore, his semantic differential provides a useful measuring instrument of attitude.

The actual measuring instrument devised by Osgood is a combination of word association and scaling techniques. In its basic form, the respondent is given a concept or social object, such as "Republican Party," and a number of polar adjective pairs, such as "good-bad," "nice-awful," "happy-sad." A scale is provided in this fashion:

REPUBLICAN PARTY Good:——:——:——:——:——:——:Bad

The respondent is asked to check the direction and intensity of his association. If he has a favorable attitude toward the Republican party, he will place a check mark to the left of the midpoint, the nearness to "good" indicating his degree of favorability. The opposite association would be recorded by a check mark to the right. The midpoint would indicate that the association was mixed or that no association was produced by the linking of the concept and the scale.

Such a scale is ordinarily scored arbitrarily on a 7 (most favorable) to 1 (least favorable) basis; each concept and polar adjective pair can be used as an individual item in an ordinary question-and-answer test. In making such an attitude test, one gathers a number of concepts which refer to or are associated with the central social object, and a number of polar adjective scales, drawn from those which have heavy loadings on the evaluative factor. Some of these include:

good-bad	pleasant-unpleasant
beautiful-ugly	sacred-profane
sweet-sour	nice-awful
clean-dirty	honest-dishonest
kind-cruel	fair-unfair

All of the pairs listed were found to have factor loadings higher than .80 on the evaluative factor, and very low loadings on the other two indentified. The significance of the high factor loadings is that almost all of the variation in response to these items is attributable to the evaluative (or attitudinal) factor.

An example of how a test of this nature operates can be provided from some of my own data. It is certainly reasonable that individuals who have chosen journalism as a profession should have a more favorable attitude toward journalism than those who have not made such a selection. Thus, their associations for a number of words related to journalism should be more in the direction of "good" than those of nonjournalists. Six polar-adjective scales were chosen, and ten concept words. Thus, a score of 42 would indicate maximum favorableness, one of 24 neutrality, and one of 6 maximum unfavorableness for a single concept word. For 41 journalism students, the mean score for the concept "writing" was 35.2, while for 30 nonjournalists the mean score was 27.1. For nine of the ten words, the scores were in the hypothesized direction. The summation over all ten concept words produced scores which differentiated journalists and nonjournalists very significantly.

Obviously, it would be quite easy to develop a test of some length with this device. Then a score would represent a summation of the scores on individual items, and would correspond to an attitude score obtained by a scaling method or by a test made up of many "direct" items.

The test does not remove the necessity of care in selecting concepts to be judged, a problem analogous to selecting questions for a Guttman scale, or statements for a Thurstone scale.[19]

But the semantic differential attitude test has several advantages. Since it can be expanded in length without difficulty, there is a greater possibility of attaining reliability through increasing the number of items. Further, it can be presented as part of a study of the meaning of words, thus disguising its attitudinal measurement purpose and restricting the possibility of responses being adjusted in the test situation to fit the questioner or the socially acceptable response. A test with a large number of items can also be given in a very short period. Subjects are encouraged to work rapidly and can handle ten to twenty items in a minute.

Another utility of the semantic differential attitude test is that because of its many similar items, memory plays little or no part in a retest. This makes possible obtaining unequivocal data on reliability. Osgood has indicated that reliabilities between .85 and .90 have been obtained.

This makes it an ideal before/after test, which does not raise the problem of developing comparable forms, a difficult task in the attitudinal field. Its greater relative sensitivity also is obviously an asset, making possible the demonstration of effects even though they are small.

Earlier it was suggested that part of the utility of the differential was the possibility of hiding its purpose from the respondents. This is related to the general concept underlying projective tests. We can say that the semantic differential can be used as a "mild" projective test. Unlike many projective tests, however, it produces results which are easy to quantify, and has given more evidence than most of being reliable.

Projective testing, however, does have some utility in the field of attitude measurement and considerable utility in personality measurement. Such devices as error choice, sentence completion, thematic apperception test, Rosenzweig picture-frustration, and others may be useful in specific communication research projects. In each of these approaches, the subject is presented with an ambiguous stimulus and is requested to respond verbally. The theory is that the individual will project his own attitudes and personality factors in responding. The problem is that the ambiguity of the stimulus, which is necessary to make the measuring instrument work, also creates ambiguity in response. Since the responses are ordinarily verbal, a difficult problem in content analysis is usually faced by the researcher who attempts to use the projective test as a measuring instrument.

The development of new measuring instruments in communication research is intimately related to the development of additional theory. As has been shown, the choice of a measuring instrument may amount to an implicit theoretical statement, even though the researcher may not have stated it explicitly and, in some cases, may not even be aware of it. Thus the two processes—development of theory and development of measuring instruments—will go hand in hand.

Since the communication process involves psychological and sociological variables, it is clear that researchers must continue to borrow and adapt measuring devices from these fields. In fact, one can say that most useful measuring instruments were originally developed in the psychological field. But as one borrows, he must remain alert to the fact that he is borrowing theory as well as instrument on most occasions.

Finally, it must be conceded that the communication process is replete with difficult and complex variables. Further, the interrelationships of these variables are often far more complex than we have imagined. Thus, the demands of the researcher are great, if he hopes to measure communication variables; this is the challenge the communication researcher must meet.

REFERENCES

1. Wilbur Schramm, *The Process and Effects of Mass Communication* (Urbana: University of Illinois Press, 1954), 3–26; Carl I. Hovland, "Social Communication," *Proceedings of the American Philosophical Society*, 92 (1948), 371–75; G. A. Miller, *Language and Communication* (New York: McGraw-Hill, 1951), 6; J. Ruesch and G. Bateson, *Communication: The Social Matrix of Society* (New York: Norton, 1951), 75; B. H. Westley and M. S. MacLean, Jr., "A Conceptual Model for Communications Research," *Audio-Visual Communication Review*, 3 (1955), 3–12.
2. W. J. Dixon and F. J. Massey, Jr., *Introduction to Statistical Analysis* (New York: McGraw-Hill, 1951), 4.
3. Bert F. Green, "Attitude Measurement," in Gardner Lindsay (ed.), *Handbook of Social Psychology* (Cambridge, Mass.: Addison-Wesley, 1954), I, 337.
4. This model is based on the Guttman method of scaling. See L. Guttman, "The Basis for Scalogram Analysis," S. A. Stouffer *et al.*, *Measurement and Prediction* ("Studies in Social Psychology," Vol. IV [Princeton: Princeton University Press, 1950]), 60–90. See also Guttman, "The Cornell Technique for Scale and Intensity Analysis," *Educational and Psychological Measurement*, 7 (1947), 247–79.
5. Helen Peak, "Problems of Objective Observation," in Leon Festinger and Daniel Katz (eds.), *Research Methods in the Behavioral Sciences* (New York: Dryden Press, 1953), 243–99.
6. Green, "Attitude Measurement," *loc. cit.*, 337.
7. The derivations are drawn from Quinn McNemar, *Psychological Statistics* (New York: Wiley, 1955), 150–61, and H. Gulliksen, *Theory of Mental Tests* (New York: Wiley, 1950), 4–27.
8. M. H. Hansen, William N. Hurwitz, and William G. Madow, *Sample Survey Methods and Theory* (New York: Wiley, 1953), I, 10.
9. Gulliksen, *Theory of Mental Tests*, 23.

10. Advertising Research Foundation, *Recommended Standards for Radio and Television Program Audience Size Measurements* (New York: Advertising Research Foundation, 1954).
11. Carl I. Hovland *et al.*, *Communication and Persuasion* (New Haven: Yale University Press, 1953).
12. D. B. Lucas and S. H. Britt, *Advertising Psychology and Research* (New York: McGraw-Hill, 1950).
13. Daniel Starch, *Factors in Readership Measurement* (New York: D. Starch, 1941).
14. Melvin S. Hattwick, *How to Use Psychology for Better Advertising* (New York: Prentice-Hall, 1950), 140.
15. Robert S. Woodworth, *Experimental Psychology* (New York: Holt, 1938), 576–94, 713–45. See also Hattwick, *How to Use Psychology for Better Advertising*.
16. Patricia Kendall, *Conflict and Mood* (Glencoe, Ill.: The Free Press, 1954).
17. Stouffer *et al.*, *Measurement and Prediction*, 138–42.
18. Charles E. Osgood, "The Nature and Measurement of Meaning," *Psychological Bulletin*, 49 (1952), 197–237.
19. See L. L. Thurstone and E. V. Chave, *The Measurement of Attitude* (Chicago: University of Chicago Press, 1929).

8

Scientific Method and Communication Research

BRUCE H. WESTLEY

THUS FAR OUR concern in this book has been with "how to conduct research." It should be obvious from the previous chapters that research is a useful tool under various circumstances and that it has various goals. Any research effort is, of course, a more or less systematic attempt to obtain dependable information about something. Research methods may be employed, for instance, to help solve some immediate problems; an example in the communication field is the readership study conducted for a particular magazine to provide its editors with information about what kinds of articles are read by what kinds of people. But research methods are also tools in the kit of scholarship not directed toward particular or immediate effects. For example, a social scientist may use them to test a hypothesis relating social strata to certain characteristic patterns of communication behavior. In this case the concern is with knowledge for its own sake. The social scientist is usually unconcerned about immediate applications of his findings in helping someone solve immediate professional problems. The scientist's work may actually have this effect, of course; his primary concern, however, is with the collection and codification of systematic theoretical knowledge.

This chapter, then, will concern itself with the basic strategy of scientific research in mass communication.[1] Research is, of course, a preoccupation of scholarship, and our concern will be only with that part of scholarship which is intended to be scientific. We have deliberately omitted a large segment of research in mass communications. This is an omission, not a rejection. The historian, the biographer, the legal scholar, and even the humanist are interested in subject matter which is closely related to journalism and which, in a sense, is part of the scholarly tradition of journalism and communications. But their investigations are not necessarily scientific, and being scientific would not necessarily make them more valuable. The point is that we are making a distinction between kinds of research—a distinction that emphasizes modes of attack on data. Preference for one or the other of these kinds of scholarship must rest with the scholar himself. However, for an understanding of the basic strategy of scientific research, it is necessary to specify further some of the fundamental distinctions between these modes of attack.

The next step, then, is to point to certain characteristics shared by all scholarship and then to develop certain further characteristics that distinguish our kind of research from others. It has recently become popular to refer to our kind as "behavioral science," a term we accept and employ in this chapter as one which is generally descriptive of the scholarly objectives of the kind of research this book has dealt with.

Quantitative, Systematic, Behavioral

We are sometimes tempted to distinguish our kind of research from others on the basis of a characteristic of the data. Our data are usually quantitative. So why not simply call it "quantitative research?" But all research of our kind is not invariably quantitative, and there is a great deal of more or less quantitative research that does not qualify as behavioral or social science research within our meaning of those terms. Raymond B. Nixon's studies [2] of ownership trends in the mass media are clearly quantitative, yet they are not behavioral science data. On the other hand Frederick Siebert's study [3] of the first three centuries of the British press is nonquantitative yet has some of the properties of the behavioral approach, since it formulates and tests hypotheses. To be sure, measurement is usually involved in behavioral science and usually demands quantification. But quantification is merely a means of employing a tool (measurement) and therefore does not seem to be the crucial distinction. Furthermore, the quantitative-qualitative dimension has always seemed a false and misleading distinction. It appears to suggest that the behavioral scientist is solely concerned with quantities, never with qualities, which is simply absurd. What he does is to quantify qualities (variables, attributes, dimensions) in order to deal with them in a more precise and systematic way.

Is *systematic* the clue we are seeking? Here the distinction would appear to turn on method in general, rather than on a characteristic of the data. But surely all scholarship must in some way be systematic. Historiography, for instance, appears to offer the scholar greater latitude, to impose fewer procedural strictures on him, to depend more on his detachment and integrity than on methods which can be replicated by any other qualified scholar. But historiography is nevertheless a more or less systematic set of rules for the study of history. It would be presumptuous to imply that only behavioral science is systematic.

Nevertheless it is worth noting that its systematic nature is crucial to Morris Cohen's widely quoted definition of science. "We reserve for the term 'Science' knowledge which is general and systematic, that is, in which specific propositions are all deduced from a few general principles."[4] Here the term systematic appears to relate specifically to the way the scientist's empirical propositions are derived. If, as we shall see, being "systematic" demands systematic observations, a systematic relation between observations and concepts, and a systematic relation between theories, hypotheses, and logic, then perhaps our kind of research is systematic or potentially systematic where others are not.

What is Productive Scholarship?

Four things may perhaps be said about productive scholarship in general:[5] (1) it is detached, objective, unemotional, nonethical; (2) it is more or less abstract; (3) it is transmissible; and (4) it is cumulative. Let us consider each of these qualities in turn.

Objectivity

Even the first of these qualities, as obvious as its terms may appear to be, is perhaps not wholly and unambiguously descriptive of all productive scholarship. While detachment and objectivity surely must characterize any pretensions to scholarship, there appear to be differences within the scholarly community over the question of the "nonethical" nature of investigation, and to some extent this is true of behavioral scientists as well. Thus we immediately come face-to-face with the problem of value, a question which appears to be important enough to deserve more detailed attention below.

Abstractness

All knowledge is, of course, abstract. Scholars do not so much manipulate reality as devise and refine abstractions about it. As this chapter will demonstrate again and again, the end product of scientific research is theory. That means abstract generalizations about the nature of reality. It may be used to anticipate reality, and the proof of its efficiency is, in fact, its power to predict. Contrary to popular opinion, all this is true of the physical and natural sciences as well. There are important differences, of course, in the kinds of abstractions social and physical scientists deal with. Some notion of the nature of the constructs employed by the behavioral sciences, their relation to logical constructs on the one hand and observed phenomena on the other, will be treated in greater detail below.

Transmissibility

Abstractions of a given kind combine into the special language of a discipline. Disciplines transcend (imperfectly, at times) natural barriers, national barriers, even language barriers. The universality of scholarly interests is made possible by its abstractness, to some extent by its freedom from value relevance, and obviously by its transmissibility.

Its Cumulative Nature

The cumulative nature of scholarship is stressed by James Conant in his definition of science: "that portion of accumulative knowledge in which new concepts are continuously developing from experiment and observation and lead to further experimentation and observation."[6] Cumulation rather obviously depends on transmissibility, which in turn depends on abstractness.

It may be somewhat less obvious that the "value posture" of the scholar is important to cumulation. Since scholars arise in various social classes and in various national states and therefore may be expected to hew to various value systems, there must be a shared scholarly value system if cumulation is to take place across national and other boundaries.

The Ways of Science

So much for a tentative listing of some qualities shared by all scholarly inquiry. We turn now to some qualities that distinguish science in general and the behavioral sciences in particular from other kinds of inquiry. The following list must be taken as tentative:

1. Science is general and theoretical.
2. It is founded on "controlled observation."
3. It is predictively oriented.
4. It seeks causal connections.
5. It is "naturalistic" and "deterministic."
6. It celebrates parsimony and strives toward "closure."

Science Is General

We have seen that all scholarly inquiry is abstract. It might be assumed therefore that it is also general. In some measure this is no doubt true. But there appears to be a marked difference between science and other branches of scholarship in the kind of generalization that is sought and even in degree. History generalizes when it labels a period "The Enlightenment." But historians by and large (Toynbee, Spengler, and Brinton are notable exceptions) do not seek to construct "constants" in history. They hesitate to group historic instances as members of a class of events, and in particular they seem to avoid constructing generalizations of an explicitly causal or conditional kind. Very specifically the traditional historian rejects the assumption of the lawfulness of history.

"Historians may formulate generalizations of limited validity which are useful in the interpretation of the past until their modification is called for by new evidence. In analyzing, selecting, and organizing their data, they make these abstractions serve their purposes as constructs or fictions based on emphasized particularities, or phases of history-in-actuality."[7] However, "attempts to discover 'laws' as exact as those now employed in the physical sciences have failed."[8]

These and other writings suggest that the historian's principal concern is not with erecting generalizations confirmable as laws but with describing events as nearly as possible in all their uniqueness.[9]

There is no error tolerance in the relation between the historian's observations of the historical record and his constructs. "The so-called 'constants' or 'repetitions' derived from the study of history ... may be ... valuable as serving analytical, comparative and descriptive purposes and as supplying guidance in the search for approximate historical patterns. ... However, they are not exact repetitions nor do they afford proof of 'laws' in history. Action based on that assumption is likely to prove erroneous."[10]

We have said that all scholarship is detached and objective. Here, too, we find a different order of objectivity in the case of historiography. For many historians, historiography is a matter of "writing history," and "every written-history represents a selection of facts and emphasis." Therefore any written history must be evaluated in light of "the possible attitudes arising from the life and circumstances of the author."[11] The scholar is charged with exercising conscious control over his own biases insofar as possible and stating his "controlling assumptions" so that fellow scholars may distinguish his "chronicles" (which are purely factual accounts of events) from his "interpretations" (which give written history meaning). Historians have specifically rejected an early "scientific" school which erred in attempting to eliminate bias by making no assumptions.[12] The characteristic position is that, since assumptions cannot be controlled, the historian should accept and try to understand the influence of his own assumptions on his observations.[13]

This digression has seemed necessary to establish that even though all scholarship is in some degree abstract and general, a crucial difference exists between the behavioral sciences and other disciplines at precisely this point. Briefly put, the scientist attempts by means of ever more securely validated generalizations from his observations to move from confirmable propositions to tentative laws. Laws, of course, are more or less confirmed propositions about some aspect of reality. But whereas "theory, or general explanation, is the ultimate objective of science,"[14] "the ideal which controls the historian in search of the utmost knowledge of the past is to achieve the most informed understanding of occurrences and personalities that available sources and discriminating imagination will permit, so as to write history with the highest possible degree of credibility."[15] In short, science seeks laws where history seeks wisdom.

Science Is Controlled Inquiry

It is often thought that the characteristic feature of science is "control." Certainly any kind of scholarly inquiry is controlled inquiry in one sense or another. Even the most speculative theology or philosophy is built under the control of the canons of logic. The periodic changes in the Marxist line must be logically related to the philosophy of the founder. In all these cases, however, what does not have to be demonstrated is the relation between the formulation and reality. The propositions of science, though derived by logical operations from general theory, must find their ultimate verification in repeated contact with the real world. It is at this point that the control characteristic of science enters the picture. What is controlled, then, is the observation. Controlled observation alone is not sufficient to yield effective scientific progress, since it cannot move us toward laws without the intervention of theory. But controlled observation is nevertheless a necessary condition.

The historian operates under conditions of controlled observation, too. He is subject to the strictures of his discipline: to approach his data with detachment, to adduce all relevant detail, whether in support of his conception of history or not, to specify sources, and of course never to falsify the record. The differences here appear to be of kind, however, rather than degree. Where the historian operates under rational control and to some extent is subject to examination by his colleagues, the behavioral scientist operates under conditions of demonstrable control. For him it is essential to demonstrate his control of any variables capable of offering an alternative explanation of his findings. And this demonstration must be based on what he did so that his controls as well as all his other procedures may be repeated by another investigator.

This is not to say that the scientist readily attains fully adequate controls. He perhaps maximizes them in the laboratory situation. But statistical controls are also available. Depending on the stage of inquiry (a matter which will be enlarged on later in this chapter) a greater or lesser degree of control may be indicated. Although conscious or rational control of bias is essential to any social scientist, the important point now is that *scientific procedures do not depend on it.* Robert K. Merton has pointed out "the virtual absence of fraud in the annals of science" and quite properly attributes it not to the moral integrity of the scientist but to the "verifiability" of science and the exacting scrutiny of his work by fellow scientists.[16] What is true of fraud is more or less true of bias.

Science Is Predictive

Aside from its generality, it is perhaps the predictive nature of science that most clearly distinguishes it from other methods. The explicitly predictive orientation of science will probably be understood fully only after we have examined in detail the complex and interdependent roles in science of theory and observation. But a few introductory statements will be attempted at this point.

Scientific propositions take an "if . . ., then . . ." form. This is the conditional form of a general statement, and to establish conditional relationships is to treat cause and effect. In science, prediction plays the significant role of demonstrating conditional relationships. Verification in science is based on the demonstration that conditional relationships consistently hold (within stated limits).

It is instructive to compare the use of instances in argumentation and in scientific "hypothesis testing." The arguer typically sets forth a general proposition and then marshals concrete observations as instances in its support. But as long as the number of possible instances is infinite and there is no assurance that the instances cited are representative of all possible instances, no number of such citations can amount to verification. Verification is possible only under conditions of genuine prediction. Repeated demonstration that a proposition successfully predicts events (under specified conditions) by methods available to others is what is meant by verification.

"It is extremely important to state the hypothesis and its consequences before any attempt at verification. . . . If we deliberately choose the hypothesis so that it will in fact be confirmed by a set of instances, we have no guarantee that it will in fact be confirmed by other instances. . . . The logical function of prediction is to permit a genuine verification of our hypotheses by indicating prior to the actual process of verification, instances which may verify them."[17]

It is worth noting that the role of prediction in science is not based solely on the actual predictive efficacy of our theories: it is not the demonstration alone but the fact that propositions are cast in a demonstrable form. Frankly we cannot wait on full demonstration of one relationship before pressing on to the investigation of another. It is not the obtained verifications but the verifiability of its methodological procedures that establishes a discipline's pretensions to scientific status.

Science Is Causal

We have seen that scientific propositions take a predictive form because only in that way may dependencies or conditional relations be established. Such conditional relations are in effect causal connections. Science does not blush at attempting to establish and confirm causal connections. When we have found invariances between classes of events and have cast them in a form in which the conditions consistently yield the predicted events, there is no reason to back away from the implication of causality. Perhaps no feature of scientific inquiry so sharply distinguishes it from other branches of scholarship.

Other areas of inquiry seem to deal with notions of cause in a more gingerly way. The historiographic "propositions" quoted above begin by rejecting supernatural cause—in fact, the derivation of cause from any "cosmology." They treat philosophical systems as the object of historical study, not as a basis for the selection and analysis of historical fact. "The term 'cause' as used by historians must be regarded as a convenient figure of speech, describing motives, influences, forces, and other antecedent interrelations not fully understood. . . . A cause never operates except as part of a series or complex."[18] Therefore single cause should be avoided, and any notion of cause should be used with circumspection.[19]

The propositions continue: "There are limiting, conditioning and determining features in a history such as the psychological, cultural, economic, biological, and physical. . . . But the precise nature, limits, and influences of such features constitute problems of knowledge and thought not easily resolved by historians. A search for such features is a valid and appropriate operation in historiography."[20] The later volume[21] takes the very different position that history cannot ignore causality because explanation requires it and that, if history ignores explanation, it is reduced to mere description. Rather than sidestep the term "cause," it argues, historians should recognize the logical demands of causal analysis and not expect "definitive results." "In the analysis of causation the true scientific spirit involves . . . the prediction of probabilities rather than certainties, the conscientious search for techniques to overcome the limitations of the evidence, and a willingness to admit that sometimes we do not have the answers." [22] Such respect for causal analysis, however, appears to fall short of determinism. Spengler and Toynbee are still in a minority among their colleagues in seeking out prime causes and inexorable sequences. A multiple and diluted causality appears to be the order of the day in history. There is nothing surprising about this fact, when one considers its subject matter and its traditional method. "Causal necessity or determinism in history is only possible in a deductively formulated social science which has a theoretical dynamics. . . . Necessary connection or determinism is not given inductively in natural history data." [23]

Does a willingness to seek causal connections demand a search for single causes? If the notion of cause necessarily connotes a single, ultimate determinacy, then "multiple causation" reduces to a logical absurdity. This is too complex and philosophical a matter to treat here. But it may be helpful to point to the distinction between necessary and sufficient conditions. C. W. Churchman and R. L. Ackoff [24] distinguish three kinds of causality employed by science. At the lowest level is *concomitant variation* (Mill's fifth canon of logic). This is the relation established by correlation. It simply says that when B occurs, there is a tendency (its strength indicated by the magnitude of the correlation) for A to occur as well. It is widely accepted that this does not establish a determinate causal connection, for the corollary of that statement is that when A occurs there is a tendency for B also to occur, giving us no answer to the question of "what is causing what." [25] In the terms of Churchman and Ackoff, correlation establishes neither a necessary nor a sufficient condition for the two events.

A *necessary* condition is established when it is shown that A produces B. It states causal direction but is a limited determinacy, since it tells us only that B tends to follow A. It does not say that *only* A produces B. (The fire could not have started had the match not been struck, but the fire was also "caused" by the presence of inflammable materials.)

A *sufficient* condition is established when it is shown that A's properties are sufficient to account for all the properties of B, and A precedes B in time. While it may be assumed that it is the aim of sciences to move toward determinacies in the nature of sufficient conditions, and it may be asserted that only a "deductively formulated science" can approach this goal, scientists, and particularly social scientists, need not despair if they must settle for lower levels of determinacy in the interim.

Naturalism and Determinism

The scientist's acceptance of both naturalism and determinism follows from the foregoing. Neither of these asserts a general philosophy, but both are related to the individual's underlying assumptions. "Naturalism" simply asserts that one views his phenomena as an aspect of nature. As one sociology textbook puts it: "To define sociology as a science means that its subject matter, human groups, is considered to be a part of nature and subject to study by the same basic methods as other natural phenomena."[26] This should not be confused with the problem of reductionism (as for instance the reduction of psychological properties to physiological terms). Essentially it is asserting that our universe of phenomena is ordered and that order is to be treated as a natural order and not, for instance, a supernatural order. This does not necessarily mean the scientist rejects the idea that the world is ordered in nonnaturalistic and more inscrutable ways. This is a matter for the individual scientist to resolve personally. What it does mean is that he sees his scientific task as unraveling the natural order in the part of that world that scientifically interests him.

Determinism is a feature of science that follows from the scientist's concern with finding the causal connections in a natural order. He simply assumes that his phenomena are ultimately determined. That is, he assumes that all the order in his phenomena can be accounted for in a causal sense. In statistical terms it means that he assumes that all the variance in his dependent variables could be accounted for by one or more independent variables if he could eliminate all errors of observation.

While determinism is not a philosophy, there is no point in ignoring its consequences for the social scientist who has become deeply committed either to a "free will" world-view or to the "rational man" philosophy of the Enlightenment. This may be particularly troublesome for the journalist interested in attacking communication behavior in a scientific way. Our "press and society" courses are largely founded, explicitly or implicitly, on the Milton-Mill-Adam Smith "rational man" assumption, which indeed has profoundly affected American political institutions. The problem is, of course, the apparent incompatibility of the idea of man's rationality with the idea that human behavior is determined. The conflict is only apparent, however, if we are careful not to confuse rationality with perfect freedom of choice. We then need assume only the lawfulness (i.e., the predictability) or rational behavior.[27]

Accepting the "deterministic assumption,"[28] however, does not require that one subscribe to "*a* determinism." Used in this sense, determinism is often a term of opprobrium. Marxists are scorned as "economic determinists," for instance, and Freud is accused of a "biological determinism." A determinism, in this sense, is an effort to subsume all manner of reality under the laws of some single discipline or some single type of determinant. Being a determinist in our sense does not require either the assumption that our slice of reality can be explained in terms of a single type of causal agent or that our type of concept can ultimately explain everything.

Parsimony and the Goal of Closure

Since theory is the goal of science and theory's task is to explain as large a slice of reality as possible in the form of predictive generalizations, it should not be too surprising that science values parsimony. *The parsimonious explanation is the one that accounts for the most variance with the fewest propositions.* This is almost directly opposed to the goal of the historian, who seeks "interpretive synthesis."[29] Any synthesis must of course sacrifice some of the reality observed, but for the historian the best explanation is the most inclusive and plausible one, not the most economical. We have seen also that history is in some measure cumulative, but it would appear that it is not cumulative "toward closure."

Like the scientist, the historian seeks regularities in his data. But his method of analysis is eclectic—he never is able to exhaust all the types of analysis he might bring to his data to draw from it ever deeper understanding. Even more importantly, his interpretive synthesis is peculiarly his. It may be concurred in by others from the force of its data and reasoning. But it nevertheless can be understood fully only in the light of his values, his orientations, his times. Each era produces its histories of past eras. So history progresses, but not toward closure.

Science, on the other hand, assumes the lawfulness of its universe and assumes that its universe is knowable. It therefore treats its task as having determinate limits, even though it must be realized that the limits are eons of patient work away. The point is that a lawful and knowable world must have a finite number of laws, even though we cannot foresee the day when all are known.

It should not be surprising, then, that scientists, almost from the beginning, have spoken of the ultimate unity of the sciences, and there exists a lively international movement dedicated to the "Unification of Science," which would wash away all our conceptual and disciplinary differences (and let us hope our methodological sins, as well).

Deduction and Induction

Is scientific inquiry basically inductive or deductive? We may perhaps best approach the problem by brief attention to one of the most ancient of philosophical controversies, rationalism versus empiricism. Although the controversy can be traced back at least to Plato and Aristotle,[30] it is typified by the positions of Descartes and Bacon. In his *Discourse on Method* Descartes sought a path to knowledge of reasonable certainty. He failed to find it either in the philosophy and science of his time or in the world of practical affairs, but he found mathematics very satisfying. Here was certainty. He therefore believed that formal reasoning held the clue to knowledge, and he laid down four rules of method. They may be summarized thus: Begin with a kind of total skepticism, eliminating from consciousness any proposition except that which "should present itself so clearly and distinctly to mind that I might have no occasion to doubt it"; then move step by step, by means of formal logic, toward the generalization of these basic "givens."

Bacon also began with total skepticism, but in place of indubitable truths he placed the evidence of the senses. "There can be only two ways of searching into and discovering truth. The one (deduction) flies from the senses and particulars to the most general axioms, and from these principles . . . proceeds to judgment. . . . The other (induction) derives axioms from the senses and particulars, rising by a gradual and unbroken ascent, so that it arrives at the most general axioms last of all." This latter, of course, is for Bacon the true way.

Roughly put, the method of Descartes is rationalism, for its basic method is the logical deduction of consequences of the most general propositions. The method of Bacon is empiricism, the logical induction of general principles from observations. Even more roughly, then, deduction moves from the general to the particular, induction from the particular to the general.

The method of science is neither inductive nor deductive but a synthesis of the two. Any particular investigation may be essentially one or the other. Inductive methods are still with us, and especially in social science they make a crucial contribution to the relative certainty of our findings. For they are heavily involved in the normative statistics through which our level of certainty is ascertained.[31] Deductive methods are still with us, too, and the extent to which they play a part in a science's procedures may be taken as an indication of that science's degree of advancement. Its crucial contribution is perhaps to the relative generality of our findings. But it has a very different function from its direct application by Descartes. Rather than depend on deduction to lead us from self-evident truths to their logical consequences, the scientist employs it in a very special way. *Its function is to guarantee the internal consistency of the parts of his theoretical system and to assure the logical connection between his theoretical structure and the empirical tests he employs to verify it.* This will here be called hypothetico-deductive empiricism.

Let us consider a man and an apple, with the apple within the sensory reach of the man. The man can observe the apple, by which we mean simply that he can apprehend it with his various sensory apparatus. He can feel it, see it, taste it, smell it, heft it. The man's pig can do all these things, too. But rational man cannot, let us assume, help taking the next step—to go beyond mere sensory contact with the apple in order to "know" apples, to understand them, ultimately it may be, to control them. In taking the next step beyond raw apprehension of this object he exercises a remarkable capacity (not shared with his pig)—the capacity to name it. This is "an apple"—an instance of the concept apple. In the crudest sense this means he has become abstract about this apple and thus has begun to move away from the tyranny of mere phenomena.

Now that he can classify objects, he can describe them, which is a first step in the direction of an even more remarkable capacity he has developed—he can "be logical" about them. As we have seen, he can follow two basic courses in this process. Working from crude deduction, for instance, he can satisfy himself that one meaning of the apple is nature's goodness. For he has a system of beliefs applicable to his whole world of phenomena which has certain "givens," a basic tenet of which is that nature is good. All things in nature are good. An apple is a thing in nature. Therefore apples are good and all their properties testify to nature's goodness. Of course there are a great many other "givens" from which our friend could proceed by way of deduction to come to understand the apple.

Another way he can "be logical" about apples is to proceed inductively. Going beyond sheer observation he begins to note regularities in apples. First they are smaller, then larger; first they are green, then red. Then some striking relationships begin to emerge. He discovers that it is more likely that if he bites into a red apple the taste will be sweet than if he bites into a green one. This very valuable finding has obvious problem-solving implications. The method also has generality. He can repeat the process in learning about other edible objects. But in each case he has to find out what is related to what (as red to sweet).

But our inquisitive friend is not satisfied. He has learned that within certain undefined limits of probability he can predict taste from color—in the case of apples, at least. He has also learned that he cannot in the case of peppers. But at least he can distinguish apples and peppers by means of classification—by setting limits on the concept "apple." By the same method he discovers that, with a somewhat lower degree of predictive power, he can relate yellow apples to a degree of sweetness greater than sour and less than sweet. This gives him the notion of a continuum of sweetness from very sweet to very sour, and he is all set to discover a new mathematical branch of logic—normative statistics—which will increase the power of his tool, inductive logic. (At this point he also stops worrying about whether sweetness is qualitative or quantitative.)

Still our friend is not satisfied. The relation between green-red color and taste seems to hold for apples and certain kinds of currants (not others) and certain kinds of plums (not others), etc. But a great many edibles seem to have this thing in common: they change not only in one observable characteristic—color—but also they vary simultaneously in another observable characteristic—taste. What he needs is a single concept that will account for all these relationships, these near-invariances. There begins to emerge a notion of "ripeness." This is a disturbing development on a number of counts.

In the first place he is not sure whether nature's goodness extends to such ideas or not. (He decides to play it safe and assume that it does, but he does not make an issue of it.) But even more disturbing is the fact that he cannot simply apprehend ripeness in the old tried and true ways—by feel, by smell, by taste, by sight, by sound. (Later he will engage in a lively argument over whether what he has hold of here is a "hypothetical construct" or an "intervening variable.") For now the problem is that ripeness is strictly something in his head, not a sensory experience but a "construct" from many sensory experiences and of different kinds at that. But the remarkable thing is that it orders a segment of his universe for him. It makes possible for him to predict the behavior of living things. This in turn gives him some measure of control over a segment of his universe. He can find uses for his knowledge, as in avoiding stomach aches. Better still, it sets him off on some exciting speculations: growth, life cycles, etc.

We have seen that our friend has tried to go beyond what his sensory equipment "told" him about an aspect of reality—in two directions. He has tried to attack his problem with pure logic, deductive logic, but this has proved to be only as fruitful as his basic "givens" are true. (And anyway it seems it is not "truth" about apples but facts about them that interest him.) He has tried another logical attack—inductive logic—and this has done some important things for him. It has created some generalizations that have power to predict some aspects of the behavior of the world around him. He suspects that these generalizations explain a lot about apples, but the strange thing is that he is not interested in apples any more. (The same thing has happened to another apple scholar with whom he has only a nodding acquaintance, the one who used to sit under apple trees watching apples fall.) He is now interested in growth, let us say.

And let us say also that he now feels there are a couple of things wrong with his method if he is really going to learn anything about growth. In the first place, he has found that if he is to predict changes on the basis of his growth theory he needs to measure these changes. He has found, for instance, that he and others cannot always agree on what is "sweet," and the question "how sweet" is even harder to deal with. The same is true of color. He needs to make precise and repeatable and agreed measurements on both sides of this relationship—color and taste. This will help him to know whether the variability in his findings is in the relationship or in the observation. Before long it will be clear to him that this is one of his central problems—he must account for variance. He is seeking out invariances in his universe, but he finds that these really do not exist in fact. There are always some variances in the relations he observes, and these can arise from two sources. One is that the relation between the two observed entities is not a perfect one. The other is in the errors his observations may contain.

So there appear to be two things he must do if he is to get on with the job. One is simply to improve his observational precision, requiring better measuring instruments. The other is to satisfy himself that he is getting somewhere by finding out whether his concepts really work. Later on, when he becomes more self-conscious about the process by which he learns new things, he will invent a term that treats both of these problems: rigor. On the one hand he is concerned with operational rigor, which has to do with the way he relates his constructs to his operations. On the other hand he is concerned with his logical rigor, which has to do with the way he relates his constructs to the rules of logic.

In short, he has used direct inductive empiricism to gain a start on his problem, but he also has pushed it near the limits of its usefulness. In the process he has revised his problem and given it focus. He is sure he is moving in the direction of worthwhile knowledge; he has found that things he has learned already have proved useful to his fellow men; but even if that were not true, he knows it is worthwhile simply because it is so exciting. (Whether his problem excites the apple man now studying "the earth's pull" is beside the point.) Furthermore, he has found it useful to devise some concepts to help in the description of his phenomena, but the elusive thing is how these concepts are related to each other. He has some hunches about what is related to what, and his continued concern with more and more descriptive and classificatory data only seems to get in the way of pursuing these hunches. He is about to take the step from one important phase of investigation, a "problem-setting," "orientation," "feeling out," exploratory, descriptive phase, to another, which we may call a hypothesis-testing, theory-building phase. He must begin to convert his hunches about relationships in his data into testable propositions about them. And he must subject them to test, which is to say that he must carry them back to the real world and find out whether they actually predict the way the real world behaves.

Now he might investigate these relationships one by one, and at first this is the thing to do. But the sooner our friend begins to try to construct a system of concepts, tentatively relating all his constructs to each other, the sooner he will begin to enjoy certain advantages. One is a matter of parsimony. An interrelated system of concepts will require fewer of them. And as long as he keeps them all at a given level, and as long as the hypothetical connections between concepts are internally consistent and obey the laws of logic, he can enjoy another economy. This is the fact that a test of only a part of the system is in a sense a test of the entire system.

A final advantage, and surely the most important, is that when the investigator meets the requirements of this method—this hypothetico-deductive empiricism—he can begin to talk about "what causes what."

Hypothetico-Deductive Empiricism

We have seen that science does not depend on inductive logic alone, nor on deductive logic alone, but moves forward by means of a synthesis of the two, sometimes described as hypothetico-deductive empiricism.

This term has within it the three basic systems that must now be distinguished and ordered. "Deductive" relates to what will here be called the "formal system," "hypothetico-" to what we will call the "theoretical system," and "empiricism" to what we will call the "reality system." Each one is essential to our method. Knowledge is a product of experience, but its utility and its certainty depend on the (theoretical) terms in which it is expressed, the (formal) logical connectedness of the terms in which it is expressed, and the capacity of its terms, when subjected to the test of *reality,* to predict events with the regularity that yields relatively secure laws in a lawful world.

Formal Systems

Exactly how do these systems differ from each other? As its name implies, the formal system is "contentless." It is completely abstract. Consisting of the logic and mathematics of relations, formal systems are systems of propositions which can be proved. They can be proved by reference to their consistency. They are founded upon agreements among users of the system as to the exact meaning of the terms employed. Two-and-two-make-four is "true" in a formal sense only and does not require verification first with apples, then peppers, etc. *It is true because we have found it useful to agree that it is true.* It is formally true because it is consistent with the logical syntax of our most precise language.

Theoretical Systems

Theoretical systems also consist of propositions. But these are not "true" until their truth is established by repeated reference to phenomena. They are not "proved," in fact, but "verified." Verification consists in the process of subjecting them to empirical test.

Reality Systems

Reality systems consist of observable aspects of the real world. This is the sense-data level where our apple man started. But all observations ideally are reducible to sense data and subject to the test of agreement. Phenomenal reality is neither "proved" nor "verified," but observations are subject to the requirement of agreement. If observers, whether directly apprehending reality through the senses or by means of instruments of one kind or another, can agree, then the observation and/or the instruments are "reliable." Reliability cannot be assumed. It must be demonstrated.

We have referred to each of these systems, implying that for each there are some orderly interrelations among their elements. Obviously the formal system must have this systematic character. It is the business of formal systems, in fact, to specify these interrelations and be consistent about them. Theoretical systems consist of concepts which are interrelated by means of hypothetical propositions. Their internal consistency, however, must be logically (formally) spelled out, and this is the clue to the relationship between formal and theoretical systems. The hypothetical propositions must be linked to formal propositions to establish their system character. Theories can be useful and still more or less presystematic. As a science advances, it tends to relate its concepts to each other by means of hypotheses, which in turn attain rigor through logical derivation from the system's elements: assumptions and postulates. Derivation does not establish the truth or the verification of the hypotheses; it merely assures their consistency with the theoretical system.

The system character of the empirical world is treated as an assumption. The point has already been made that the behavioral scientist assumes the orderedness of his universe and then sets his task as finding out the nature of the order in his kind of data. His experience with scientific method has repeatedly indicated that this assumption is a safe one, intuitively. But since it is a sort of gross, underlying assumption, not usually stated in his theoretical system, this is an assumption that is not often subjected to direct test. But in another sense it is tested every time scientists in any given universe of phenomena find order and connectedness in that universe. In summary, then, the system aspect of his formal system is something the formal system must contain; the system aspect of his theoretical system is something he must construct in consistency with both his logic and his phenomena; the system aspect of his empirical system is something he must assume.

Two Kinds of Rigor

We have seen that the connections the scientist constructs between these systems are crucial to hypothetico-deductive empiricism. It is in establishing these connections that he meets the requirements of rigor. We turn now to a brief examination of the demands of these two kinds of rigor.

Standing between the phenomenal system and the theoretical system is the problem of measurement. Obviously, if an observation is to represent a concept and a concept is to represent a class of observations, a precise "mapping" is necessary between the observation and the concept. Let us say our friend has a proposition that says the redder the apple the sweeter the taste. He needs measurements of both redness and sweetness. Usually he must reduce these qualities to quantities. Notice that he has drawn from his formal system the concept "greater than." This is a purely formal concept, one that states nothing more than a relation. Now he is applying this relation to his observations of particular classes of events, and it is necessary to devise operations by which he consistently orders his data according to these relations.

The doctrine of operationism is fairly new to social science.[32] It seems to be crucial to the element of behaviorism in the notion of behavioral science.[33] It will be recalled that the behavioral scientist demands rigor at the points of contact between his observations and his constructs. Operationism attempts to achieve this rigor by assuring that a construct is nothing more than the operations to which it is tied. To the operationist the villain of the piece is "surplus meaning." Social scientists have usually begun with terms in common usage. These have acquired associative meanings that are far from exceptionless. *Rigor demands exceptionless meanings.* Operationism's answer is constructs that are exceptionless because they contain nothing more than certain repeatable operations. An average readership score is nothing more than the averaged answers of a population of persons to the questions in a particular method of readership study. The term "readership" may be heavily weighted with variable meanings: knowledge of, interest in, or simply valence for some kind of communication content. And these accumulated semantic connections may actually be of value to the theorist in thinking about readership. But the investigator of the behavior of readers cannot be various in his use of the concept. He may employ its surplus meanings in exploring and finally testing relations between this concept and others that everyday wisdom suggests may be empirically related to it. He must not confuse "readership" and "interest" with each other, but he may very well investigate the empirical connections between readership and interest, provided he can define them independently (and operationally).

Also in the interest of rigor the investigator is concerned with another connection between his systems—another "mapping" between concepts in two systematic realms. He is concerned with the derivation of his hypotheses. Here the problem is one of making a precise mapping between his theoretical constructs and his underlying logical or formal system. Such a system consists of a set of primitives or undefined terms, a set of unproved statements called postulates or axioms, and all the theorems that may be deduced from the axioms by use of the laws of logic. Since these are wholly formal statements of relations, it is possible to map theoretical content to these formal propositions. The richest of these logical systems are mathematical models. "A mathematical model is a mathematical system whose primitives and postulates correspond to entities and rules governing them." [34] Thus a mathematical model is a formal system to which the elements of a theoretical system may be mapped in a one-to-one relationship.

But is not there only *one* mathematical system? [35] There are many, each a logical system with an internally consistent set of primitives and axioms together with an exhaustible but usually incomplete set of theorems. A wide choice of mathematical models is already available, and some have already proved useful in attacking communications problems. For instance, the Shannon-Wiener information-theory-cybernetics model has been employed by Wilson Taylor [36] in the development of a new readability measure. Frank Harary and Robert Norman [37] have pointed out the usefulness of graph theory in work on communication nets by several investigators. Melvin De Fleur [38] has used the Weber-Fechner law as a model in a study of message diffusion of air-dropped leaflets.

To the advantages of mathematical models already implied in discussing the formal system in general (they assure the logical interrelatedness of our theoretical constructs, and they help contribute precision to our measurements) must now be added another. "If the postulates are sufficiently rich, it is possible to deduce many consequences about the concrete system (note: in our terms the theoretical system) of which one may not have been aware." [39] In other words, a mathematical model may suggest relationships within the theoretical system that our concepts, prior research, and plain intuitions have missed.[40]

Levels and Stages of Inquiry

In an effort to summarize what has been said so far, a tentative outline is presented in Chart 1 in an effort to relate most of the concepts used in this discussion in a broad scheme of levels (or stages) of inquiry. The three systems discussed above have been entered across the top, together with the mapping devices that connect them with each other. Arrayed vertically are the levels or stages. The previous discussion has attempted to justify the idea that these are levels of empirical investigation, with deductively formulated science rating a more sophisticated level than inductive empiricism. But these are also labeled "stages" in the belief that any science moves through these phases consecutively.[41] In general it seems apparent that a science moves from acute observation, common-sense wisdom,

CHART 1

A Schematic Representation of Three Levels of Empirical Investigation *

Level (Stage)	Purpose	Formal System	← " Mapping " Devices →	Theoretical System	← " Mapping " Devices →	Reality System	Approached " End Product "
I Orientation, Problem-Setting	Orientation: problem-setting, " hypothesis hunching." Intuitive (no certainty) knowledge of loosely defined segment of reality.	" Common sense." Inductive logic.	" Common sense."	Fragmentary, intuitive constructs. Plausible hypotheses and explanations. " Interpretations."	Verbal definitions. Subjective relations between observations and constructs.	Sweeping, inclusive, holistic, interpretive observations (wholly uncontrolled).	Description; insight, " wisdom." Orientation.
II Inductive Empiricism	Orientation: problem-setting, hypothesis formulating. Conceptual clarity. Low certainty knowledge of a more or less defined segment of reality.	Inductive logic.	Concepts loosely related to formal properties.	Hypothetical constructs of increasing refinement. Emerging hypotheses.	Measurement of attributes. (Operational definitions?) Normative (probability) statistics.	Observations defined by operations (statistical control).	" Observed dependencies " leading to testable hypotheses.
III Hypothetico-Deductive Empiricism	Dependable (high certainty) knowledge of a strictly defined segment of reality.	Deductive logic.	Formal derivation.	Assumptions, postulates and derived hypotheses.	Measurement of attributes. Operational definitions. Normative and non-normative statistics.	Observations strictly defined by operations. Controlled observation (statistical and/or laboratory controls).	Verified generalizations, statable as laws, and inferring causal connections.

* This may also be treated as stages in the development of a science or as stages in the advancement of a particular investigation.

shrewd hunches, and other unsystematic exercises of the senses and the intellect to the method of induction, which cannot emerge until such preliminary efforts have been invested in the problem. In turn, inductive methods advance a science by beginning to draw on phenomena and beginning to give it order and focus by classifying, generalizing, and ordering the objects of its inquiry. This method, in turn, is handicapped in its ability to carry us to more satisfying levels of knowledge, particularly the level of causal connections. Hypothetico-deductive methods carry us to this higher level and more advanced stage. But just as deduction had to wait on a preliminary feeling-out of the subject matter—a pure empirical stage—so deductively formulated science must wait on the preliminary phase of an inductive narrowing, focusing, clarifying, problem-setting stage.

For "a science of communications," toward which it will be assumed we are jointly striving,[42] this notion of stages in the advancement of inquiry may be useful. For a long time our "knowledge" of communications has derived from the practical wisdom of reporters and news editors and from a wealth of descriptive detail and interpretation of journalism's past. In relatively recent years some investigators have moved in the direction of the cumulation of more systematic knowledge of our universe of discourse by means of essentially inductive methods. Readership studies are a case in point, and so are content analysis and readability studies. It is a moot question whether this stage has been sufficiently advanced to warrant taking the next step. However, as seen in Chapter 3, careful experimental studies are beginning to appear in our literature, and there is evidence that we are at least on the threshold of hypothetico-deductive methods.

Of course, to sketch out rough stages of inquiry does not imply that a science moves suddenly and completely from one stage to another. It would appear that we are in a stage of development where much inductive work is still needed but where the gradual introduction of more fruitful methods is not premature. Perhaps there is a significant clue in the recent emergence in our literature of conceptual models of communication processes.[43] Conceptual models are efforts to stake out significant concepts in the field, to codify scattering findings of the past and weave them into a single conceptual framework which will help give direction and focus to future work. Such efforts may be seen as building a bridge between Stages II and

III in our diagram. A conceptual model is not a mathematical model, for it contains no formal system of relations. It is not even a theory, and it cannot become a theory until its postulates have been spelled out and a start has been made in deriving hypotheses. It may, however, take an important preliminary step toward general theory.

Some Illustrations

A brief illustration from the literature of mass communications may help to clarify work at the three levels laid out in the chart. The first stage need not be illustrated. A great many different kinds of data fall in this category: the wisdom of the elder statesmen of our craft, the "chronicles" of our historians of journalism, many thoughtful but purely intuitive analyses of our problems. This is the domain of what may be excellent but "prescientific" scholarship.

The second stage is illustrated rather neatly by Charles Swanson's[44] prodigious effort to find some order in the data of the Continuing Study of Newspaper Reading. The problem was frightening. In the first place, the basic data had been drawn prior to any formulation of even tentative hypotheses (at least by Swanson and others who carried out this analysis). Further, it was in a condition to preclude any very positive findings, owing to certain features of the original data-gathering method. Yet it seemed likely that some order could be found and that, if it were isolated, it could form the empirical basis for some future hypotheses.

Of course Swanson had some hypotheses about what dimensions of newspapers might predict certain features of the order he was seeking. But in advance of well-formulated theory the best solution was to include everything available in an all but purely empirical exercise, in order that no possibilities would be overlooked. Among the data not available were the social class of the respondents and the depth of reading of any item. But there were dependable data on the subject matter of the stories, the sex of the respondents, the size of the page, the visual form of the item, the geographical origin of the news stories, etc. There was nothing to do but put it all on punched cards and see what was related to what. Swanson contributed a useful analytical device to compare the attention given various categories of content by the editors with the attention given the same categories by the readers. (For instance, comics accounted for 4.7 per cent of all the items in all the papers but 13.2 per cent of all the readership of all the respondents.)

This study is here chosen to illustrate inductive processes because its circumstances intensified the difficulties of this method. Actually much more satisfying use of the method is demonstrated repeatedly in our journals. But despite its cumulative, pretheory utility, the reader may judge for himself the distance it leaves us from organized knowledge of relatively high certainty.

Another communication study illustrates Phase III in Chart 1. De Fleur [45] was confronted with a problem of predicting the effectiveness of air-dropped leaflets in communicating information to a population deprived of the information in other media. He narrowed it to the researchable problem of the relation between the number of leaflets dropped to the magnitude of the message diffusion. In so doing he worked first at our Stages I and II, assembling the wisdom and the data that had been brought to bear on the influence of the magnitude of the stimulus on the size of the response in mass communication. The literature search was largely unproductive. But casting the problem in this determinate form led to a mathematical model with which psychophysics has dealt with analogous problems. The Weber-Fechner law states a mathematical relation between stimulus intensity and response magnitude. De Fleur first presents the equation in its basic form and then transforms it algebraically into a form which permits him to make a one-to-one correspondence between his operations in the field and the terms of the derived relationship. The mathematical derivation allowed him to draw a curve representing the theoretical expectation of the effect of the leaflets. Then leaflets were actually dropped on eight approximately equated towns.[46] Two tests of their effect were conducted. One provided sample survey information on the number of persons who knew the leaflet's message; the other was based on compliance with the leaflet's directions to "fill out and mail in" the leaflets themselves. In both cases the obtained percentages could be plotted against the theoretical curve. A test of "goodness of fit" between the obtained and theoretical curves yielded an estimate of the likelihood that the obtained fit could be attributed to chance. (See Chart 2.)

There are grounds on which this study may be criticized, but it serves well as an illustration of the advantages to be obtained from use of a mathematical model. The advantages in terms of certainty and precision would appear to be obvious. Another advantage may be somewhat less obvious. This is that by linking the investigation to a widely used psychophysical model a vast literature is tapped which may well suggest other stimulus-response relationships worthy of empirical test in the mass communication setting. But the investigator need not be tied down to these aspects of the problem, for his basic data, if he has done his work well, should be just as productive of fruitful insights as if his methods had been purely inductive. His research has thus gained both in certainty and in richness.

CHART 2

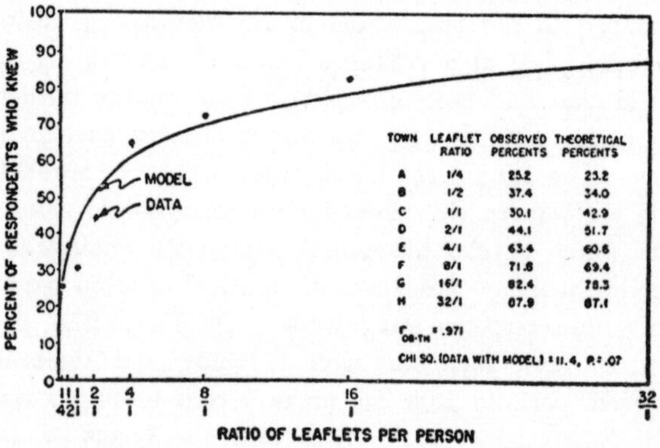
PERCENT OF RESPONDENTS WHO KNEW
100
90
80
70
60
50
40
30
20
10
0
MODEL
DATA
TOWN LEAFLET RATIO OBSERVED PERCENTS THEORETICAL PERCENTS
A 1/4 25.2 23.2
B 1/2 37.4 34.0
C 1/1 30.1 42.9
D 2/1 44.1 51.7
E 4/1 63.4 60.6
F 8/1 71.8 69.4
G 16/1 82.4 78.3
H 32/1 87.9 87.1
r OB-TH = .971
CHI SQ. (DATA WITH MODEL) = 11.4, P. = .07
1/4 1/2 1/1 2/1 4/1 8/1 16/1 32/1
RATIO OF LEAFLETS PER PERSON

(Courtesy of *Sociometry*)

PER CENT OF RESPONDENTS WHO KNEW MESSAGE FOR EACH LEAFLET RATIO

Values and the Social Scientist

Now that we have rounded out a tentative picture of what behavioral science is, we must return to the first problem raised in this discussion—the investigator's detachment, his objectivity, in the words of Max Weber his "ethical neutrality."[47] Here we find something less than perfect agreement among scientists. But on one point there can be little dissent. Science as such has never been concerned with the problem of ethics, with what is right. Ever since it made a clean break with metaphysics its concern has been not with what is right but, first, with what is, and later what happens when. . . .[48]

For the physical scientist, recognition of the nonethical nature of his task provided a simple solution to the problem of value: science and values were antithetical. But for the social sciences, as they evolved under the subject-matter influences of social philosophy and the methodological influences of natural science, the problem was more complicated. Must a scientific posture in the social field also require treating values as irrelevant? It soon became apparent that attitudes, value systems, ideologies lay at the heart of the subject matter of social science, that value legitimately could become an object of analysis for the social scientist as long as his method adequately took account of the problem of the value bias of the observer.

We have seen that history rejected the solution of the "scientific historians," who attempted to control their biases by an effort of will. History's solution has been one of the relativity of value—the historian's observations and interpretations are weighed in the light of the observer's probable bias, inferred from his times, his cultural setting, and his intellectual heritage.

The scientist's solution is neither to depend on will power nor on the relativity solution, but rather to depend on what Morris Cohen and Ernest Nagel have called the "self-corrective nature of science."[49] The scientist's primary dependence is on replication: If he fears that the mote in the eye of the observer has influenced the content of the observation, he can set up the same conditions and repeat the observation. As previous chapters show, he rarely observes "with the naked eye" anyway. His instruments ideally not only aid in making his observations more precise; they even contain built-in means of estimating the magnitude of observational error. Adequately invoked, these means can help the scientist control (if never eradicate) faulty observation tracing to the scientist's values.

Scientific Values

A characteristic solution to the problem of values in social science—by no means a universally accepted one—distinguishes scientific values from values in general. Scientific values may derive from values in general and thus cannot perfectly transcend them. Like all value systems, they are founded on shared experience, but it is experience shared with other scientists that shapes scientific values. Thus, scientific values tend to ignore national boundaries and to some extent cut across religious beliefs and other products of a particular culture.

Scientific values are ordinarily organized around some central conception of the problem of knowledge. But for the individual scientist they include not only the importance of discovering new knowledge but also the relative value to be placed on kinds of knowledge and a set of preferences about what kinds of data and what kinds of methods will facilitate the discovery of new knowledge. And it is strictly up to the individual scientist to work out a careful synthesis between his own scientific and general-value systems—or to keep them almost wholly distinct. A theoretical physicist may see no relation between his work and the times in which he lives, as long as they leave him alone to pursue the search for knowledge. Or a social psychologist may have worked out a careful synthesis between those values he considers to be scientifically and socially compelling, as did Kurt Lewin. Sometimes scientific and secular events conspire to force some sort of synthesis between the scholar's scientific and general-value systems, as in the case of nuclear physicists after their work led to the development of an atom bomb.

"Pure" and "Applied"

Characteristically the scientist makes a distinction between "pure" and "applied" science, or "basic science" and "technology." In the example just mentioned science did not, of course, "produce the atom bomb"; technology did. The scientific work that made the bomb technologically possible was done long before its applications to warfare were dreamed of—in pursuit of knowledge of the ultimate physical nature of matter.

The same distinction may readily be made in the social sciences.[50] Psychology and anthropology, for instance, have pursued respectively the conditions of learning and the nature of culture, regardless of the uses to which this cumulative knowledge might be put by others. But just as natural science has made technology possible, so educationists have labored to use advances in learning theory to solve their problems in the world of affairs,[51] and "applied anthropologists" have used their knowledge of cultures to guide policy in occupied lands.

It is important that the "pure science" orientation does not disparage such uses of knowledge. Characteristically, however, it does guard jealously against the possibility that concern for applications will divert scientific effort from the pursuit of knowledge for its own sake. In other words, the scientist wants scientific values and not values in general to select the problems of scientific work.

Now it should be clear that we have moved from a consideration of values as a biasing factor *at the level of observation* to a consideration of values as determiners of *what the scientist shall investigate.* The scientific community may be said to be a unique combination of discipline and anarchy. For the individual investigator, what his fellow men think of his work is all but irrelevant in relation to what his fellow scientists think of it. But even the approval of his fellow scientists is of qualified importance to him. If he persists in a theory that has been disproved, he knows he cannot survive the scorn of his fellow workers. To falsify data is all but unthinkable. But what he considers important to investigate is another matter. To the layman's typical value question his answer is unequivocal: he investigates what he considers scientifically valuable. He knows from the record of the past that what is trivial today may be crucial tomorrow. He cannot even trust the main stream of his own discipline. His best guide is that which excites him. The discipline, then, is exerted over *how* he investigates and how he reports, and is decisive in guaranteeing the self-corrective nature of his method. The anarchy lies in *what* interests him enough to investigate and is decisive in permitting and encouraging creativity.

Two Dissents

For students who find what William James called the "tough mindedness" of the scientist unattractive, it should be pointed out that there is by no means perfect agreement on these points among social scientists. Two other views seem to predominate among the dissents from the purist position just stated. One centers around the issue of the legitimate *ends* of scientific work and contends that seeking solutions to present-day social problems is a perfectly proper and useful goal of the scientist. The other specifies the observer's values in the scientific orientation itself and makes them an integral part of the investigation.

The first of these positions may be called the "action research" or "social engineering" approach. The basic premise here is that pure theory and action goals may be served simultaneously if only we are aware of what each demands. (This is a position not uncommonly found among communications people, who have tended to come to the communication problem from a desire to improve communication effectiveness or to diminish the alleged toxic effects of the media.) That this position is widely shared in the social sciences is indicated by the presence of action-research journals among the traditional disciplines. A variant of this position is the "policy sciences"[52] approach, which recognizes the extent to which social scientists are being called on as experts to advise social institutions on matters of policy. It proposes systematizing a sort of superscience of public policy and is as interested in the process of interaction between policymaker and social scientist as it is interested in action research aimed at solving public problems.

The other position also values action research as such but emphasizes the reconciliation of the personal and scientific values of the social scientist. As expressed by Gunnar Myrdal,[53] this view is that the social scientist cannot escape the consequences of his own value position and its impact on his work, whether or not this is possible for his colleagues in the natural sciences. Rather than profess detachment, he should make his value assumptions a central part of his theoretical position. Let them not slip into his work surreptitiously or unconsciously; let them rather be positioned among his stated underlying assumptions, and let him then be frank in stating that his findings stand only to the extent that and for as long as his value position can be defended.

Social scientists have increasingly become aware of profound recent changes in the sources of their support. Most of it still comes from sources as disinterested as they try to be: educational institutions and the great foundations. But increasing support of both applied and basic research is now coming from the government, the military, business, and industry. Usually in accepting it they give up a measure of independence in the selection of their problems, even if such "tainted" sources cannot and do not wish to interfere with the objectivity of their contact with data.

Toward Disciplinary Status

This, of course, and the whole question of the relative value of pure and applied research is a matter for the individual investigator to work out for himself. In a field closely associated with the profession and industries of communications, the problem has special meaning. This is an area in which compromise has been effectively demonstrated. For instance, academically based research organizations have accepted government or private funds on the understanding that part of the support is to be earmarked for basic research, even though most of it is oriented toward some legitimate policy objective. There are many instances of this in our own field. Important basic work on readership at Minnesota by Ralph Nafziger and his associates and successors was sponsored by a newspaper organization and by one of the armed services. Significant theoretical advances have been made at Illinois with assistance from the National Institutes of Health. The leaflet-diffusion study cited previously was supported in part by military funds. Such instances are not hard to find.

But in each of these cases it is worth noting that the investigator did not wait for a problem to turn up and then apply his method to the problem as presented by an action agency. *He had already isolated a theoretical problem.* Then when an engineering problem was presented, he found ways of setting up a research effort that satisfied both. Use of the engineering problem as a means of "sharpening up tools" can be justified to a point. But scholarship, the pursuit of new knowledge, moves ahead, not as rapidly as research methods move ahead, but as rapidly as it develops testable and tested theory.

At the risk of elaborating the obvious, this point of view has been developed at some length because of the peculiar situation in which the study of mass communication may be found at the present time. This volume has been written by and for journalists, although its authors also share an interest in mass communications as the subject of research and a behavioral science orientation as a methodological approach. Yet journalism's short life in the university has been very largely as an applied field. Journalism's even shorter span as a contributor to knowledge of mass communication functions and processes has been largely "problem-oriented" or applied. We can hardly claim to have established a discipline in the usual sense. When we have used research techniques, we have used them largely to help solve immediate mass communication problems.

Meanwhile others have been working in the same vineyard. Sociologists, psychologists, historians, political scientists, and others have done work in the area of public opinion, mass communication effects, etc., but this work has had the advantage of being anchored in their respective disciplines. The question then arises whether communication research by journalism must continue to address itself to the immediate problems of the profession and business of journalism. Such a question cannot be legislated, of course. But there does seem to be a growing feeling in our field that we are well on the way toward developing the unique set of phenomena, the unique types of problems, the sufficiently sophisticated methodology, and the dawning of an idea of *what is basic* that signals the approach of disciplinary status.[54]

Science Demands Creativity

There is danger, perhaps, after outlining an "ideal type" behavioral science framework for research in mass communications, that the reader will be left with some false impressions. Two of them must be considered briefly.

The first concerns how the scientist actually proceeds. The neatness of the pattern this chapter has tried to draw belies the surface chaos through which the research practitioner actually moves. But nothing needs to be added to Percy Tannenbaum's treatment of the subject in Chapter 3. The present chapter attempts a reconstruction, as does everything written about science—a reconstruction drawn from what scientists do and inferring their aims from what they do. Without doubt, the scientist's world is less orderly and less antiseptic than this account implies.

The second and more significant point relates to what kinds of skills scientific effort demands. In implying an orderly, purposive attack on some problem of knowledge, we are in danger of inferring that there is a scientific cookbook ("take two tbsp. analysis of variance, add a pinch of interjudge reliability . . .") that anyone can use if he but learns the language of the scientific cuisine. The danger is that this thought may imply that where other modes of scholarship require originality, interpretive wisdom, creative thought, and intellectual sensitivity, behavioral science requires rigor above all else and only methodological sophistication after that. This would be an unfortunate impression; for the best scientific effort requires all the creativity, sensitivity, and ingenuity available to the most original minds. This point has been stressed by the psychologist Skinner, the physicist Einstein, the physiologist Cannon, the anthropologist Malinowski, the sociologist Merton, and undoubtedly many others, and does not need to be documented here. Creative insights are demanded at every level of science, from the first germ of an idea for a conceptual restructuring that begins to find some shape or order in an apparently shapeless mass of data or of seemingly conflicting reports, to the creative use of analytical devices to feel out hidden richness in new data, to the brilliance required in interpretive insights in the writing of final research reports, pointing to hitherto untapped relationships and probing implications for future research. Scientific work is demanding in terms of the special skills it requires of competent practitioners. But it is vastly more demanding in the realm of ideas than of skills. Two favorite adjectives of scientists are "elegant" and "exciting." Scientific method provides a model for elegance, but only the richness of its creativity can provide the excitement.

REFERENCES

1. Earlier chapters have dealt with tactics; this chapter attempts to treat strategy. For a similar usage see James B. Conant, *On Understanding Science* (New Haven: Yale University Press, 1947; New York: New American Library, 1951).
2. Raymond B. Nixon, "Concentration and Absenteeism in Daily Newspaper Ownership," *Journalism Quarterly*, 22 (1945), 97–114.
3. Frederick S. Siebert, *Freedom of the Press in England, 1476–1776* (Urbana: University of Illinois Press, 1952), especially introduction, 1–13.
4. Morris R. Cohen and Ernest Nagel, *An Introduction to Logic and Scientific Method* (New York: Harcourt, Brace, 1954), 191. The writer knows no single source that equals this one in transmitting understanding of the "philosophy of science." Chaps. 10, 11, 14, 19, and 20 are recommended especially.
5. By "productive scholarship" we mean scholarship in the sense of searching actively for *new* knowledge. It should not be confused with erudition, which is at best a qualification for and precondition of scholarship.
6. Conant, *On Understanding Science*, (New American Library ed.), 102. This little book is a helpful introduction to the nature of science from the viewpoint of one of America's most noted scholars. It is richly anecdotal rather than systematic, however, and de-emphasizes the contribution of general theory to the advancement of a science.
7. *Theory and Practice in Historical Study: A Report of the Committee on Historiography* (New York: Social Science Research Council [SSRC Bulletin No. 54], 1946), 138. This bulletin, produced by a special

SSRC committee under the chairmanship of Merle Curti, contains a concise and systematic set of " Propositions " " stating the historian's position on nearly every imaginable point of methodology.

8. *Ibid.*
9. A recent instance is Raymond Aron's exceptionally clear-headed discussion of the evidence-inference process in history. " The object of history (not to be confused with the social sciences) is reality, which by its nature is and will never again be. The decline of the Roman Empire occurred once and once only. It was unique." Raymond Aron, " Evidence and Inference in History," in Daniel Lerner, ed., *Evidence and Inference* (Glencoe, Ill.: The Free Press, 1958), 20.
10. SSRC Bulletin No. 54 (note 7 *supra*), 137.
11. *Ibid.*, 135.
12. It is interesting to notice, however, that a more recent report of the same committee seems to take a very different position. Cf. *The Social Sciences in Historical Study: A Report of the Committee on Historiography* (New York: Social Science Research Council [SSRC Bulletin No. 64], 1954). Here, for instance, the position of " certain German historiographers " that " all historical phenomena are unique and the corollary that no general statements whatsoever may be made about historical processes " is rejected (p. 26). " From the point of view of the social scientist every historical event shares traits with other historical events of the same general type " (p. 26 n.). There are in this volume many other indications of a growing convergence between the methodology positions of the historian and the behavioral scientist. See especially " Process of Historical Research," 23–30; chap. 4, " Problems of Historical Analysis "; and chap. 6, " Methods: Theory and Practice."
13. For a particularly stimulating comparison of scientific method and other modes of investigation, see Cohen and Nagel, *An Introduction to Logic and Scientific Method,* especially chap. 17, " Probable Inference in History and Allied Inquiries."
14. Melvin H. Marx, " The General Nature of Theory Construction," in M. H. Marx (ed.), *Psychological Theory* (New York: Macmillan, 1951), 5.
15. Bulletin 54 (note 7 *supra*), 138.
16. Robert K. Merton,, *Social Theory and Social Structure* (Glencoe, Ill.: The Free Press, 1949), 314.
17. Cohen and Nagel, *An Introduction to Logic and Scientific Method,* 210.
18. Bulletin 54 (note 7 *supra*), 137.
19. An interesting dissent from this position by Charles A. Beard and Alfred Vagts urges the total elimination of the idea of cause from historical writing. They believe history's concern is with " consequential and coexisting relations between events and personalities and interests which are intimate in nature and have the appearance of necessity," but appear to be rejecting the concept of causality on grounds of ambiguity. *Ibid.*, 136.

20. *Ibid.*, 137.
21. Bulletin 64 (note 12 *supra*); cf. chap. 4, "Problems of Historical Analysis."
22. *Ibid.*, 86 ff. Aron (note 9 *supra*) takes a similar view. "The search for laws in the natural, or even behavioral, sciences postulates the determinism which it strives to elaborate. The search for causes, in history and especially human history, presupposes contingency (which does not mean indeterminism), i. e., the appearance at a point in time and space of a datum which was not the necessary result of laws." (p. 29) In history "the aim of causal inquiry . . . is to reveal the structure of the course of history, to disentangle the skein of great underlying causes and particular events." (p. 31) But "irrefutable proof is impossible. We cannot repeat the experiment. . . . Hence, when we assert a causal relation between a situation and a past event our assertion is no more indisputable than is the forecast of such an event." (p. 32)
23. F. S. C. Northrop, *The Logic of the Sciences and the Humanities* (New York: Macmillan, 1947), 260. Although some of Northrop's views are rather "special," particularly in the matter of values, the serious student of scientific method will find this work understandable and profitable. The first seven chapters are especially recommended.
24. C. West Churchman and Russell L. Ackoff, *Methods of Inquiry* (St. Louis: Educational Publishers, 1950), 338 f. This excellent textbook in the philosophy of science is especially helpful in relating scientific methods to philosophical systems. See especially their chapters on the contributions of pragmatism and logical positivism.
25. For an excellent discussion of the risks of inferring causality from correlation, see Eleanor Maccoby's review in *Public Opinion Quarterly*, 20 (1956), 347–50.
26. Ronald Freedman *et al.*, *Principles of Sociology* (New York: Holt, 1952), 5. Chap. 1 is an extremely successful short introductory statement of the nature of behavioral science.
27. Tolman's "purposive behaviorism" represents a classic resolution of a very similar problem in psychology. See Edward C. Tolman, *Purposive Behavior in Animals and Men* (New York: Century, 1932). The relevant excerpts may be found in Marx (ed.), *Psychological Theory*, 410–28. Economics characteristically treats rational behavior in terms of a group or an individual "seeking to maximize some quantity," as a "utility." In basic assumptions this is not unlike Tolman's "behavior at a choice point." The "theory of games" expresses rational choice behavior in terms of probability distributions. In all these cases the lawfulness of purposive and rational behavior may readily be assumed. See Kenneth F. Arrow, "Mathematical Models in the Social Sciences," in Daniel Lerner and Harold D. Lasswell (eds.), *The Policy Sciences: Recent Developments in Scope and Method* (Stanford: Stanford University Press, 1951), especially "The Principle of Rationality," 135–39.
28. The historian's antipathy for determinism is stated cogently if uncharit-

ably by Arthur Schlesinger, Jr., in a book review in *The Reporter*, December 15, 1955, pp. 45–48. Schlesinger equates determinism with fatalism.

29. Bulletin 64 (note 12 *supra*), 140.

30. Churchman and Ackoff, in *Methods of Inquiry*, have presented an excellent summary of the origins of rationalism and empiricism. See especially chaps. 2 and 3.

31. "The theory of statistical inference . . . is precisely the mathematical expression of the logic of induction." Arrow, note 27 *supra*.

32. The classic statement of "operationism" is C. W. Bridgman, *The Logic of Modern Physics* (New York: Macmillan, 1928). Its implications for behavioral science are well stated in S. S. Stevens, "Psychology and the Science of Science," *Psychological Bulletin*, 36 (1939), 221–63, reprinted in Marx (ed.), *Psychological Theory*, 21–54. Besides a readable statement of what operationism is and is not, this essay relates operationism to logical positivism, the philosophical movement with which it is so closely associated. See also E. G. Boring *et al.*, "Symposium on Operationism," *Psychological Review*, 52 (1945), 241–94.

33. The "behaviorism" to which this essay adheres in referring to "behavioral" science owes a debt to, but is not by any means identical with, the behaviorism in psychology to which Watson's name is linked. Nor is it limited to psychology. Any scholarship which takes a systematic, theoretical-empirical, predictive, and nonethical approach to the study of behavior phenomena, human and nonhuman, individual and social, is behavioral science for our purposes. This would appear to be the case in just about all of psychology, most of sociology and anthropology, and much of economics. It overlaps the biological sciences and may be found in history, political science, journalism, education, and speech.

34. Frank Harary and Robert Z. Norman, *Graph Theory as a Mathematical Model in Social Science* (Ann Arbor: Institute for Social Research, 1953).

35. When most of us think of mathematics we think of the "whole numbers" we manipulated in arithmetic. This fact seems to account for much of the typical objection to quantification of social science. Ratio scales, for instance, are powerful but inappropriate models because of the difficulty we encounter in making one-to-one mappings between them and our kind of data. The assumptions of the probability calculus underlying statistics are easier to meet. Nonparametric or "distribution-free" statistics are gaining popularity in social science because, while less powerful as a model than normative statistics (based on the normal distribution), they require assumptions still more easily met. For an excellent discussion of the formal properties of scales consult S. S. Stevens, "Mathematics, Measurement, and Psychophysics," in S. S. Steven (ed.), *Handbook of Experimental Psychology* (New York: Wiley, 1951), especially 1–30, 44–49.

36. Wilson L. Taylor, "'Cloze Procedure': A New Tool for Measuring Readability," *Journalism Quarterly*, 30 (1953), 415–33.

37. Note 34 *supra*, chap. 3.
38. Melvin L. De Fleur, "A Mass Communication Model of Stimulus Response Relationships: An Experiment in Leaflet Message Diffusion," *Sociometry*, 19 (1956), 12–25.
39. Harary and Norman, *Graph Theory as a Mathematical Model in Social Science*, 2.
40. It is possible to touch barely on mathematical models here. For a wholly nontechnical treatment of the subject which summarizes and describes a number of them, consult Abraham Kaplan, "Sociology Learns the Language of Mathematics," *Commentary*, 14 (1952), 274–84. Only slightly more technical are Kenneth J. Arrow, "Mathematical Models in the Social Sciences," in *The Policy Sciences* (note 27 *supra*), 129–54, and Alphonse Chapanis, "Men, Machines, and Models, *American Psychologist*, 16 (1961), 113–31. Wilbur Schramm, "Information Theory and Mass Communication," *Journalism Quarterly*, 32 (1955), 131–46, presents a nontechnical exposition of information theory and suggests some of the ways its postulates may be used to uncover interesting problems in mass communications.
41. The notion of stages in the advancement of a science appears to be accepted widely in the literature of the "science of science." Northrop's stages of "problem analysis," "natural history," and "deductively formulated theory" are much like the three stages employed in this scheme; see note 23 *supra*, chaps. 2, 3, and 4.
42. That this is not unanimously agreed on by systematic students of communication phenomena may be seen in a bitter attack on "scientism" by one of the most effective of our Stage II investigators. See Dallas W. Smythe, "Some Observations on Communications Theory," *A-V Communication Review*, 2 (1954), 24–37. Smythe's principal villain, however, proves to be not the social scientist as here described but the methods-facile "social engineer."
43. Comprehensive conceptual models have been published by Wilbur Schramm, "How Communication Works," in Wilbur Schramm (ed.), *The Process and Effects of Mass Communication* (Urbana: University of Illinois Press, 1954); Bruce H. Westley and Malcolm S. MacLean, Jr., "A Conceptual Model for Communications Research," *AV Communication Review*, 3 (1955), 3–12; George Gerbner, "Toward a General Model of Communication," *AV Communication Review*, 4 (1956), 171–99; David K. Berlo, *The Process of Communication* (New York: Holt, Rinehart and Winston, 1960); and Chilton R. Bush, "The Communication Process," in *The Art of News Communication* (New York: Appleton-Century-Crofts, 1954). Note the pervasive influence of a mathematical model in these formulations; information theory concepts appear in various forms in all of them.
44. Charles E. Swanson, "What They Read in 130 Daily Newspapers," *Journalism Quarterly*, 32 (1955), 411–21.
45. Note 38 *supra*.

46. For details on these and other controls, see the original article.
47. Max Weber, "The Meaning of 'Ethical Neutrality' in Sociology and Economics," originally published in 1917. Even more relevant is Weber's "'Objectivity' in Social Science and Social Policy" (1904). Both are reprinted in translation in Max Weber, *The Methodology of the Social Sciences* (Glencoe, Ill.: The Free Press, 1949).
48. "When the normatively valid is the object of empirical investigation, its normative validity is disregarded. Its 'existence' and not its 'validity' is what concerns the investigator." *Ibid.*, 39.
49. Note 4 *supra*, 395.
50. For a more detailed development of this problem and others raised in this section, see William J. Goode and Paul K. Hatt, *Methods of Social Research* (New York: McGraw-Hill, 1952), especially chaps. 1–4.
51. The classic statement in opposition to the pure-science, knowledge-for-its-own-sake position is probably Robert S. Lynd, *Knowledge for What? The Place of Social Science in American Culture* (Princeton: Princeton University Press, 1939).
52. Consult Harold D. Lasswell, "The Policy Orientation," in *The Policy Sciences* (note 27 *supra*), 3–15.
53. Gunnar Myrdal *et al.*, *An American Dilemma: The Negro Problem and Modern Democracy* (New York: Harper, 1944), Methodological Appendix.
54. There is encouragement, too, in the beginnings of a philosophical-methodological "dialogue" in our field, for example Jay W. Jensen's unpublished paper read at the 1960 convention of the Association for Education in Journalism, "Perspectives in Communication Research: a Critique" and Wayne Danielson's reply. There is another unpublished "reply" to Jensen, also as yet unpublished: Edwin B. Parker, "Scientific Method in Communication Research," which takes a similar position to that of this chapter but devotes more attention to philosophical issues. Copies of all three papers are available from the authors.

Name Index

Subject Index